THE PLEASURES
OF POETRY

THE PLEASURES
OF POETRY

Donald Hall
UNIVERSITY OF MICHIGAN

Harper & Row, Publishers
NEW YORK   EVANSTON   SAN FRANCISCO   LONDON

THE PLEASURES OF POETRY

Copyright © 1971 by Donald Hall

STANDARD BOOK NUMBER: 06-042604-7

LIBRARY OF CONGRESS CATALOG CARD NUMBER: 70-123934

ACKNOWLEDGMENTS

CLARK

"Like Musical Instruments." From *Stones*, by Tom Clark. Copyright © 1967 by Tom Clark. Reprinted by permission of Harper & Row, Publishers.

CRANE

"Voyages II." From *Complete Poems & Selected Letters & Prose of Hart Crane*. Reprinted by permission of Liveright Publishers, New York. Copyright 1933, © 1955, 1966 by Liveright Publishing Corp.

CUMMINGS

"Poem, or Beauty Hurts Mr. Vinal." Copyright 1926 by Horace Liveright; renewed 1954 by E. E. Cummings. Reprinted from his volume, *Poems 1923-1954* by permission of Harcourt, Brace & World, Inc.

DICKINSON

"After Great Pain." From *The Complete Poems of Emily Dickinson*, ed. Thomas H. Johnson, by permission of Little, Brown and Co. Copyright 1929, © 1957 by Mary L. Hampson. "I Cannot Live With You" and "A Narrow Fellow in the Grass." Reprinted by permission of the publishers and the Trustees of Amherst College from Thomas H. Johnson, Editor, *The Poems of Emily Dickinson*, Cambridge, Mass.: The Belknap Press of Harvard University Press, Copyright, 1951, 1955, by The President and Fellows of Harvard College.

EBERHART

"The Groundhog." From *Collected Poems, 1930-1960*, by Richard Eberhart. Copyright © 1960 by Richard Eberhart. Reprinted by permission of Oxford University Press, Inc. and Chatto and Windus Ltd.

ELIOT

"Journey of the Magi" and "The Waste Land." From *Collected Poems 1909-1962*, by T. S. Eliot. Copyright 1936 by Harcourt, Brace & World, Inc.; copyright © 1963, 1964 by T. S. Eliot. Reprinted by permission of the publisher and Faber & Faber Ltd.

FROST

"The Gift Outright," "Out, Out—," "To Earthward," and "The Most of It." From *The Poetry of Robert Frost*, ed. Edward Connery

Lathem. Copyright 1916, 1923 by Holt, Rinehart and Winston, Inc. Copyright 1942, 1944, 1951 by Robert Frost. Copyright © 1970 by Lesley Frost Ballantine. Reprinted by permission of Holt, Rinehart and Winston, Inc.

GINSBERG

"America." From *Howl and Other Poems*. Copyright © 1956, 1959 by Allen Ginsberg. Reprinted by permission of City Lights Books.

GRAVES

"In Broken Images." From *Collected Poems*. Copyright © 1955 by Robert Graves. Reprinted by permission of Collins-Knowlton-Wing, Inc.

HARDY

"The Oxen," "The Ruined Maid," "During Wind and Rain," and "Transformation." From *Collected Poems of Thomas Hardy*, by Thomas Hardy, by permission of his Estate; Macmillan & Co. Ltd., London; and The Macmillan Company of Canada Ltd. Reprinted by permission of The Macmillan Company. Copyright 1925 by The Macmillan Company.

HILL

"Of Commerce and Society." From *For the Unfallen*, by Geoffrey Hill. Reprinted by permission of André Deutsch Ltd.

HOPKINS

"Spring and Fall," "The Windhover," "I Wake and Feel the Fell of Dark." From *Poems of Gerard Manley Hopkins*, 4th ed., Oxford University Press, Inc., 1967.

HOUSMAN

"To an Athlete Dying Young." From "A Shropshire Lad"—Authorised Edition—from *The Collected Poems of A. E. Housman*. Copyright 1939, 1940, © 1959 by Holt, Rinehart and Winston, Inc. Copyright © 1967, 1968 by Robert E. Symons. Reprinted by permission of Holt, Rinehart and Winston, Inc. and The Society of Authors as the literary representative of the Estate of A. E. Housman, and Jonathan Cape Ltd., publishers of A. E. Housman's *Collected Poems*.

MUIR

"The Horses." From *Collected Poems 1921–1958*, by Edwin Muir. Copyright © 1960 by Willa Muir. Reprinted by permission of Oxford University Press, Inc. and Faber & Faber Ltd.

PLATH

"Lady Lazarus." From *Ariel*, by Sylvia Plath. Copyright © 1963 by Ted Hughes. Reprinted by permission of Harper & Row, Publishers, and Olwyn Hughes.

POUND

"Hugh Selwyn Mauberley" IV, "The Return," and "The River-Merchant's Wife: A Letter." From *Personae*, by Ezra Pound. Copyright 1926 by Ezra Pound. Reprinted by permission of New Directions Publishing Corporation.

RANSOM

"Captain Carpenter." Copyright 1924 by Alfred A. Knopf, Inc. and renewed 1952 by John Crowe Ransom. Reprinted from *Selected Poems*, 3rd rev. ed., by John Crowe Ransom, by permission of the publisher.

ROBINSON

"Eros Turannos" and "Hillcrest." Reprinted with permission of The Macmillan Company from *Collected Poems*, by Edward Arlington Robinson. Copyright 1916 by Edward Arlington Robinson, renewed 1944 by Ruth Nivison.
"Mr. Flood's Party." Reprinted with permission of The Macmillan Company from *Collected Poems*, by Edward Arlington Robinson. Copyright 1921 by Edward Arlington Robinson, renewed 1949 by Ruth Nivison.

ROETHKE

Reprinted by permission of Doubleday & Co., Inc. From *The Collected Poems of Theodore Roethke*. "Cuttings" and "Orchids," Copyright 1948 by Theodore Roethke; "Big Wind," Copyright 1947 by The United Chapter of Phi Beta Kappa; "My Papa's Waltz," Copyright 1942 by Hearst Magazine, Inc.; "The Visitant," Copyright 1950 by Theodore Roethke; "Elegy for Jane," Copyright 1950 by Theodore Roethke; "I Knew A Woman," Copyright 1954 by Theodore Roethke; "The Rose," and "The Meadow Mouse," Copyright © 1963 by Beatrice Roethke as Administratrix of the estate of Theodore Roethke.

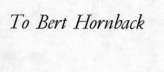

To Bert Hornback

CONTENTS

*Page references refer to poems quoted and discussed in the text.

ONE HUNDRED POEMS

*Names in small capitals represent poets whose works appear in the preceding
section, "Ten Great Poets."

PREFACE

This text and anthology is intended to introduce poetry to the beginner. The text concentrates on feelings that are especially appropriate to poetry, feelings that begin in the mouth and that end in resolutions of wit, or in discoveries of inward life.

In the crib a baby croons noises which mean nothing but feel good in his mouth. Poems begin from this crooning, and end in *King Lear* and "Birches." The baby is always there, in all of us, all the time. If we cannot, in our adult lives, reconnect with this baby and his pleasures, we cannot read poems.

This book tries to do many things: It talks about technique, it talks about ideas in poems. But where it differs from most introductions to poetry is in its emphasis on the relationship of poetry to man's emotions, rather than to his intellect.

The anthology is in three parts. "Ten Great Poets" (English and American)—is an arbitrary selection but may please readers who prefer an extended selection of works by particular poets. "One Hundred Poems" can serve as a brief survey of the history of poetry in our language, and can be supplemented by larger anthologies and by collected works. The poems are arranged chronologically, so that in the first section one can observe the development of particular poets and in the second section one can discern changes in English poetry.

The final section of the anthology consists of a few selections of rock poetry by the Beatles. (The limitation to the Beatles is arbitrary. Other folk and rock lyrics are fine, but some are not available for reprinting.) For the first time in several hundred years, the lyrics of songs partake of the pleasures of poetry. I suspect that no single rock lyric, as of this moment, is a great poem. But passages of some of them are superb poetry. In these lines, a generation has grown up on fantasy, metaphor, sensual sound, and other poetic pleasures.

D. H.

October, 1970

THE PLEASURES
OF POETRY

1
PLEASURE AND
THE WORDS OF POEMS

Poetry is a pleasure, like making love. This book is for people who have not experienced poetry, and who are therefore deprived of this pleasure. I do not believe that people *should* like poems. Most of us have Puritan ideas about "culture"; we make the sensual pleasures of art sound like a boring activity, like attending graduation exercises. Poetry is a pleasure, and man is an animal that seeks pleasures; the more pleasures we open ourselves to, the more human we are.

Poetry is a pleasure that requires understanding and familiarity, or it will be no pleasure at all. All of us receive some signals more clearly than we receive others—I can receive sculpture and painting relatively easily, but I am full of static when it comes to music. Yet all of us can improve our sensitivity to particular stimuli; even a colorblind man can learn to enjoy the shapes of painting.

The pleasures of poetry vary. One poem amuses us, another moves us to tears; one poem delights us with its aptness, another has us floating in a daze of sensual enjoyment. The poems that please me the most are journeys of the imagination, explorations of areas inside ourselves which are mostly dark, but which a poem illuminates with its own strange light. There is also a poetry of sheer intelligent force, a revelation of depth by organized wisdom. Particular poems may please us in one way or another, and each possible way requires a particular sort of sensitivity or a particular awakening of our senses. Once we are used to the requirements of one type of poem, we are ready to enjoy it in its many embodiments. When we are not familiar with the specific pleasure, we usually call the poem obscure, or poetry dull, or ourselves unable to read poetry. But if we persevere into familiarity, we will be able to read anything—and the pleasures of poetry will be open to us. Anyone who loves music or painting knows these delights; think of adding another. The epicure is the man who schools himself to appreciate all things, to enlarge his enjoyment of the world.

Poems happen mostly in the mouth. Poems happen in the brain also, but the brain is not the *place* of poetry. Painting can tell a story, but storytelling is not the *point* of painting. A story can distract us from the real point of a painting. In the same way, ideas can be distractions in poems; many of us tend to overvalue their importance to the poem and therefore miss what really happens in the collision of words that makes the poem.

Some poems make it difficult for us to spoil them by making them intellectual. They resist interpretation by their simplicity. Here is a poem by Thomas Hardy (1840–1928) that I love, called "During Wind and Rain":

They sing their dearest songs—
He, she, all of them—yea,
Treble and tenor and bass,
    And one to play;
With the candles mooning each face . . .
    Ah, no; the years O!
How the sick leaves reel down in throngs!

They clear the creeping moss—
Elders and juniors—aye,
Making the pathway neat
    And the garden gay;
And they build a shady seat . . .
    Ah, no; the years, the years;
See, the white storm-birds wing across!

They are blithely breakfasting all—
Men and maidens—yea,
Under the summer tree,
    With a glimpse of the bay,
While pet fowl come to the knee . . .
    Ah, no; the years O!
And the rotten rose is ript from the wall.

They change to a high new house,
He, she, all of them—aye,
Clocks and carpets, and chairs
    On the lawn all day,

And brightest things that are theirs . . .
    Ah, no; the years, the years;
Down their carved names the rain-drop ploughs.

If we had to paraphrase "During Wind and Rain," we would have to say something like: "People have a good time, especially families, but then they get old and die. Times four." The paraphrase is a cliché, a commonplace, something that everyone takes for granted. But the poem is certainly not a cliché. If we think it a cliché, we are looking not at the poem itself; instead, we are looking at our paraphrase of the poem and evaluating our paraphrase. People who *miss* poetry frequently make this tactical error: They react to (discuss, think about) not the poem, but their paraphrase of the poem.

The poem moves us in a way that cannot be explained by its ostensible content. Therefore, in its own way, it is obscure. We cannot name, to our genuine satisfaction, the sources in the poem of the feelings we experience when we read it. I suppose this statement is true, to some degree, of all good poems—there is something about them which exceeds our explanations—and so all good poems are obscure or mysterious.

When a poem is more intellectual, it is easier to talk about. Ideas are easier for most people to talk about than feelings are, and so poems in which ideas predominate get talked about more than unintellectual poems like "During Wind and Rain." As a result, the teaching and the criticism of literature tend to misrepresent the body of poetry by making it appear more intellectual than it is. Many a teacher who enjoys "During Wind and Rain" himself will not teach it in class because he has so little to say about it.

When we try to talk about "During Wind and Rain," we run out of ideas as soon as we start, and we are driven to talk about things like rhythm and imagery. We may notice how percussive the rhythm of the last line is—all those loud sounds in a row:

/   /   /   / /   /
Down their carved names the rain-drop ploughs.

(Even "their" is a *bit* loud.) The line requires us to say it slowly, and relish it on our tongues. To relish is to take pleasure, which can lead us to notice something else: Despite the depressing nature of the ostensible content of the poem, the poem pleases us instead of depressing us. It pleases us by its sounds—"While pet fowl come to the knee"—and by its shape, the intricate form of the stanza, with its rhymes and its repetitions and its near-repetitions. There is a joy in the art—an art which makes a shape in the air, as actual as a piece of marble—which is as real as the sadness of its statement, and maybe a good deal more real simply because it is less immediately noticeable. This shapeliness is common to all good poems, even when they lack rhyme and meter. The great poet W. B. Yeats said that a perfectly made poem made a sound like the click of the lid of a perfectly made box. The sense of wholeness, of everything coming together, of resolution—is one of the primary pleasures of poetry.

The more we look at the words of "During Wind and Rain," the more we see how intricately constructed it is. ". . . the candles mooning each face" is astronomically accurate; the real moon shines by reflecting the light of the burning sun; so the candles (little suns) turn the four family faces into little moons, each face reflecting candlelight.

The last line is especially poignant. In the first part of the last stanza, the poet recollects moving day, and then wakes himself up, reminding himself again, "Ah, no; the years, the years." Then, magically, he sees the family names "carved"; the members of the family are long dead, their names engraved in stone. Then the line elongates, with its slow pace, until time seems to extend over centuries. The word "plough" has a great force; it brings to mind the country scene (this is no city family) and then makes us think of centuries of time, because it would take centuries for raindrops to carve furroughs in granite. The poet's vision has carried him from the recent past into the remote future.

This sense of "ploughs" is not on the surface; it is a metaphor. An experienced reader of poetry, hearing this line, doesn't think out a paragraph like my paragraph above. He *feels* time stretch out and doesn't explain to himself the reasons for his feeling; he is content simply to feel it. But if you ask him why he feels what he feels, he will look at the line for a while, and then tell you. The beginning reader of poetry needs to learn to inquire of words, to interrogate them until they open their fullness to him. He must learn to ask, "What's *happening* with 'plough'?" and he must see the granite furrowed like a field, the raindrop like the bright steel edge of a horse-drawn plough. Eventually, he will not need such interrogation, because it will become second nature to read deeply, to feel the texture of words—their insides, and their literalness.

But at first, he must explore words consciously, over and over, the way an athlete practices the same motion a thousand times until he seems to do it by instinct. It is important to realize that these motions are acquired and not inborn; they seem instinctual because they are eventually habitual.

Taking words literally, and not intellectually, is one of the main keys to the pleasures of poetry. Shakespeare has Hamlet talk about taking arms against a sea of troubles. We can read the phrase, "to take arms against a sea of troubles," and translate it as "futility," and we will have understood the phrase intellectually. *But we will have missed the poetry and the power and the pleasure.* If we read the line slowly and deeply, we don't translate it at all, ever. We take Shakespeare's image into our heads and we see something like a knight in armor wading into the surf, swinging wildly against the waves with his broadsword. We *feel* the futility from *seeing* the image; we don't *think*, in any conventional sense, at all. But we are reading a poem, and we are responding sensually to images.

The distinction between the literal and the figurative is hard to learn at first. From the age of nine or ten, all of us have been taught to intellectualize, to abstract, and to rationalize the sensual and the instinctual. To read poetry well (and—I believe—to feel, respond, and live well), we must learn to perform this act of abstraction only when it is necessary, and not all the time. Poetry is therapeutic because it requires, and leads to, a resurrection of the instinctual life.

In one of his sonnets, E. A. Robinson refers to a man as "blind"; nine out of ten beginning readers jump to the idea that the man is obtuse; he is figuratively "blind," as in "blind to the fact that his employees are stealing his goods." But if we read the poem modestly enough to hear what the poet actually says, we will understand that the poet is talking about a blind man. I remember reading a poem in school about a man who had climbed a mountain. Our teacher asked us what the poem meant. A number of us offered various solutions: He had come to the end of his life, he had achieved a great ambition, he had reached maturity. The teacher finally cut us off, and told us, "It means he climbed a mountain!" Again, if you ask a group of students what Frost means by "sleep," when he writes, "And miles to go before I sleep," only the rare student will guess that he might mean "sleep." Most students will leap to suggest that Frost is talking about death. But if he had been talking about death, in any direct way, he would have changed the rhyme and written:

And things to do before I die,
And things to do before I die.

The fact that he says, "And miles to go before I sleep," is something that we as readers ought to respect.

Of course no one with any sense would say that Frost's "sleep" is *only* "sleep," either. It starts out as sleep and then, in conjunction with other images in the poem, it takes on implications of oblivion in general: It says something like, "sometimes I'd rather not be conscious of anything at all."

A horrible phrase often turns up in literature classes, when the student or the teacher says of the poet, "What is he *trying* to say?" One immediately sees the image of the poet as a fumbling, inarticulate idiot, unable to talk plainly or say what he means. Something is wrong with this picture. T. S. Eliot was once asked by a college student, "Sir, in 'Ash Wednesday,' what do you mean when you say, 'Lady, three white leopards sat under a juniper-tree'?" Mr. Eliot answered, "Lady, three white leopards sat under a juniper-tree."

Intellectualizing (treating our paraphrase as if it were the poem; hunting ideas; thinking "futility," instead of seeing the knight wade into the ocean) serves a purpose for us. It keeps emotions at a distance. Avoiding the literal meanings of words is one of the most effective ways of avoiding the feelings—the scarey pleasures —of poetry. When we read Blake saying, "O Rose, thou art sick!" we ought to be shocked. If we think, "Now, what does 'rose' mean; what does 'sick' mean?" we are using intellect to evade feeling. We think we are being intelligent by asking these questions, but really we are protecting ourselves from the shock of imagining a rose that is sick. When we turn Blake's rose into a symbol of something—instead of considering it a red flower that is an invalid—it has no smell to it, it is not real, and we are protected from the dangers of feeling. We are protected from the life of feeling, from the instinctual life, and from the sensual life.

To discriminate between literal statement and general implication takes tact—which is a result of experience. But a wise rule is always to start with the literal: See and feel the reality of every image; let the implications grow out of the realities.

Bad poets often fail because they don't see the insides of words. Sometimes they make mixed metaphors by using clichés without seeing what they are actually saying:

He was anchored to the spot
And chose to cast his lot
With her who drove a wedge
Between him and his pledge.

In the first line the man is a ship; in the second he is an ancient priest practicing divination; then the lady splits wood—part of the wood is the ship-priest-man and the other part is an avowal of honor, both treated as parts of the same material.

That example is unfair, because I made it up. But once I was reviewing a book of poetry which I didn't like, and I found a genuine example. The poet was a highly intelligent man, but he lacked a sensitivity to the insides of words. He wrote things that _looked_ like poems, from a distance, but when you bit into one you could tell that it was made of sawdust and chemicals dripping from retorts in laboratories; it was like supermarket bread. In order to make my point in the review, I looked for and found an example of his insensitivity. In describing a dance, "in one serene continuum," he used the line:

To ape the greater body of the dance

He was not trying to be funny. Tone-deaf to the insides of words, unable to see words for what they literally say, this poet used the word "ape" as if it were a synonym for "imitate," or "copy," or "emulate." And so, to the adequate reader of poetry, he has made a grotesque double image: The grace of a dancer lies super-imposed upon the shape of a hulking, knuckle-dragging, King Kong of a gorilla.

There are no true synonyms. Words resemble each other in meaning, but they are not identical. Poetry happens in the minute differences. In newspaper writing, it may not make much differ-ence whether you describe a wall as off-white, grey, oyster-colored, dirty white—or whatever. In a poem the feelings we convey are bound up in the precise words we use. Suppose we take Hardy's first stanza, and change every word that we can change, but try to stay as close to the original as possible—try to use synonyms, in fact.

They sing the songs they like best—
Men and women, the whole family,
Soprano and alto and bass,
    And another playing the piano;
With the light reflecting on their faces . . .
    No. Time. No.
Look at how the dead leaves fall to the ground!

There is no rhyme, the meter is gone, the lines are surely less pleasing to hear. But it is not only a matter of sound. Hardy's words are more exact in their images (". . . the candles mooning each face") and more economical (". . . dearest," ". . . one to play") and more evocative: "Ah, no; the years O!" "How the sick leaves reel down in throngs!" Sound has something to do with the sense of economy, and with evocation. But also look at that word "reel," which is having an effect on us of which we are probably not conscious. The word can mean a fishing reel, but that meaning makes no sense here; the context effectively cancels out this possible interpretation. "Reel" also means to stagger, and this meaning is evoked in the line, especially by "sick" but also by "down"— we see the faltering, lurching motion of a falling leaf—and by "throngs"—where we see a crowd of staggerers. Then, deeper and less obvious and less meaningful, I suggest there is another meaning of "reel" at work; "reel" is also a word used in what the English call "country dancing," which is like our square dancing. The small scene of the singing group may bring to mind, ever so dimly, another group activity associated with music—and of which the leaves' dying motion ironically reminds us.

So the pleasure of "During Wind and Rain" lies in its shapely particularity, its sounds in the mouth, and the unending implications of its specific words. There are no synonyms, and the poem in its own identity is an endless passage into the self. We can read "During Wind and Rain" every year of our lives, and we shall never come to the end of it.

2
VARIETIES OF PLEASURE

When I called Hardy's poem obscure, I was making a paradox, because the poem is apparently so simple. But all good poems, I said, are obscure in some sense or other. Modern poems have a special reputation for being obscure, but everything new has been called obscure at first; people's eyes are used to the shapes of old things, so new things seem shapeless. Here is a modern poem, in translation from the German, which I suppose most admirers of Hardy, if they stopped reading poetry with the sort of poetry Hardy wrote, would find difficult and therefore unpleasant. It was written in 1952 by a Rumanian Jew who had spent time in German concentration camps during World War II. The translator is an English poet named Christopher Middleton. The poem is "Fugue of Death" by Paul Celan (1920–   ):

Black milk of daybreak we drink it at nightfall
we drink it at noon in the morning we drink it at night
drink it and drink it
we are digging a grave in the sky it is ample to lie there
A man in the house he plays with the serpents he writes
he writes when the night falls to Germany your golden hair
  Margarete
he writes it and walks from the house the stars glitter he
  whistles his dogs up
he whistles his Jews out and orders a grave to be dug in
  the earth
he commands us now on with the dance

Black milk of daybreak we drink you at night
we drink in the mornings at noon we drink you at nightfall
drink you and drink you
A man in the house he plays with the serpents he writes

he writes when the night falls to Germany your golden hair
      Margarete
Your ashen hair Shulamith we are digging a grave in the sky
      it is ample to lie there

He shouts stab deeper in earth you there you others you
      sing and you play
he grabs at the iron in his belt and swings it and blue
      are his eyes
stab deeper your spades you there and you others play
      on for the dancing

Black milk of daybreak we drink you at night
we drink you at noon in the mornings we drink you at
      nightfall
drink you and drink you
a man in the house your golden hair Margarete
your ashen hair Shulamith he plays with the serpents

He shouts play sweeter death's music death comes as a
      master from Germany
he shouts stroke darker the strings and as smoke you shall
      climb to the sky
then you'll have a grave in the clouds it is ample to lie
      there

Black milk of daybreak we drink you at night
we drink you at noon death comes as a master from Germany
we drink you at nightfall and morning we drink you and
      drink you
a master from Germany death comes with eyes that are blue
with a bullet of lead he will hit in the mark he will
      hit you
a man in the house your golden hair Margarete
he hunts us down with his dogs in the sky he gives us a grave
he plays with the serpents and dreams death comes as a master
      from Germany

your golden hair Margarete
your ashen hair Shulamith

Because "there are no synonyms," poetry is untranslatable. Yet
some poems are more translatable than others, especially poems
that work through images, rather than through wit or argument.
Because the poem is a translation, I will talk not about the inti-
macies of word and rhythm, but of the images and how they

combine to make the whole. "Schwartze milch," after all, is pretty definitely "black milk." We could try "dark milk"; but that substitution will not work; it is too much a diminishment. One translator of this poem—another man with no sense of the insides of words—translated the phrase as "coal-black milk." He gave us the color all right, but he ruined the plain simplicity of the phrase, and he brought in a whole irrelevant world of coal mines, coal miners, geology, fires, and Newcastle.

A fugue is a musical form in which different voices of melody interweave simultaneously. In a poem there is no way actually to be simultaneous, because one word has to follow another. But sometimes the poet can achieve an effect of simultaneity by repetition, and certainly he can interweave various voices in sequence —for example, the "black milk," the "man in the house" who "writes" "your golden hair Margarete," and the "smoke," and the "serpents" and "Shulamith." The words are mixed up in the sense that there seems to be no conventional sequence of phrases. The lack of punctuation leads the reader headlong from image to image, and increases his sense that one phrase lies superimposed on another. Celan is able, with his semimusical form, to repeat part of a phrase late in the poem that recalls the fuller phrase spoken earlier; in this way the last two lines are a coda and a summation of all previous lines in the poem.

If we tried to paraphrase this poem, what would we come up with? I can think of nothing more adequate than a scream of horror trailing off into a sigh. But noises are not generally accepted paraphrases. (Maybe they should be, together with gestures and facial expressions; these reactions probably resemble more closely the feelings of a poem than any intellectual account.) At any rate, let us see what we can say about the poem. The scene is a concentration camp. The important German (camp commandant? we don't know for sure) writes sentimental letters to the ideal of German beauty while the inmates under his command suffer and ultimately die. The German's sentimental feelings for one distant person contrast with the brutality of his present actions.

That last sentence of mine is not actually a lie—as far as I can tell, it represents something that is in the poem—but how inadequate it is to this horrifying, deeply moving poem. The "contrast"—mere intellectual word—is expressed in that first, repeated phrase, "black milk" which "we drink" continuously. If we must be intellectual about it, we can explain that the blackness of this white, life-giving, maternal sustenance is a symbol of the aberration and unnaturalness of Nazi concentration camps. But the explanation almost serves to rob the phrase of its feeling. We need such explanations in a book like this, only to assure ourselves that we are talking about approximately the same feelings—and, since the feelings are the poem, approximately the same poem.

"Fugue of Death" is a simple poem like "During Wind and Rain" —no paraphrase can dress it up in grand ideas; and it is obscure like "During Wind and Rain"—no explanation will solve the question of why a phrase like "black milk" should move us so. There is the added obscurity of the unconventionality of its writing, but this obscurity is superficial. If we read the poem a few times, without being upset by its lack of punctuation, we grow accustomed to the headlong thrust of its images, and we find that the poem will read as smoothly as Hardy's. It is a matter of getting used to a style, and nothing more.

This poem appears to be figurative at first (and remains figurative to a considerable degree), but it becomes more literal as we get to know it better. "A grave in the sky" becomes literal when we remember that the burned bodies rose as smoke in the air. ". . . he plays with the serpents" takes on a literal level when we think of the Nazi swastika, which was often represented by Hitler's enemies as intertwined snakes. Even the phrase "black milk" has its realistic source, though I needed to have this fact pointed out to me; the phrase "schwartze milch" was actually used by inmates of concentration camps to describe the condition of the milk that their guards occasionally doled out to them.

I chose to talk about Paul Celan right after Hardy because I thought the poems looked deceptively different in their levels of obscurity and complexity, literal and figurative—but were really not so different after all. Both deal mainly with a simple contrast: one poem talks of fulfillment and of death; the other talks of sentimentality and suffering. So many poems work by measuring one thing against another. Hardy balances the first five lines of each stanza against the last two. Celan mixes throughout, making a frightening series of juxtapositions. One thing a poem cannot do, and remain any good, is to go *all in one direction*.

For that matter, neither can a person. If anyone ever says to you: "I love you wholly and totally; I would lay down my life for you; I'm a hundred percent certain of hundred percent pure hundred percent love"—there is only one thing to do: run and hide.

He must mean you harm; you are the one who is to lay down your life.

Feelings are always ambivalent. We may love someone, but there is always an underside, which is sometimes hate or distress, sometimes fear, sometimes even malice; the names do not matter. We may abhor someone, detest him; but some part of us is admiring him, or in some way moving toward him as well as away from him. Even Celan's Nazis are rather beautiful, in a sinister way to be sure, with their blue eyes and blond hair; and they are hugely powerful. Because poetry is the embodiment of feelings, and because it is the nature of human feeling to be ambivalent, poems are ambivalent.

Some poems pretend not to be. George Gordon, Lord Byron, was a fine poet (especially when he was satirical), but on occasion he wrote a lyric that claimed an innocence which it is hard for a sane man to believe in. The last stanza of "She Walks in Beauty" goes:

And on that cheek, and o'er that brow,
  So soft, so calm, yet eloquent,
The smiles that win, the tints that glow,
  But tell of days in goodness spent,
A mind at peace with all below,
  A heart whose love is innocent!

Nobody believes junk like this. Nobody ever has, really. A lady might like to fool herself that someone had such ideas about her, but I believe that part of her would know that it was a hoax—that the poet might be hoaxing himself, that she might be hoaxing herself, or some of each, but at any rate that the feelings were not real, human feelings. A poet might con himself into thinking that he had such feelings—doubtless in order to deprive the lady of the innocence he professes to prize—but a deep part of him would know that the anatomy he describes is pure fudge. He is not *really* writing a poem about a lovely, innocent lady; he is writing a poem to show a poet in a romantic attitude, a poet making an insincere speech about a lady. The poem is looking at itself in a mirror. So even this poem, which pretends to be a hundred percent, is ambivalent in a sense; love is a disguise for self-love.

Ambivalence is not a matter of being on both sides of a question. It is a matter of feelings pulling us in both ways at once, which they always are, if we are honest, intelligent, and sane enough to understand them. Most bad poems fail, I think, because the complexity of the real feeling does not come through; parts of the feeling are suppressed or distorted by the poet's inability to understand himself, or by his fear that he might understand himself.

Sir Thomas Wyatt (1503–1542) wrote a poem in anger which is usually called by its first phrase, "They Flee from Me."

They flee from me, that sometime did me seek,
With naked foot, stalking in my chamber.
I have seen them, gentle, tame, and meek,
That now are wild, and do not remember
That sometime they put themselves in danger
To take bread at my hand; and now they range,
Busily seeking with a continual change.

Thanked be fortune, it hath been otherwise
Twenty times better; but once, in special,
In thin array, after a pleasant guise,
When her loose gown from her shoulders did fall,
And she me caught in her arms long and small,
Therewithal sweetly did me kiss,
And softly said, "Dear heart, how like you this?"

It was no dream; I lay broad waking.
But all is turned, thorough my gentleness,
Into a strange pattern of forsaking;
And I have leave to go, of her goodness,
And she also to use new-fangledness.
But since that I so kindely am served,
I would fain know what she hath deserved.

I said Wyatt wrote in anger and surely he did. The end of the poem (which is hard to read, because 450 years have diminished the freshness and even the senses of words like "new-fangledness" and "kindely") splutters with sarcasm. And the beginning is hurt pride, the man pitying himself in his abandonment. But the middle is a scene between lovers which is tender and erotic. Suppose the poem were only the first stanza followed by the third, resentment followed by sarcasm. The poem then would be a straight line of complaint, and therefore boring. We would have nothing against which to contrast the loneliness of the poet's present condition, nothing to support his hurt and his anger. Black night is simply nothingness; a single candle shows up the darkness around it.

When we know that "once, in special,/In thin array" (the detail of her light clothing begins the sensuality), "after a pleasant guise" (perhaps after a masquerade; perhaps after a time of teasing), "When her loose gown from her shoulders did fall,/And she me caught in her arms long and small" (her very frailty is feminine and appealing; something about the word "small" suggests the feminine, as in the poem on page 184); and when we read that she "Therewith all sweetly" (as I read it) "did me kiss / And softly said, "Dear heart, how like you this?"—when we read this anecdote, we feel the intimacy of the past which makes the present so unbearably lonely. The candle illuminates the dark.

At the same time—and this point is hard to accept if we are sentimental—he is making a pun, a play on words which ties together the different parts of his poem. It takes a sense of Wyatt's times, I suspect, to catch the pun. History is important to poems when it becomes a part of the vocabulary. Probably the most important tool, in reading old poems, is a knowledge of the history of words—what they meant at various times. Therefore, in order to read old poems, we have to *know* something; as we have to know our own language to read contemporary poems, we have to know something of the past in order to feel the pleasures of old poetry. The huge Oxford English Dictionary, twelve volume with a supplement, provides the senses in which words were used at different times. Thus "kindely" tends to mean something like "naturally." And "heart," which of course means an organ in our chest and a term of endearment, can also mean "hart" or "deer"— which is also spelled "dear."

Look back at the first stanza for a moment. "They flee from me, that sometime did me seek." Who? From the poem as a whole, we can clearly answer, "People. One woman especially." But in this first stanza, "They" are not really described as people. We must look closely at the insides of the words, taking them as literally as possible. "I have seen them, gentle, tame, and meek, / That now are wild. . . ." "Tame" and "wild" especially lead us to think of animals, and then we may remember "stalking" as well. And ". . . they put themselves in danger / To take bread at my hand. . . ." So they were animals that he fed, though they were fearful of him. ". . . and now they range, / Busily seeking with a continual change." "Range" is an animal word too. They no longer come to his hand but flee from him, and presumably go to other hands instead.

In England, there are still deer parks preserved from the Middle

Ages. Magdelene College at Oxford has a pretty one, where handsome deer range behind fences, occasionally approaching a tourist who offers a portion of his sandwich. In the sixteenth century all the great estates had deer parks, occupied by relatively tame herds that were attractive to watch and, in days before refrigeration, handy for slaughter. (That Wyatt thinks of women as deer may tell us something about the social position of women at that time.) It is the perfect image for his complaint at the start of the poem: They were pretty, compliant, they accepted favors—and now they go to others. Then, when he tells us his tender recollection in the second stanza, he links it to the first stanza with "Deer hart."

Few readers immediately see the deer in the first stanza when they look at the poem. But if a reader had no sense of animals at all, he was reading poorly; if he thought of lions or humming birds, he was missing the quality of the feeling, but he was getting the animal sense to a degree. If he caught "deer" immediately, either he is a sensitive reader of poetry, or he came to the poem with some fresh knowledge of Tudor deer parks.

When we notice the pun, it helps to know a little history too. The older a poem is, as a general rule, the more problems we have in reading it. Most of us live in a small present, geographically and historically provincial; a pun is something to hold one's nose at. But obviously puns were not odious for Wyatt, nor for Shakespeare a few years later. Shakespeare used them in the middle of passionate speeches. For the sixteenth-century man, a pun was a verbal connection which was perhaps clever but which was not necessarily an attempt to raise a laugh. The connection of "Dear heart" with the deer imagery in the first stanza is not comic; neither is the connection that all the lines make by being written in meter.

Of course, many old poems give us small problem (and others require that you be a scholar to read them at all). Another old poet who loved women was Robert Herrick (1591–1674), who wrote "Upon Julia's Clothes" about a hundred years after Wyatt.

Whenas in silks my Julia goes,
Then, then, methinks, how sweetly flows
The liquefaction of her clothes.

Next, when I cast mine eyes, and see
That brave vibration, each way free,
O, how that glittering taketh me!

There is not much trouble with history or vocabulary here. Reading "brave vibration, each way free"—to describe the sweet swing of a woman's hips—we are not inclined to take "brave" as the reverse of "cowardly," but to realize that there is an older sense of the word, which is certainly a word of praise. But, by accident, the heroic overtones of "brave" are amusing and pleasing. What remains, and probably works on us more than we know, is the sound of the long "a" in the middle of "brave" and "vibration." For that matter, it is really a three-letter repetition, a noise we could spell as "bray." We put a kind of *hold* on these sounds—the vowel is long to say—so that we savor it in our mouths, a sensual pleasure, which resembles the pleasure of our eyes in watching Julia.

A paraphrase of "Upon Julia's Clothes" might simply run: "I take great pleasure in seeing Julia dressed in silk and walking." Maybe that is what the poem *says*, insofar as we can separate the saying from the doing, but there is more to the poem. Herrick loves women but he also loves words; here he loves women through words. The sensual pleasure of the language embodies the sensual pleasure of looking at pretty women. Silk shines and glimmers like water, so there "flows / The liquefaction of her clothes." "Flows" and "liquefaction" go together as an image (the way Wyatt's animals and "deer hart" went together), which is a pleasure, but it is more than that: The word "liquefaction" is a pleasure both to the intellect and to the mouth. It "flows" smoothly, and seems—because of the context—to imitate what it describes. Also, it is almost funny: the use of this Latinate word among all the simple words like "flows" and "clothes" to describe such a delicate thing. It is like an old scholar attending a children's party. It is all these things and more—and it is a pleasure of words in motion, which is separate from the pleasure of a real Julia, but analogous to it.

Poems exist to describe things and to embody feelings. They also exist simply to *be* things. Everyone can accept that a found object —like a stone worn smooth by the sea—can be a pleasant *thing*, with no intellectual message for us. So can a stone which a sculptor has carved. So can a well-made spoon, or a staircase. Because poems are made of words, and because we seem to use words for their contents mostly, we tend to overlook the way in which some gatherings of words—poems especially—exist as objects, as handsome things to be fondled and appreciated. We overlook the object-side of poems also because poems usually *do* say things; it is confusing. But if we look at what the poem is saying, and then at what our reaction is, there is usually a disparity. If we are looking for a secret passage in an old house and we find that one wall appears to be five feet thick, we may get a trifle suspicious. If our pleasure in "Upon Julia's Clothes" is greater than we might be expected to receive from this ordinary message, then what we are liking is the poem as form/shape/object, the pleasure of the words in "That brave vibration, each way free."

The existence of the poem as object is most clear in poems that virtually have no message or story at all, like some poems which are pure nonsense (Lewis Carroll's "Jabberwocky," p. 245) or like surrealism. But all poems have this separate existence as formed things—separate from *any* content, obvious or covert—or they are not good poems. This object-side of poems helps explain why many poems, like Hardy's "During Wind and Rain," that are about depressing themes actually give us pleasure. The material may be dark, in a familiar way—we all know that we will die—but the shape that the words make is a pleasure to us in itself. A poem about a pretty woman, or a poem about growing old and dying—both are also "about" the pleasures of words in motion.

A poem by a contemporary American poet, Louis Simpson (1923–   ), called "Early in the Morning," illustrates this sort of doubleness.

Early in the morning
The dark Queen said,
"The trumpets are warning
There's trouble ahead."
Spent with carousing,
With wine-soaked wits,
Antony drowsing
Whispered, "It's
Too cold a morning
To get out of bed."

The army's retreating,
The fleet has fled,
Caesar is beating
His drums through the dead.
"Antony, horses!
We'll get away,
Gather our forces
For another day . . ."

"It's a cold morning,"
Antony said.

Caesar Augustus
Cleared his phlegm.
"Corpses disgust us.
Cover them."
Caesar Augustus
In his time lay
Dying, and just as
Cold as they,
On the cold morning
Of a cold day.

This poem is about Antony and Cleopatra and about how everybody has to die sooner or later. But also, I think it is about the dance of its own syllables. It is about how a line of two stresses manages to sound natural even though the poet rhymes all the lines. It is about rhyming "carousing" with "drowsing," "wits" with "It's," and "Augustus/disgust us/just as." It is about its own rhythm, the way it uses the delicate pauses at the ends of short lines—I love the slight hesitation after "It's" in the first stanza—and it is a gloomy poem which gives pleasures to anyone who reads it. The pleasing-object side of the poem comes through louder and clearer than its overt message.

So here are four representatives of the variety of poetry—two old, two new, two apparently complex, two apparently simple, all carrying feeling, in different degrees, and even ideas—and all with a poetic shape which has its own existence and its own justification.

3

IMAGE AND METAPHOR

·

The best thing to do, if we want to find pleasure in poetry, is to concentrate on whole poems. But there comes a time when we must detach ourselves for a while from whole poems, and concentrate on the material of the medium of poetry: images and metaphors on the one hand, and sounds on the other. These qualities are like canvas and pigment in painting.

An image is a piece of sense—any of the senses. "Brown cow" is an image. So is "while pet fowl come to the knee." These are visual images. We use the same visual word—"image"—to describe phrases that appeal to other senses. Visual images dominate poetry, but there are images of touch (cool, smooth; grasp, caress); of smell, of taste and of hearing. An image of hearing ("a late lark twitters") is not to be confused with the sound the poem makes, though it may be combined with it. "Liquefaction" is a visual image, but it is also audibly descriptive.

Then there is metaphor, which often makes an image too. In the line, "With the candles mooning each face . . . ," faces are not moons, but they are compared to moons, in the logical and astronomical way that I explained. In the process of the comparison, the poet makes a precise picture. He could have made the comparison explicit if he had wanted to—"with candles like suns, making the faces like moons"—and the image would not have changed. I think that the distinction between simile (when we say "like" or "as") and metaphor (when we do not) is trivial; but generally I think a metaphor is more intense and direct; a simile seems more of a literary performance, as if it called attention to its own wit.

A great deal of our casual language is metaphorical, though we are not aware of it. We speak in dead metaphors, old comparisons from which familiarity has drained the reality and the literalness.

If I say, "I was anchored to the spot," the cliché simply communicates that I felt unable to move. When the inventor first spoke the phrase, it was colorful; he said that he was a ship, that the floor (or wherever he stood immobile) was the sea, and that he felt as if he had dropped a great iron chain to the sea floor, dragging an anchor to a spot where it caught and fixed him. But when *I* say it now, I am using a once-colorful word that has diminished into the black and white of abstraction. I am not using the potential of the language. I am speaking inefficiently.

In the last paragraph I attempted to resuscitate a dead metaphor, to move a spectrum into "color" by saying "black and white." I don't know whether I succeeded in raising the dead, but it has been done. The novelist Peter de Vries likes to invent witty sentences in which characters inadvertently revive dead metaphors: "Penicillin is a drug on the market"; "Top soil is dirt cheap in Connecticut."

The new metaphor is a miracle, like the creation of life. Robert Frost used to say that once a man had known the pleasure of making a metaphor, it unfitted him for all other work. He was making a conscious and funny excuse for being lazy, but he was also reporting the real pleasure of making something new. The pleasure the reader takes in discovering a metaphor that is new and exact—to take arms against a sea, to moon a face—is the receiving end of the poet's creative pleasure.

Images and metaphors are mixed together and in reading closely we do not make distinctions between them, any more than we paraphrase or intellectualize. But it is just as well to *know*, with one part of our minds, the various distinctions; such knowledge, buried in our heads until we are no longer conscious of it, helps us to read with greater pleasure. "Down their carved names the rain-drop. . . ." So far the line is all image—a direction, a headstone with letters incised, a raindrop—and then comes the word ". . . ploughs," which is image as metaphor. Gravestone becomes field, raindrop becomes steel-edge cutting dirt, and the *expressiveness* of the metaphor lies in the sense of extended time, of the centuries it would take for the raindrops to act on granite, the way ploughs act on fields.

Metaphors are typically expressive; so are images, when they are fantastic. "Black milk" is an image, not a metaphor, but it is an image of an unheard-of object. Granted that the phrase was used in the concentration camps in reality, it affects the reader not as a reminiscence of the actual, but as a new combination of the adjective "black," which he knows from a thousand contexts and of the noun "milk," which he has known from the time he began to talk. The combination makes a new object, not a metaphor because nothing is being compared to anything else, but a phrase which contains and transmits feeling through the fantastic, or through the dream world to which we all have access. This new creation becomes a genuine image in the floating self of the reader, and it embodies horror. "Ploughs" involves fantasy too. The sense of time suddenly lengthening out is a dreamlike experience. All expressiveness, whether through metaphor or image, involves fantasy, involves reaching past the boundaries of the ordinary (the ego, the rational mind) into the state of dream, or what psychologists call primary process thinking. Expressiveness comes about through magic—transformations, metamorphoses, time-and space-shifts.

Anyone can invent fantastic images mechanically, simply by combining words that do not ordinarily go together. The lawn mower paints telegrams for supper. It can be fun to do—and may be good exercise for brains bored by ordinary chores—but the images will not be genuinely expressive of feeling unless they come from some dreaming place inside the self, and are more than mechanical.

Other poems in the first two chapters, besides the two I have been quoting, abound in examples of images and metaphors. The sense we receive of animals in Wyatt's first stanza—from "tame" and "wild" and "take bread at my hand"—is metaphorical, and I mentioned how the comparison of women to deer was expressive of an historical attitude toward women. I do not have to repeat or explain the images of touch in the second stanza. Herrick's poem is visual in its imagery, and in the first stanza makes an extended metaphor of silk as liquid. Louis Simpson's "cold morning/Of a cold day" is an image of touch which is expressive of desolation and death.

Talking about images and metaphors, one is of course not talking about whole poems. To end the chapter, I propose to use two handsome sonnets by Shakespeare as vehicles for talking about metaphor and image. Shakespeare's greatness lies in the incredible fertility of his mind in inventing new metaphors. If I open a page of the plays at random, I find enough inventive metaphor in the speeches of a few characters to keep a lesser poet busy for a lifetime. Shakespeare seems to have had the looseness of mind to set down a stream of expressive metaphors at will, developing character, furthering plot, and all the time giving us the liberating pleasure of the created metaphor. When he wrote the sonnets in particular, he set the metaphors down in an orderly fashion. For example:

When to the sessions of sweet silent thought
I summon up remembrance of things past,
I sigh the lack of many a thing I sought,
And with old woes new wail my dear time's waste:
Then can I drown an eye, unus'd to flow,
For precious friends hid in death's dateless night,
And weep afresh love's long since cancell'd woe,
And moan the expense of many a vanish'd sight:
Then can I grieve at grievances foregone,
And heavily from woe to woe tell o'er
The sad account of fore-bemoaned moan,
Which I new pay as if not paid before.
    But if the while I think on thee, dear friend,
    All losses are restor'd and sorrows end.

Of course Shakespeare is talking about memory. But—because I am discussing metaphor—the question is, in what *terms* is he talking about memory? In the first line, the word "sessions" has for us the general meaning of intervals of time; it can also have special associations, as in sessions of group therapy, and the sessions of a court: "The court is in session." All the possibilities of a word are ready to be realized by its context, providing we remain alert to its insides. The courtroom side of sessions is activated by the verb-phrase of the second line, "I summon up." We are well enough aware of the legal usage of "summons."

As we look through the poem as a whole, we see more legal words, and words relevant to financial matters. The metaphorical *area* of the poem is a court of law concerned with finances: "cancell'd," "expense," "grievances," "account," "pay" and "paid," and "losses." Memory is 'like' debt and guilt. (You have to pay your dues.) I used the phrase "metaphorical *area*." Sometimes a poet will use a metaphor just once, as Hardy does with his candles mooning faces, at other times a poet will connect two things extensively, as John Donne loved to do (see pp. 101–108) and as Wyatt does to a degree with his deer-women. But many times a poet will suggest a large—loose, but limited—area within which he will make his comparisons. Sometimes this metaphorical area will be as tight as Shakespeare's court/finances, and at other times as loose as up-and-down metaphors combined with natural-world metaphors, with nothing horizontal or indoors allowed—trees but not sofas.

Another of Shakespeare's sonnets is simpler in some ways and more complicated in others.

That time of year thou mayst in me behold
When yellow leaves, or none, or few, do hang
Upon those boughs which shake against the cold,
Bare ruin'ed choirs, where late the sweet birds sang:
In me thou seest the twilight of such day
As after sunset fadeth in the west;
Which by and by black night doth take away,
Death's second self, that seals up all in rest:
In me thou seest the glowing of such fire
That on the ashes of his youth doth lie,
As the death-bed whereon it must expire,
Consumed with that which it was nourish'd by.
    This thou perceiv'st which makes thy love more strong,
    To love that well which thou must leave ere long.

The subject is old age, and the three quatrains (four line stanzas; here rhymed ABAB) talk about the ends of things: the year, the day, and a fire. That part is simple. We even have contemporary cliches—"the autumn of his years," "the sunset of life," "he's all burned out"—to prove the naturalness and commoness of these metaphors. (No one has ever claimed that memory-as-a-debtors'-court was a common metaphor.) But Shakespeare does a variety of complicated things with these obvious metaphors.

First comes the autumnal image. Note the arrangement of the adjectives in the second line—"yellow" for autumn, "none" for the sudden glimpse into the future of total barrenness, "or few" to snatch us back to the shreds remaining of vitality. ". . . those boughs which shake against the cold" enforces the image of the tree as an old man shaking in a real cold, or in the throes of death. Of course the shaking of the tree, in a cool autumn wind, is what rips leaves from branches. Then Shakespeare does an extraordinary thing; having established one set of terms of comparison—"I am like a tree in autumn"—he then compares the comparison—the boughs of this tree are like empty, roofless, choirlofts.

To understand "Bare ruin'd choirs" we need a little history-as-vocabulary, or common sense and a dictionary. First, the choirs here are not groups of singers but the places where they sing, choir-lofts in churches. "Choirs" is an architectural term, then, and because they are *things* (carved of wood, generally), choirs are not so distinct from trees, in their metaphorical area, as we might at first think, if we conjured up an image of a group of robed singers.

The differences are huge: A choir loft is a man-made object, and religious, and a tree is neither. But similarities exist also. These choirs are bare—as the tree is, or will be, bare of leaves—and ruined, like the tree at winter and the man at death. Then we find that knowledge of English history comes in handy. In Shakespeare's landscape there were many bare, ruined churches and monasteries, without roofs and despoiled, opened to the cold wind and to the rain and snow of winter—bare of protection and ruined by weather. The Reformation, and gradual reforms before it, had taken much wealth from the church and had emptied many a religious house, which then fell into ruins.

". . . the sweet birds" are of course the real birds that sang in the tree until the cold forced them south; they are also the high-voiced choir boys who sang in the choirs that the tree is compared to; and then, since both the tree and (through it) the despoiled churches are compared to the man speaking, the "sweet birds" in terms of his life are the happy utterances or spontaneous flights of feeling which he associates with his youth. On the outer edges of implication, we may remember that one of the traditional symbols of a poem is song, and even birds' song; so we may wonder if the man is lamenting the loss of his poetic voice together with the loss of his hair and his vitality. Many a fine poem has been written about the poet's inability to write a poem.

The second quatrain is less complicated, though it makes a little leap that can remind us of the big leap, from tree to church, in the first quatrain. In the fifth line, we move from the large unit of the year to the small unit of the day, emphasizing that we are comparing the man not to the units themselves but to the stage at which each unit is described. Here we are at the sunset of the day, and night is like winter.

The little leap I referred to is the movement from "night" to "Death's second self"—four syllables with the same rhythm as "Bare ruin'd choirs"—which leaves the comparison behind, this time not to go to another physical realm for a further comparison, but to explain it abstractly with the noun "Death." There is a small comparison of night and death to people, because the word "self" is used, but it hardly surfaces as a metaphor. And then night and death are all included in the idea of "rest" or sleep.

Sleep—like the thoughts we may have of spring or dawn—can hold out hope. But the fire in the third stanza consumes itself entirely, and when it burns itself out, there is no hope for its revival. Ashes are youth; the glowing coals of age lie on the burned-out past, and youth is (paradoxically) compared to the deathbed of the aged. To live is, necessarily, to progress toward death. Without living there is no death. We burn ourselves up by being alive in the first place, "Consumed with that" life that we were nourished by. Life is hopeless, but there is a certain heroism and grandeur to it also. As often happens in Shakespeare's sonnets, the couplet which ends the sonnet is not the best part of the poem and bears little metaphorical relationship to the rest; but "leave" is mentioned, and might remind us of trees as well as of absence.

But what is the metaphorical relationship of the three quatrains, the three main metaphors? Obviously the most important thing is what we have been seeing all along: here are three *endings* of things. Then there is the difference—the two natural units, both of which could have implied rebirth or second life, and the man-made fire which is totally consumed. So there is a relationship between them in their identity, and then in their dissimilarity—which is like a giving and then a taking away of hope.

What else differentiates them and binds them? Always in talking about poetry we concern ourselves with the unity that holds things together and the diversity that distinguishes them. The combination of identity and dissimilarity is something we find beautiful. (We can see this effect clearly in meter, and in rhyme, of which there will be more in the next chapter.) One great diversity is size—from year to day to fire. Though we move from time to space, we are moving from the large to the small and to the smaller still. (A fire *can* be large, and *can* be kept alight for centuries; but in poetry, we are dealing with the probable rather than the possible.) A further—and more tenuous—unity is color. I think this is a small matter in this fine poem, but it is a subtle and usually overlooked bit of unity which is genuinely pleasing, whether we notice it consciously or not: yellow leaves, yellow sunset, yellow-gold embers.

4
THE NOISES POEMS MAKE

If poems happen in the mouth, we must learn to pay attention to the sounds that poems make; loud, soft, harsh, sweet, high, low, fast, slow. We must learn to notice how our tongues and lips play with the words of poems. Mostly I will talk about rhythm and meter, but also I want to pay attention to rhyme, and to free verse, and to particular ways of combining consonants and vowels.

We have to realize that the sound of a poem is never perceived by us *purely*—unless we are hearing a foreign language far removed from us, like Chinese—and that our minds cannot divest words entirely of their meanings, to hear the sound by itself. "The music of poetry," if it were just music, would be boring and monotonous. We continue to use that trite metaphor—"the music of poetry"—because we try to explain or express this simultaneous blending of different things, things as different as sound and meaning.

When we talk about the noises of poems, we are talking about at least two different *kinds* of thing. There is sound in motion, the movement of words down the page, slight hitches at the ends of lines, and perhaps a pleasing argument between arbitrary line structure and meaningful sentence structure. In some poems this kind of noise is almost all that we hear; in other poems, which are slow moving and have pauses at the ends of each line, we do not hear much sound-in-motion. This second sort of noise is almost (but I am being metaphorical) spatial rather than temporal. If draws attention to the rubbing together of adjacent sounds, frequently long vowels and consonants which our voices can hold—words like "warm" and "farm."

Most poems include examples of both sorts of noise, but I think it important to consider them as separate effects, though both are audible and both appeal to our ears, or probably more accurately to our mouths. John Milton was especially good at the first kind of sound, his blank verse (unrhymed iambic pentameter) line galloping and pausing down the page:

Of man's first disobedience, and the fruit
Of that forbidden tree, whose mortal taste
Brought death into the world, and all our woe,
With loss of Eden, till one greater Man
Restore us, and regain the blissful seat,
Sing, Heavenly Muse, that on the secret top
Of Oreb, or of Sinai, didst inspire
That shepherd . . .

For a momentary example of the slow, cadenced noise, we can recall the end of "During Wind and Rain," "Down their carved names the rain-drop ploughs." The percussiveness slows us down, and so does the structure of the consonants. To get from "carved" to "names," we have to travel across a "v" and a "d" and into an "n." The repetition of the same vowel sound in "names" and "rain" is a pleasure, and so is the repetition of "z" sounds at the end of "names" and "ploughs." Almost all the words, by the length of the vowel or the combination of vowels and consonants, take a long time to say. The line *has* rhythm (it is slow and percussive) and it has meter—iambic tetrameter—but it gives mouth-pleasure in its slow adjacent sounds rather than in any headlong rush.

Rhythm and meter are wholly different things—which is like saying that "the earth" and "carrots" are different things. Rhythm is a large, loose, and inclusive word. Rhythm is things like fast and slow, staccato and smooth. Free verse has rhythm, prose has rhythm, speech has rhythm. Any series of words, from a sonnet to a sentence spoken in anger, has a rhythm; whether it is pleasing or adequate is another matter. Meter, on the other hand, is a repeated number of something. The word "meter" comes from the Greek word for measure, and in different languages poetic meter measures and adds up different qualities of speech. Meter indicates a form of arithmetic; we add something, and we find the same number of it in another line. English syllables take different lengths of time to say—"it" is short; "warm" is long—and this fact is important to the noise of a poem and even to its rhythm; a line of long sounds is slower to say, and is therefore different in rhythm. But English *meter* (not rhythm) takes no account of the length of the syllable, with exceptions infrequent enough to be overlooked. In Greek poetry, on the other hand, the length of syllable was what counted, measured, added up, or "metered." The original Greek iambus, marked ∪—, was a short syllable followed by a long one. (The convention stated that there were two lengths of syllable, one half as long as the other; it would be impossible to defend such a proposition about English.) Greek iambic pentameter was ∪–∪–∪–∪–∪–.

Some other languages measure just the *number of syllables*, like French Alexandrines—twelve syllables with a pause in the middle. Other languages meter pitch, or volume. English measures mostly volume or loudness. Often the prominence is called accent, which may not be such a bad idea; some scholars seem to have shown that we occasionally give importance to a syllable by pitch or duration, and not just by loudness, so maybe "accent" is a better word than "loud" because it is less specific. But the names of English meter are frequently miscalled short and long, which is surely inaccurate.

English does *not* measure absolute loudness or accent, as if there were a special class of loud syllables and soft ones, like Greek with its long and short. A word like "softer" can be pronounced only with the first syllable louder than the second; that is true. And we distinguish between the two meanings of CONtent and conTENT by changing which ever syllable is the louder. (In fact the pitch also changes, and the accented syllable takes longer to say; so actually we are changing three things.) But with a monosyllable like "soft" or "I," there can be no absolute rule: the monosyllable can be softer or louder depending on its position in the line.

Soft*er*, loud*er*. That is the key. English meter, as defined by the usage of the poets, is a matter of *relative* accent. The English iambus, which we write ∪ / to distinguish it from the Greek, tells us only that the first syllable is softer than the second. They might be both loud or both soft. It does not matter, *metrically*. Of course everything matters rhythmically. What matters metrically, what is *measured*, is the pair of syllables of which one is at least a little louder than the other.

Of good English verse written in meter—that is, free verse and prose poems excluded—I suppose that more than 90 percent is iambic. More than half is iambic pentameter (iambus five-measure), including the blank verse of Shakespeare, Milton, Wordsworth, Tennyson, and Frost. Another large proportion is written in iambic tetrameter (four-measure), and a trifle in trimeter or other feet. (There is a list of these feet in a note at the end of this chapter.) Here, when I talk about meter, I will talk about iambic pentameter only, and anything I say about it can be applied, one way or another, to the study or analysis of other English meters.

The marking of a line of regular iambic pentameter is $\cup/\cup/\cup/$ $\cup/\cup/$. Most of the lines written by the great poets are regular. Visually, the diagram looks monotonous. When beaten like a drum on the edge of a chair—*duh*-DUM[5]—the rhythm is monotonous indeed. But the lines of the great poems are not monotonous. That is because these marks record the metrical unity of the poem (which is real; the DUMs are all relatively louder than the *duh*s) but do not represent the rhythmical variety. This contrast of rhythm and meter is a perfect example of beauty as unity in variety. The wittiest meter occurs when the lines are so natural and lackadaisical in tone and rhythm that they do not seem to be regular—but they are. Here is a passage from "The Gift Outright," the poem Robert Frost read at the inauguration of President Kennedy. The first line is so regular it is almost monotonous. Then the meter becomes witty, but it always scans:

The land was ours before we were the land's.
She was our land more than a hundred years
Before we were her people. She was ours
In Massachusetts, in Virginia,
But we were England's, still colonials, . . .

The meter is always the unity, and the rhythm is the variety. Lines vastly different in their rhythmical structure, in the noise they actually make, scan exactly the same way, have the same meter. But we cannot preceive the similarity between these two vastly different lines unless we are able to perceive meter. And that is why it is worth our time to talk about English meter.

Every now and then a poem contains a line which is actually monotonous—all the even syllables are about equally accented and all the odd syllables are about equally unaccented—and a poet can put such a line in his poem every now and then without trouble. "I saw a man who sat and sketched a hill." But if he did it several times in a row we would fall asleep. He must keep to the meter, and he must provide variety, which almost goes without saying, but he provides it within the boundary of meter. One of the strongest conventions of art is that if the artist starts with a condition he abides by it; free verse is fine, and has its own strange consistency, but that is another matter.

The poet provides variety within meter by using the relativity of stress. In most lines of iambic pentameter, there are only three or four really loud noises. Another one or two are loud only relative to the neighbor in the same foot. When I began teaching I noticed that my university was a perfect iambic pentameter line: "The University of Michigan"—ten syllables, in the precise order necessary. The last syllable, "-gan" is soft, but it is louder than the miniscule "-i-" which comes before it. The fact that "-gan" is softer by far than "Mich-" is wholly irrelevant to the meter. *Rhythmically* the fact that the line has only two really loud noises is of course to the point; it is the special thing about the line. *Metrically* the line is a regular $\cup/\cup/\cup/\cup/\cup/$. For rhythm—if for a moment we violate English metrical signs and make $/$ mean loud and $\cup$ mean not-loud—"The University of Michigan" could be scored $\cup\cup\cup/\cup\cup\cup/\cup\cup$. The second marking (which some people confuse with meter) is the sort of advice on pronunciation which a director might give an actor: "Hit that word. Throw away the rest of the line." It is like underlining, and indicates emphasis, and therefore it is a part of rhythm. It has nothing to do with meter.

Though meter exists independent of emphasis (emphasis is a matter of meaning, and meaning is not *measured;* relative volume is measured), it can *contribute* to emphasis. Meter cannot change the pronunciation of words; no way of arranging the line could get us to say mich-EYE-gn. But if the poet is clever, he can occasionally (only occasionally) use meter to reinforce an emphasis that is already implicit, or at least potential, in his words. A typical line of iambic pentameter, with three loud noises, is Macbeth's line, "Tomorrow and tomorrow and tomorrow," which scans $\cup/\cup/\cup/\cup/\cup/\cup$. (Do not worry about the final unaccented syllable. It is called a feminine ending, and by the agreement of poets it is not irregular; the extra soft sound dangles into the pause at the end of a line, hardly noticeable as extra.) The "and"s are not very loud, but they are a bit louder than the "-ow"s of the "tomorrow"s, so they receive relative stress. In order to hear the line as iambic pentameter, one has to pronounce the "and"s fairly distinctly. By no means are they *equally* as loud as the "mor"s of "tomorrow" but they are not slurred over, either; in normally slovenly speech we might say "Tomorrow'n tomorrow'n tomorrow." But the *meter* leads us to modify in a particular way the pronunciation and therefore the emphasis of the line, and to say the "and"s distinctly, and thus to add to the sense—the interminable empty repetitiousness of human life—that the line contains. Sound and meaning walk hand in hand.

But they walk hand in hand only for a reader who hears the poem metrically. We do not have to count on our fingers to tell if a poem is metered. We hear it as if by instinct. Something inside us, that we are not aware of, is doing the counting. And if the poet makes a mistake, as beginners will, and we find a line with one foot too many or one foot too few, we nearly break a leg; it is like going down a staircase in the dark and finding one step more or less than we had expected.

Here is another example of the way in which meter *occasionally* lends a hand to meaning. In "To Autumn," Keats writes:

> . . . to set budding more
> And still more later flowers for the bees. . . .

Counting "flowers" as two syllables (which Keats does here; usually poets count it as one) the second line has ten syllables and is iambic pentameter. Actually, we cannot tell if a poem is in iambic pentameter just by looking at one line of it, because the meter is only what all the lines have in common. If all Keats's lines had ten syllables but did not occur in a softer-louder iambic foot pattern, the meter (measure) would be simply that each line had ten syllables.

Look at the first four syllables of the second line, "And still more late- . . ."; obviously syllables two, three and four could each be loud, but not all at once, in a line of iambics. We could either say MORE, / And still MORE later flowers . . ." or we could say "MORE / And STILL more LATEr FLOWers." But in the first alternative, we cannot come up with five feet. And if we do not come up with five feet we lie sprawled on the cement floor of the cellar. So that convention of meter gives us a musical (or directorial) notation here, saying, "Pronounce 'STILL' and 'LATE-' louder than the second 'more,' please." The difference in emphasis, I suppose, is a tiny difference in meaning, though I would not know how to describe the difference.

In this example, we came upon another way of adding rhythmical variety within metrical sameness. Before, I described how we could have feet in which both syllables were quite soft, but one was relatively louder, so that we came up with lines like, "The University of Michigan" or "Tomorrow and tomorrow and tomorrow." The converse is true: We can have an iambic foot in which both syllables are loud, but one is relatively louder than the other, like "more LATE-" or, in the line before, "set BUD-".

Milton wrote nearly a whole line of loud syllables: "Rocks, caves, lakes, fens, bogs, dens, and shades of death." We could pronounce this line in a variety of ways. Other metrical contexts could provide different things to count. We could count the number of syllables, or the number of loud noises, and call the measure syllabic or accentual, ten-syllable or eight-accent. Or we could pronounce it: "rocks, caves, LAKES, fens, bogs, DENS, and SHADES of DEATH." This kind of grouping makes as much emphatic sense as any other. But if we read it with the first three syllables, and then the next three, united with a single terminal stress on the third and sixth syllable, we have a line which is divided into four feet rather than five: ∪∪/∪∪/∪/∪/. There we are again, sprawling on the floor.

Here, emphasis does not help us scan (scansion is what we do when we mark the meter of a line), but scanning enforces emphasis, or at least grouping. When we read this line, we have already read 1418 lines of Milton's iambic pentameter. The one *unity* linking all these lines in our ears is that all of them can be said with a five-spaced rise and fall of accent. Therefore, our ears or our mouths, automatically, without thinking and without counting, sort the line according to twos; the first six syllables are all noisy. But we keep time, and we read them giving a little more noise to the second, the fourth, and the sixth: "Rocks, CAVES, lakes, FENS, bogs, DENS, and SHADES of DEATH." A perfectly permissible and metrical reading would raise the volume on *each* of the first six syllables, so that the second was louder than the first, the fourth louder than the third, and the sixth louder than the fifth. It would still be marked ∪/∪/∪/∪/∪/, relatively. The particular way in which we achieve the relative loudness is not important; what is important is that we count by twos. Otherwise we miss the unity of finding five of something.

Only five lines away from this line in *Paradise Lost* is the line: "Abominable, inutterable, and worse." Milton pronounced "abominable" "abom'nable," and "inutterable" "inutt'rable," so the line scans regularly, just like "Rocks, caves, lakes, fens, bogs, dens, and shades of death." The metrical wit of John Milton lies in the identity and the diversity of these two lines. The mystery of how the iambic pentameter remains ∪/∪/∪/∪/∪/ but is not monotonous is, therefore, no mystery. When two lines as different as those I have quoted are both marked ∪/∪/∪/∪/∪/, there can be no monotony. Many readers of poetry, who understand the ideas and who respond to the images, miss the pleasure of this paradoxical unity in diversity. Missing a pleasure is at least a minor disaster, which is why I spend so much time talking about meter. Any reader sees the rhythmical differences between the two lines, or sees some of them; but anyone who cannot feel the metrical identity cannot sense the ghostly framework from which the diverse rhythms depart.

Every line I have mentioned so far is regular and involves no departure from the metrical norm. A number of departures from the norm are so common that they are really—in the minds of poets and sophisticated readers—not departures at all. There can be an extra syllable in a foot, usually if it is quick to say, and usually if there are not too many of them. (But a poem sets up its own little world, with its own laws and conventions. A given poem might use a good many extra syllables.) A line like E. A. Robinson's "For no man else in Tilbury Town to hear," reads ∪/∪/ ∪/∪ ∪/∪/. (The second, third, and fourth syllables are all quite accented—but relative stress sorts them into iambics.) The fourth foot, ". . . -bury Town . . .," if we pronounce the town "TIL-bur-y" —and not "TIL-b'ry" the way some New Englanders would—has a tiny extra syllable in it. No matter—it is easy to say. It is a common metrical variation, which makes us take a little rhythmic quick step in saying the line.

Syllables are omitted far less frequently. When a syllable is missing, it is usually the first unaccented syllable in the line. Some people call this a headless line; an example would be: "University of Michigan." We seem to be able to endure the missing syllable more easily when it happens during the slight pause that exists between lines:

The student sat at his small desk and wrote,
"University of Michigan"
Across the spine of every book he owned. . . .

This headless line is easier to take than a line which has a syllable omitted in the middle, like:

I saw "University of Maine"

When an omitted syllable in the middle of the line sounds acceptable to us, we usually find that it comes after a pause—and thus is like the headless line, with the omitted syllable taking place in the pause itself:

I paused. "University of Maine,"
The road sign said. . . .

But it seldom happens, as a matter of fact.

   The most common variation from ∪/∪/∪/∪/∪/ is the reversal of the order of louder and softer syllables in one foot of the line, often in the first foot:

   ∪ / ∪   /   / ∪ ∪ /   ∪   /
Old Eben Flood, climbing alone one night

/ ∪ ∪ / ∪ /   ∪ /   ∪ /
Over the hill between the town below. . . .

In the second line, the first four syllables form a familiar configuration. There is no doubt about the pronunciation of the first word. No one could say "oVER"; the word is not in our language. Therefore the first foot is inverted and the second foot rights itself, like a child's toy which, when we knock it over, balances itself upright again. This pattern, /∪∪/, has a little dance step to it which is one of the familiar variations in the regular order of the pentameter. We get used to it, as we might to the dancing habits of a partner who liked to do a particular twirl every now and then, not at regular intervals, but in time with the music. Every now and then, the poem goes: DUM *duh duh* DUM. Usually those two *duhs* are quite quick to say, also. Usually, this rhythm occurs at the beginning of the line; but when it does not, as with omitted syllables, it usually occurs after a pause. For example, in the first of the two lines just quoted, Robinson inverts the order of louder and softer in the word "climbing," so that "climbing alone," /∪∪/, is another example of that particular rhythmic figure which is the noise of metrical inversion.

   That is really all we need to know; we pick up the refinements as we read more poems. Now might be a good time to mark the whole of "Mister Flood's Party" (page 252). (I print my marking of this poem in a note at the end of this chapter, but it would be best not to look at it until you have made your own decisions.) Sometimes one reading of a phrase seems almost as good as another, so two readings are given. But usually, if we can pronounce either the odd syllable or the even syllable louder than the other, the expectation—which would be the even syllable—wins out. It *is* important, to preserve the penta-part of the pentameter, that we chose one syllable or the other. For centuries, people have talked about feet like ∪∪ and // in English, but they are really bad ideas for the analysis of meter. They name, approximately, something true for rhythm—two rather soft syllables often precede two rather loud syllables, for instance—but they confuse rhythm and meter. In Andrew Marvell's famous couplet,

Annihilating all that's made
To a green thought in a green shade. . . .

the marks are regular (tetrameter) in the first line ∪/∪/∪/∪/, and there are two inversions in the second line, but in the second line there are still four groups of syllables arranged relatively as feet /∪∪//∪∪/. No one could deny that "green" is louder than "To"; but the difference is metrically irrelevant. What is metrically relevant is that each group of two syllables contains one syllable that is louder than the other.

Rhyme is a less frequent, and less important, feature of poetry, but it is common enough to bear looking at. A satisfying rhyme fulfills the same formula which makes for satisfying meter—the paradox of unity within variety. With rhyme, the unity is the similarity of sounds, and the variety is the difference between words. Cliché rhymes in English are combinations like fire/desire womb/tomb, and breath/death. These rhymes are clichés not just because poets have used them so frequently, but because something in the nature of each pair of words suggests the other, either because of similarity (fire/desire) or because of opposition, which is another kind of similarity (breath/death, womb/tomb).

Conversely, the most witty and effective rhyme brings words together which we would not expect to fit together. In the first place, these words do not remind the reader of each other, and therefore the rhyme word (which, in practice, leads us to think of the other one of the pair) usually comes as a surprise. But there are more ways to contrast words than merely to contrast meaning. We can contrast words grammatically, by rhyming a noun with a preposition (store/for) or, more commonly, by rhyming a noun or an adjective with a verb (struck/truck). Or we can contrast parts of speech, together with spelling and number of syllables in a word (almanac/black). Or we can do all these things, and we can also contrast different types of words, or the kind of language the words come from (paradox/locks) or, for that matter, "wits/It's", or "Augustus/disgust us/just as."

Except in a poem which consistently tries to be witty, all rhymes will rarely be as varied as my examples. Some of them will be, but if all of them are, the rhyme begins to draw attention to itself, which in many poems would be a detriment. There is a middle ground between the outlandish rhyme—like Ogden Nash's "Boomerang/kangeroo-meringue"—and the cliché rhyme of "June/moon." If we look back at the Hardy poem, we see that most of the rhymes are what we might call neutral; we hear them, they please us, but they do not point to themselves and say: "Look, I'm a nifty rhyme."

A lot of the best poetry, especially modern poetry, is not written in meter at all. Meter is what free verse is free of. Each free verse poem is a new invention, an improvised form. Yet a poet feels as much resolution and exactness—Yeats's click of the box—in a free verse poem as he does in a perfect sonnet, and the sophisticated reader feels it too. Robert Frost, who always wrote in meter, and who felt a professional enmity to free verse, used to say that he would as soon write free verse as he would play tennis without a net. It is a good debater's point, but a bad analogy. When you write free verse, you make up a new net every time you hit the tennis ball.

Of all the people who have tried, no one has so far been able to demonstrate a theory of free verse which explains how it arrives at this sense of exactness and finish. Free verse is a negative description of a form. If we say that a poem is written in free verse, all we are saying is that it is not unified by any sort of measure, any numerical count. It may be the long rhetoric of Walt Whitman, or the more measured, shorter lines of T. S. Eliot, or the very short, enjambed lines of William Carlos Williams. (Enjambment is the technical term for the movement of the sense of a sentence over the break between lines, as in my example from the beginning of Milton's *Paradise Lost*.) To begin with, it may be worth while to make some broad distinctions of types of free verse. Here is some Whitman, for instance:

Coffin that passes through lanes and streets,
Through day and night with the great cloud darkening
    the land,
With the pomp of the inloop'd flags with the cities
    draped in black,
With the show of the States themselves as of
    crape-veil'd women standing,
With processions long and winding and the flambeaus of
    the night,

With the countless torches lit, with the silent sea of
    faces and the unbared heads,
With the waiting depot, the arriving coffin, and the
    somber faces,
With dirges through the night, with the thousand voices
    rising strong and solemn,
With all the mournful voices of the dirges pour'd
    around the coffin,
The dim-lit churches and the shuddering organs—where
    amid these you journey.
With the tolling tolling bells' perpetual clang,
Here, coffin that slowly passes,
I give you my sprig of lilac.

Here the closest familiar form (when we are in strange country
we look for recognizable forms: there is a church, that looks like
a store) is prose, only prose which has a lot of rhythmical orga-
nization, like the prose of the King James version of the Bible or
the prose of political oratory. To say that a poem's rhythmic struc-
ture is close to prose is not to rate it low as poetry—Whitman is
one of the great poets of our language. It is only to say which old
form lies behind this new form. The lines are end-stopped, and
some of them are even small paragraphs. Often grammatical or
rhetorical repetition reinforces the rhythm. But these few charac-
teristics only begin to describe it.

Other forms of free verse have different old forms lurking behind
them. T. S. Eliot first described this phenomenon when he said
that late Jacobean blank verse was behind his free verse, which
usually had three stresses a line (the approximate number of
genuinely loud noises we expect in old blank verse) and which
ran from eight to thirteen syllables. Eliot's free verse *looks* like
blank verse, but it is not, quite; the only thing missing is the
metrical structure of five feet. Here is a patch of *The Waste Land*,
in which the lines tend toward four stresses, though the syllables
do vary from eight to thirteen:

At the violet hour, when the eyes and back
Turn upward from the desk, when the human engine waits
Like a taxi throbbing waiting,
I, Tiresias, though blind, throbbing between two lives,
Old man with wrinkled female breasts, can see
At the violet hour. . . .

Another sort of free verse is the kind we see the most of, and
to many readers it seems to be the typical form of free verse—

short-lined, fast-moving, with a lot of percussion and therefore many monosyllables, and with considerable enjambment. William Carlos Williams (see page 261) is one of the masters, and even inventors, of this sort of free verse. Often this rhythmical structure goes together with a pure and simple diction, like this poem by Williams:

This Is Just To Say

I have eaten
the plums
that were in
the icebox

and which
you were probably
saving
for breakfast

Forgive me
they were delicious
so sweet
and so cold

One feels certain—but one will never know—that Williams really did leave this note for his wife. But the skill that shaped the poem is not so easy as it looks. Let me take another poem in reverse, starting with a prose sentence and arriving at the real line-structure only at the end. First, suppose we came across this sentence: "So much depends upon a red wheelbarrow, glazed with rain water, beside the white chickens." I do not think we would pay much attention to it. There are things to notice in it, but nothing about the sentence especially draws our interest. Suppose that we then space it into lines, first by the most obvious pattern of its clauses:

So much depends upon
a red wheelbarrow
glazed with rain water
beside the white chickens.

Now the sentence becomes at least a little more interesting. We have a first line which is a sort of indicator, asking us to pay attention to what follows; it almost might have a colon at the end of it. Then we have three particularities, or small collections of particularities, each ending with a noun. We learn the color of an object in one line, the particular sheen of this color and how it gets that way in another line, and its position next to other objects in the final line. The fact that each of the last three lines ends with a noun draws attention to the "thinginess" of our perceptions. Of course the emotion of the poem comes partly from the claim on our attention which in the first line makes. But our willingness to grant emotion to these lines also depends upon the sound of the lines. By making mandatory pauses—by using lines instead of paragraph form—the poet slows down the order of our perceptions. (If a reader hears no difference between this version and the prose version, he is reading too fast and paying no attention to line-structure.) We see the nouns as nouns, and their thinginess is emphasized because they dangle out into space on the right-hand side of the page, into the white space of the page which is the blank time-pause in our reading or hearing.

But this is how William Carlos Williams actually spaced the poem:

so much depends
upon

a red wheel
barrow

glazed with rain
water

beside the white
chickens

Now a lot is happening, and all because of line structure—a visual device which indicates a way to speak or to hear the poem. Therefore, the poem becomes a pleasure to the mouth. In the first phrase, there is a kind of etymological wit. Etymology is the study of the origins of words, and poets, with their sensitivity to the insides of words, frequently play with the history of a word. The word "depends" is from the Latin "de-pendo," or "hang from." Here the "upon," isolated as a single word in the second line underneath the longer first line, hangs from the word "depend." The visual and audible arrangement plays with the etymology, and also makes us see the usually compound phrase "depends upon" as composed of two different words. In saying it, we normally drop our voice with "upon." Here the word "depends" stays high in pitch because we need to emphasize it in order to indicate the end of the line. This increases the emphatic or emotional meaning of the phrase from which, in a real sense, the rest of the poem "depends."

The second pair of lines visually (and therefore audibly) resembles the first, and then we notice that so do the final two groups of lines. Williams has improvised a highly symmetrical form. It is free verse because it is a one-time-only experiment. It is unfree in the sense that it imitates itself. The "meter" of this poem can be described, short as it is: There are eight lines separated into four groups of two; the first lines of each of the four groups (or stanzas) contain three words, each followed by a one-word line; the three-word line has either three or four syllables, and the one-word line has two syllables invariably. With some room for argument, one could assert that the first lines each have two loud noises, and the second lines each have one.

Also, the second lines of each stanza have, in the last three instances, a downward motion of stress and unstress. The first instance, "upon," which is unique in being a preposition and not a noun, has an upward motion as it focuses our attention on the thinginess of the poem. The other words have a downward motion, and come to rest in nouns.

In the second stanza, there is another example of etymological wit, which leads toward the intellectual point of the poem. The familiar compound word "wheelbarrow" is broken up into the two words from which it was made. We get two nouns in place of one. "Wheel," at the end of a line, gets considerable emphasis; but "barrow," in a line all by itself, gets even more. The word "red," virtually beginning the line, also gets considerable emphasis. By the economy of these short lines, and especially by splitting the compound noun into its components, Williams focuses concentrated attention on the minute particularity of the scene, exemplifying what he had before asserted—that "So much depends/upon" it.

The third stanza does something similar. We are used to "rain water" as a near-compound, or even as a real one. By splitting the two words over the line break, Williams again draws our attention to the two separate nouns. Rain becomes more rain, because we pause after it; it is not merely an attribute of water, it is rain itself. But also, and perhaps ultimately more important to the emotion of the poem, the separation of "rain" and "water" emphasizes the assonance.

Assonance is the repetition of vowel sounds, which is especially noticeable when the vowel sounds are long, like the "a" of "glazed" and the "a" of "rain." Because of the prominence granted by line structure, we tend here to dwell upon them, to *hold* them, especially when we come to the second. Assonance together with the line break changes the reading, the noise we make, from my prose version, and even from my four-line version. It slows it down further, it brings it more sensually into our mouths, and it adds a mysterious quality of attention to these visual details. The poem has moved into the mouth, and it has done it mostly by the arrangement of the lines.

The same effect continues in the final stanza, where the long "i"s of "beside" and "white" give us more assonance. In the first two stanzas, Williams uses etymological wit; the third stanza continues the split of the compound, but moves into the area of assonance; the third no longer splits compounds, but continues in assonance, and of course draws attention to the whiteness of the chickens by isolating the word "white" at the end of a line. In the progress from the prose version to this final poetic version, Williams has changed what seemed to be a silly statement into a moving insistence on the beauty and actual existence of the external world.

The assonance, after the wit of etymology, seems to introduce and sustain a deeper and more emotional tone. Both assonance and etymology, as they are embodied, make pictures of the wheelbarrow more vivid, but I believe that the poem seems to move inside when the vowels start coming together in our mouths. In free verse the coincidence of assonance and percussion is often an emotional thing. Of course regular verse has as much assonance as free verse. With less percussion, assonance is sometimes less noticeable. Sometimes poets have used it in an interlocking fashion. Take this line from a sonnet by Robert Lowell, an American contemporary (see page 299):

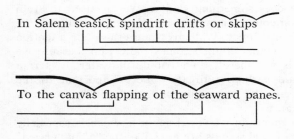

There is a lot of alliteration, with all the "s"s, which I show above the line. (Alliteration is the repetition of consonant sounds.) The extraordinary thing is the interlocking assonance. Lowell did not invent this way of writing. All the best poets move into it, especially at their most heightened moments. John Keats, for instance, makes some of the most satisfying noises—or most mouth-pleasing sounds—of any poet in our language. When we are able to identify meter, and when we become sensitive to nuances of rhythm and the repetition of sounds in words, we can be wholly responsive to a dimension of the art of poetry which passes most people by. A good exercise at this time might be an analysis of the last stanza of Keats's *To Autumn*:

Where are the songs of Spring? Ay, where are they?
   Think not of them, thou has thy music too,—
While barrèd clouds bloom the soft-dying day,
   And touch the stubble-plains with rosy hue;
Then in a wailful choir, the small gnats mourn
     Among the river sallows, borne aloft
      Or sinking as the light wind lives or dies;
And full-grown lambs loud bleat from hilly bourn;
    Hedge-crickets sing; and now with treble soft
    The redbreast whistles from a garden-croft,
     And gathering swallows twitter in the skies.

So many aspects of the sound of poetry—the noises a poem makes —are present in these lines: meter, rhyme, rhythm, assonance, alliteration, and all the other things which we have to make up names for, because the critics have not been able to make up the names themselves.

TERMS

Feet:

Iambic: a softer syllable followed by a louder: desPAIR

Trochaic: a louder syllable followed by a softer: HAPPy

Dactylic: a louder syllable followed by two softer ones: CHANGE-able

Anapestic: two softer syllables followed by a louder one: in the HOUSE

Pyrric and Spondaic: These are terms prominently used in classical meter, which really do not apply in English. When used, pyrric means two soft sounds in a row and spondaic, or a spondee, two loud syllables in a row. In English, these effects are rhythmic and not metrical.

Length of line:
Monometer: one foot
Dimeter: two feet
Trimeter: three feet
Tetrameter: four feet
Pentameter: five feet
Hexameter (or the Alexandrine): six feet

Meter of "Mr. Flood's Party" (page 252)

1.
```
U/U//UU/U/
/UU/U/U/U/
/UU/U/U/U/
U/U/U/U/U/
U/U/U/U/U/
U/U/U/U/U/
U/U/U/U/U/
U/U/U/UU/U/
```

2.
```
       (U/)
/UU/U/U/U/
U/U/U/U/U/
U/U/U/U/U/
U/U/U/U/U/
       (U/)
/UU/U/U/U/
U/U/U/U/U/
       (U/)
U/U/U//UU/
U/U/U/U/U/
```

3.
```
U/U/U/U/U/
U/U/U/U/U/
       (/U)
U/U/U/U/U/
U/U//UU/U/
U/U/U/U/U/
U/U/U/U/U/
U/U/U/U/U/
```

4.
```
/UU/U/U/U/
U/U//UU/U/
U/U/U/U/U/
U/U//UU/U/
U/U/U/U/U/
U/U/U/U/U/
U/U/U/U/U/
U/U/U/U/U/
```

5.
```
       (U/)
/UU/U/U/U/
/UU/U/UU/U/
U/U/U/U/U/
U/U/U/U/U/
U/UU/U/U/U/
       (/U)
U/U/U/U/U/
U/U/U/U/U/
       (U/)
/UU/U/U/U/
```

6.
```
/UU/U/U/U/
U/U/U/U/U/
/UU/U/U/U/
U/U/U/U/U/
U/U/U/U/U/
U/U/U/U/U/
U/U/U/U/U/
U/U/U/UU/U/
```

7.

```
U/U/U/U/U/
U/U/U/U/U/
U/U/U/U/U/
U/U/U/U/U/
U/U/U/U/U/
U/U/U/U/U/
U/U/U/U/U/
U/U/U/U/U/
```

5
THE ICEBERG
OF POETIC INTENT

The title of this chapter comes from a student who let me read his notebook, in which he referred to the fact that the greatest part of an iceberg is reputed to hide under water. Much of a poet's intention, I believe, is usually hidden. It is hidden not only from the reader, but from the poet as well. This generalization may be easier to accept if we realize that a poem is not, commonly, a mechanically realized object of a conscious purpose. At least, there are large portions of poems which exist outside intentions, the way a man saying one thing may communicate something else— perhaps the opposite, perhaps a reservation—by his facial expression or his gesture.

Such a realization dispels a false but prevalent idea—that there is a real, single "meaning" to a poem, the discovery of which is our object in reading. If we ask someone to define what this "meaning" is, chances are that his reply will be some variation of a phrase like "what the poet was trying to say," or "what he had in mind before he wrote the poem," or simply "the poet's intention."

This idea is psychologically naive. If someone interprets his own dream for us, we do not necessarily believe him. It may occur to us that he might have good reasons for misinterpreting his own dream. A poet usually is aware that he is not in total control of his poem—not in total *conscious* control, that is; some less lighted part of his mind may be controlling the poem firmly. Today's general acceptance of the idea of the unconscious mind has encouraged many poets to feel that the dark parts of their mind write the best poetry, and so they try to do away with light by automatic writing and other methods of suppressing rational thought.

But even poets who are dedicated to presenting a reasonable surface realize that other things are happening inside their poems. Even after he had written his "Four Quartets," with all their religious content, T. S. Eliot said that in poetry all content was only ostensible content; that if the poem had a real life, probably something was going on of which the poet was unaware. So the idea that conscious intentions create the "meaning" of a poem is merely silly. Our knowledge is restricted to the words on the page and history-as-vocabulary. If the same day he wrote a poem, the poet himself swore out an affidavit headed "This is what I was trying to say," I would immediately disbelieve him. I would think, "Who is *he* to tell *me?* He must be trying to cover something up. I will take a closer look at his poem."

The reasons for the secret life in poems do not lie in the art of poetry but in human life itself. We are all complicated and our feelings are many sided—so many sided that we cannot identify, or know consciously, all sides. The same ambiguity that inhabits an honest poem (a dishonest poem is frequently one which a frightened man has overcontrolled into single-mindedness) inhabits our daily lives and shows up in our dreams, our verbal slips, our changes of mind and heart, and our sense that our lives are not clear and singly directed, but are rather a shifting combination of opposing forces. No one is *wholly* aware of the motives behind any serious action, any more than a poet is wholly aware of what makes his poem.

I would like to draw on my own experience for illustration. When I was twenty-five or twenty-six, I wrote a poem called "The Sleeping Giant," which is the name of a hill in Hamden, Connecticut, where I grew up. From certain angles the hill *does* look like a sleeping giant—head, neck, chest, waist, the legs trailing off. One day I happened to think of the Sleeping Giant and either remembered or invented the thought that a small child, hearing his father say, "There's the Sleeping Giant," might believe that the hill was a real sleeping giant, and be frightened.

At that time in my life as a poet, I needed to feel wholly in control of a poem. I knew before I started writing where I was going to go in the poem. (In retrospect, it now seems to me that the better poems of that period always went places I didn't know they were going. The ones that did what I told them to, like obedient children, are all deplorable.) I decided to write a poem about a child being frightened of the Sleeping Giant, and then getting older—going to school perhaps—and realizing that the giant was not real. It was a poem about illusion and reality, I told myself.

The poem took a long time to write. First, I tried writing four-line stanzas of blank verse. I made the story come out right, but I was still dissatisfied with the feel of the poem—it lacked the click of the box. I decided that, for some reason I could not understand, it was the *sort* of poem that had to be rhymed. I took it apart and rhymed the second and fourth lines of each stanza. It began to sound better. After six or eight months of intermittent work, the poem was in good shape, I thought—except for the last line. It would not come right. I needed an image that would give a time span during which the illusion could be dispelled, that would kill the giant, that would be an outdoor scene and thus continue the metaphorical area of the poem, and that could be part of a child's world—all at once. One morning I was copying the poem out and I watched—with amazement and gratitude—while my right hand, all by itself with no apparent help from my brain, wrote the line that I wanted. Here is the poem that I finished that day:

The whole day long, under the walking sun
That poised an eye on me from its high floor,
Holding my toy beside the clapboard house
I looked for him, the summer I was four.

I was afraid the waking arm would break
From the loose earth and rub against his eyes
A fist of trees, and the whole country tremble
In the exultant labor of his rise;

Then he with giant steps in the small streets
Would stagger, cutting off the sky, to seize
The roofs from house and home because we had
Covered his shape with dirt and planted trees;

And then kneel down and rip with fingernails
A trench to pour the enemy Atlantic
Into our basin, and the water rush,
With the streets full and all the voices frantic.

That was the summer I expected him.
Later the high and watchful sun instead
Walked low behind the house, and school began,
And winter pulled a sheet over his head.

My hand had written the whole poem, without the help of my brain, because it was not the "little thing about illusion and reality" that I thought it was. But years went by before I discovered the real content of the poem.

At first, I was pleased in a small way with what I had written and I sent the poem to the *New Yorker*, which printed it, and I included it in my first book, and then people began to praise it and editors began to anthologize it. I gradually became offended for my other, more serious (I thought) poems. I began to dislike "The Sleeping Giant" as one might resent the one child whom one's friends preferred to one's other children. I could not see what people saw in it.

Five years later I read an article which a poet had written about my poems. He pointed out that I had often written about the relationship between fathers and sons; but the best of these poems, he said, was "The Sleeping Giant."

I felt the chills on my spine that one feels when something hits home; I suddenly saw that my fear of the giant was a dream representation of the baby's fear of adults. Every culture contains myths of giants, as if giants once did inhabit the earth—and indeed they did and do. When a baby is two feet long, the creatures who stand over his crib are giants, and something inside him remembers them until he dies.

I looked at the poem more closely and saw that it was classically Oedipal; the boy in the poem was afraid of the giant ". . . because we had/Covered his shape with dirt. . . ." The boy assumed that "we" had buried the giant; the fear of killing and the fear of being killed are simultaneous feelings in the psyche, the two sides of the Oedipal terror. Without knowing what I was doing, I had rehearsed an ancient story. The primitive engine had made the poem go, for me, and—I am sure without most of them knowing it—for my readers too.

It is rare, in my experience, that a critic points out an unconscious content which a poet can accept. Often the poet does not want to admit to himself feelings of which he might be ashamed. At the time I wrote "The Sleeping Giant," I would not have admitted the feelings that made the poem. What is more, if I had been aware of them, I could not have written them down—so my blindness was helpful to me. Now when I write a poem, I *know* I don't know what I am revealing or discovering, so my poems are often fantastic or nonsensical on the surface. (I no longer need, or even want, an ostensible content, a neat little argument, or a story about "illusion and reality.") But frequently when I have finished a poem I see the inner content—or I think I do, or I see at least part of it. That is how I can tell I have finished a poem.

Sometimes, of course, the disparity between ostensible content and inner content is small, or difficult to discern, or at least hard to define. In Hardy's "During Wind and Rain," for instance, the ostensible content is depressing in the extreme, but the feeling of the poem is inwardly comforting and warm. One can say little more. But in some other poems, one can sometimes identify covert meanings which are comically at variance with the ostensible content. Frequently in such cases the inner meaning is sexual, and it does not *seem* at any rate that the poet was aware, when he talked about birch trees or violins, that his words applied with considerable consistency to masturbation. But one of my favorite examples of this kind of disparity is not sexual. William Wordsworth (1770–1850), who loved the English countryside and its flowers, wrote a handsome poem which is usually called "Daffodils" and is sometimes called by its first line:

I wandered lonely as a cloud
That floats on high o'er vales and hills,
When all at once I saw a crowd,
A host, of golden daffodils,
Beside the lake, beneath the trees
Fluttering and dancing in the breeze.

Continuous as the stars that shine
And twinkle on the Milky Way,
They stretched in never-ending line
Along the margin of a bay:
Ten thousand saw I at a glance
Tossing their heads in sprightly dance.

The waves beside them danced, but they
Outdid the sparkling waves in glee:
A poet could not but be gay
In such a jocund company!
I gazed—and gazed—but little thought
What wealth the show to me had brought:

For oft, when on my couch I lie
In vacant or in pensive mood,
They flash upon that inward eye

Which is the bliss of solitude;
And then my heart with pleasure fills,
And dances with the daffodils.

The poem *is*, of course, about daffodils, and shows a joy in the flowers which is surely genuine. Yet there is another side to the poem, which exists in the words and can be derived from the words by close attention, and which belongs to a world entirely different from the world of nature and daffodils.

For many years I read the poem with pleasure, but with a dim sense that something was happening in it which I did not understand. Finally I took a closer look at it. Really, Wordsworth is rather odd about these daffodils. Indeed he emphasizes the pleasure they gave him. But in describing the flowers themselves, he does two unusual things. First, he does not talk about a single daffodil, which one might want to isolate and contemplate; rather, he emphasizes the *quantity* of the daffodils. Even before we have the name of the flower, we have "a crowd,/A host." Then the imagery multiplies them: "Continuous as the stars . . . on the Milky Way" and ". . . never-ending line," and finally he names a falsely specific large number. (False specificity is a common tradition of lively speech and of poetry.) "Ten thousand."

Second, Wordsworth talks in a *peculiar* way about the color of the flowers. Daffodils are yellow, indeed, and in his first reference to the daffodils Wordsworth uses the alternative word, "golden." It is a perfectly fine word, but there is no such thing as a synonym, and there are various ways in which "yellow" and "golden" differ. Some of the differences are trivial, perhaps, but some are certainly not. The difference that Wordsworth chooses to exploit is the metallic overtone in "golden"—an overtone which is an intimation of riches. Words like "shine" and "twinkle" would not seem normally appropriate to daffodils. (Those numerous stars have intervened; but what applies to stars must apply to daffodils as well.)

"Shine" and "twinkle" work in this poem because of the metallic connotation of "golden." "Sparkling" continues the image, and then Wordsworth ends the third stanza with extraordinary skill by bringing together in one metaphor his two themes of quantity and gold: What happens if you have a lot of this metal? You're rich, that's what happens. "I gazed—and gazed—but little thought/What wealth the show to me had brought." Wordsworth makes inescapable his comparison: Looking at the daffodils was like suddenly inheriting a great deal of money. It takes great skill to combine two different lines of imagery, two remote metaphorical areas (one of color, and one of quantity) and to bring them together in a single word, so that they are welded together inescapably. The word "wealth" performs just this act of skill. I am virtually certain that Wordsworth was unaware of his economic metaphor; therefore, we have an example of superb technical skill which is unconscious.

Wordsworth carries the comparison further. He asks himself, "What does a sensible person do when he suddenly acquires a great deal of money?" and he answers, "He invests it, and lives on the income." For a moment, look again at the fourth and final stanza of the poem:

For oft, when on my couch I lie
In vacant or in pensive mood,
They flash upon that inward eye
Which is the bliss of solitude;
And then my heart with pleasure fills,
And dances with the daffodils.

Let me set an arithmetic problem: 10,000 daffodils at 6 percent is how many daydreams a year?

Ever since I noticed this covert meaning to the poem—that it is about money at least as much as it is about flowers—I have delighted in telling people about it, and I once described it in an article. Some people think I am joking, possibly satirizing a sort of criticism, and many others are outraged at what they consider a sacrilege. I *do* think that the disparity between the two levels of the poem is comical, but I am not making a joke. (If I were interested in trying to be funny, I could assert that "the margin of a bay" was a reference to buying on the margin.) I truly believe that this meaning exists in the poem as a result of the unconscious intention of the poet. Far from ruining the poem, this further level increases its fascination. The first few times we read the poem with this covert meaning in mind, the comic disparity may split our vision a trifle, but eventually we can hold both meanings in mind at once, and appreciate the poem as the complicated act of a human psyche.

Unconscious content is unconscious for strong reasons, because we do not wish to acknowledge it. Here Wordsworth writes a poem in praise of money and investment. Wordsworth's England was

Marx's England, the England of child labor and the slums of Manchester. Wordsworth turned his back on the slums, the child labor, and the factories. They were ugly and nasty, and he could not bear to see them. He could look at London only before the day's work had started.

But there is a strange justice in the psyche: If you live in the country to forget that your prosperity derives from exploitation, you will look at flowers and praise them in terms of money. I remember the anecdote that gave John O'Hara the title of a novel: The old Sultan, noticing the figure of Death lurking in his courtyard, hurriedly departs for Samara to hide from him. Another person seeing Death stops for a chat, but Death says he has no time to talk; he has an appointment in Samara.

Anyone who feels that his appreciation of the poem is harmed by this reading never appreciated it in the first place; he is thinking only of some picture postcard of the English countryside which a teacher substituted for the poem. Postcards are easier to handle than poems, which are as complicated as people. If we read the poem openly, it seems to me, the daffodils are still there, and the imagination that walks among them dreams of them later. But the imagination is specifically capitalist, not feudal or socialist, and as the daffodils move in the breeze and touch each other, they make a clinking sound.

When I published some of these paragraphs, I received a deluge of letters from outraged Wordsworthians. One lady told me that the only clinking sound was in my head. Another letter made me realize that unconscious intentions exist in literary articles too, and not just in poems—or that they probably do—I will never know for sure. When I was about sixteen I had an English teacher with whom I often had great quarrels. A few days after my article had been published, I received a letter from him enclosing a postcard of daffodils in the lake country. He said that my fingerprints were still on the card. I did not remember, and still do not, that he handed the postcard around in my class. But I have a strong suspicion that he did, and that some part of me knew it, and that my phrase, "some picture postcard . . . which a teacher substituted for the poem," which I thought I just made up, was really a piece of long-term revenge.

Although I like the poem, I am not sure that this disjunction in Wordsworth's mind was a good thing. Maybe his lack of self-knowledge was what kept him from being a poet as great as

Shakespeare, or, I think, as great as Keats or Blake. In suggesting this reason, I am on shaky ground; but the only way to avoid shaky ground is to stand still. I suggest that Blake or Keats would indeed write without being aware of their whole meaning, like any poet of talent, but that their intelligence and integrity extended even into their unconscious minds; that they wrote with a more whole and enlarged intelligence; that they dreamed with their eyes open, in the same way that we should read poetry. They fail neither by excessive control or rationality (a disease which is actually a neurotic fear of the dark) nor by imitation of the looseness of the baby, who is all instinct and no brains.

For a poem combining intelligence and unconscious power, a poem that is surely generally "intended" yet has a content greater than what is merely ostensible, look at William Blake's (1757–1827) "London."

I wander thro' each chartered street,
Near where the chartered Thames does flow,
And mark in every face I meet
Marks of weakness, marks of woe.

In every cry of every Man,
In every Infant's cry of fear,
In every voice, in every ban,
The mind-forged manacles I hear.

How the Chimney-sweeper's cry
Every black'ning Church appalls;
And the hapless Soldier's sigh
Runs in blood down Palace walls.

But most thro' midnight streets I hear
How the youthful Harlot's curse
Blasts the new born Infant's tear,
And blights with plagues the Marriage hearse.

The "I" of the poem begins with an action, a special kind of unpurposeful movement called wandering—an action which is not ego-bound or practical. Yet he wanders through "chartered streets," and the word "charter" is repeated in the next line. When I first read the poem, sloppily, I thought of the streets as "charted" or mapped, rather than "chartered." Maybe "charted" or "mapped" underlies the real word as a sort of pun and thus reinforces it, for a map is a purposeful construct of the intellect. But the word is "chartered," and we must ask ourselves what a charter is, and why Blake uses it here. A charter is a legal document—like the Magna Carta—in which a King grants rights or properties to his subjects. As early as 1386 (the Oxford English Dictionary quotes Chaucer), a charter was an agreement between men about the ownership of property. Here is an example of the usefulness of a great dictionary, because it tells us what a word *could* mean at a particular time. The word "charter" ultimately came to mean a legal document specifying personal ownership, and therefore implying restriction or overt control. Now we see that the first line contains a struggle between opposites (whether *intentionally* or not is unknowable and even uninteresting)—the looseness of "wander" stands out against the tightness and control of "chartered." We begin to see that London is the scene of a struggle between the unplanned and the planned.

The second line makes the paradox more violent, because though a street is man-made, a river is usually a geological accident. In "Near where the chartered Thames does flow," "chartered" and "flow" immediately stand out against each other. The very idea of a river, embodied in the name of the Thames and in the memory of the poets who have written of its gentle waters, argues with its commercial exploitation. Consulting the Oxford English Dictionary, we see that a charter is sometimes "a contract between owners and merchants for the hire of a ship and the safe delivery of the cargo. . . ." At the end of the eighteenth century, when Blake wrote this poem, English merchantmen, aided by English militia, were selling the products of English mills throughout the world, in the growing British Empire.

Blake sees in his London a conflict between what is natural and what is legally or financially restricted. The result ". . . in every face I meet" is "Marks of weakness, marks of woe." He says he "marks" or "remarks" (notices) these signs; yet the verb "marks" can also mean to cause a mark, as if to make a scar. Maybe, in a small way, the poet is saying that he may share responsibility for the signs of weakness and woe that he sees. But the main thing to notice here is the connection between the conflict in the first two lines and the result in the second two. The connection is mostly emotional and implied, not intellectual or argued. However, the word "mark" has some interesting connotations which make for some intellectual connection; not only is a man's mark his signature, which he may affix to a charter, a mark is more importantly a legal seal—like a notary public's—which indicates that a document is valid. So "Marks of weakness, marks of woe," while first indeed referring to the actual facial expressions of oppressed Londoners—*never forget the literal*—is the precise word to use for the signs in this line. Facial expressions are described by a word that can belong to the metaphorical area of legal documents.

In the second stanza, Blake moves from visual "marks" to audible cries. Man and child, the child fearing something unnamed, both indicate their unhappiness. But then the sound is not only the sound of crying, it is the sound of any voice at all—"in every voice"—just as the marks earlier existed "in every face." The latter half of this third line sends us back to the dictionary. Even before we look, we can think of "ban" as a prohibition, as some sort of voiced forbidding, which restricts our freedom as charters do. But Blake's term had more precise meanings, especially as a sort of curse or ecclesiastical *ban*-ishment. Though often secularized, as a "prohibitory command or edict," the word retained a religious overtone. Thus the Church begins subtly to enter "London" as another institution which causes the "marks," which are opposed to the flowing. Finally, any reader in Blake's time, and an experienced reader in our own, will necessarily think of another spelling. "Banns" comes from the same word, and is the ecclesiastical proclamation of "an intended marriage, in order that those who know of any impediment thereto may have opportunity of lodging objections." For Blake the lodging of an objection to love was like the chartering of the Thames. The very sounding of banns —which were called out in the churches—was therefore a cry inviting and representing potential restriction.

The final line of the second stanza tells us overtly, but with a great deal of feeling which we cannot sum up in a paraphrase, the name of the disease of London which Blake is diagnosing. Manacles (handcuffs) restrict us, like the bans or charters, and these restrictions are what he sees marked in the faces and in the voices of Londoners. These manacles are created by the mind. As we look carefully at the implications of all his words, we can see that by "mind" he means what we might call "reason"—the part of human life responsible for charters and bans, the institutionalized ego. And he *hears* these manacles—horrid iron things made in the blast furnace of the mind—clanking in the cries, the voices, and the bans. Of course "manacles" is a visual image too.

The third stanza hangs grammatically from the second. "I hear" "... the Chimney-sweeper's cry" and later "... the hapless Soldier's sigh." Chimney-sweepers were exploited labor in England at the beginning of the industrial revolution—they were either small boys or stunted men who could squeeze into narrow chimneys and they breathed soot all day. They walked through the chartered streets of London advertising their trade by the cry of "Sweep, sweep, sweep," which is nearly the same as, "Weep, weep, weep." Also, for Blake, their "cry" was their hopeless sinking into an early death. One would think that the Christian church might have shown concern for the sufferings of exploited children—but Blake did not find any. He says that the "cry" "appalls" the "blackening Church." We think of "appalls" as "shocks": "I was appalled to learn of conditions in. . . ." Yet we seldom use the verb as "X appalls Y" the way Blake does. Actually, once we have consulted our historical sense and our dictionary we can see that he is doing something else entirely: "To appall" means to "make pale."

The line is complex, and the first thing to do is to take it as literally as possible. The churches are first described as "blackening," and most of us are satisfied to take "blackening" as a conventional symbol for "worsening." But the fact is that the churches in England, in Blake's day, were turning black. Coal smoke from growing industry, and from the concentration of people in the cities which was an effect of industry, entered the porous English stone and turned the churches black. (Some buildings in northern England today, if they have not recently been cleaned, look as if they had been carved from lumps of coal.) The same coal smoke that literally blackened the churches literally caused the chimney-sweepers to cry "sweep." The sweepers, by lessening the amount of coal dust in chimneys, may literally have paled the churches a bit, or slowed down the blackening. But at any rate the darkening churches *should* have turned pale at the sight of the suffering to which, as a result of the complicity of all institutions (state, church, and industry), it was bound.

The government is named in the last pair of lines in this stanza. Soldiers were not dying in England at this time. They were dying in the American colonies, trying to repress the desire for local determination. They were dying in India and they were dying in Africa, trying to defend the crown and to open markets for the coal-burning factories. The blood of the unlucky soldier figuratively stains the palace walls red, just as the chimney-sweeper's cry changed the color of the church. In both cases an audible image—a cry of pain or protest, a sigh of expiring life—turns into something visual. Blake involves a variety of senses in his political and moral assault on the London he sees, hears, and feels.

In the final stanza Blake's attack rises to a shriek. We return to the situation of the wanderer in the street; we return to hearing and what we hear is the curse (the ban) of the youthful prostitute. The harlot is the most immediate and horrifying embodiment of a "chartered Thames," for she is a young woman who has allowed the sex which is a natural and flowing thing to be exploited for financial gain, directed and ordered from the mind (which forged these manacles) to earn her living by perverting her nature. Prostitution is an economic institution which has debased a natural thing, and is thus perhaps parallel to man's relationship to his land (chartered, Palace) and to Church; it is the worst perversion of all.

"The new born Infant" is the most innocent of things (though its natural "tear," in these surroundings, takes us back to the earlier "Infant's cry of fear"), yet it is already blasted, or damned, by this midnight curse. The innocent offspring of legitimate love is damned by the perversions of its society. It is also true—on a distant and tenuous level of verbal echo—that the word "Blasts" can remind us not only of damnation to hell but of blast furnaces, industry, and the shop where we manufacture the "mind-forged manacles."

In the final line Blake heaps his anger in a series of words of great power. The innocent antecedent to the innocent Infant would be the innocent marriage. But in this London the perverted curse of the institution of prostitution "Blights" (plant diseases) with "plagues" (animal diseases, which thus destroy the whole natural world) "the Marriage hearse." Almost as in a film the carriage of the wedding couples changes, under the assault of Blake's imprecation, into a more appropriate funeral carriage. (There is a literal side to "plagues" too; prostitution increased the spread of venereal disease, and syphilis could convert love to death and bring forth children already syphilitic.) The final line rises to a pitch of corruption and disease—the chartering has corrupted the wandering and the flowing—and ends with the corpse of the manacled society.

Perhaps many of the puns or tiny echoes which I feel in this poem, like "charted" and "blast furnace," never occurred to Blake. Maybe they will not occur to another reader. Yet they are possible, and consistent with the poem, and so I think they are *there*, whether Blake consciously thought of them or not. On the other hand, the main thrust of the poem, its attack on the venality of institutions and the restrictions of reason, is clear and overt. There is no hidden subplot as there was in Wordsworth, and so in a way the poem is, paradoxically, more rational than Wordsworth's.

6

THE DARK VOYAGE AND THE COOL OF WIT

I have been talking about different kinds of poetry. I think the variety of poetry is infinite, increased by a unit of one each time a good new poem is written. Still, there are various poles by which one can define some of the differing pleasures of poetry, and thus the title of this chapter.

The cool of wit is the pleasure we take in exquisite phrasing, and in the happy fulfillment of formal demands. It is the same kind of pleasure we take in sharp conversation, or in a comedian's well-timed joke, or in card games, or in a sports writer's elegance of expression. The delight in verbal wit at times seems to flourish in a particular region. Elizabethan England certainly valued extravagant speech—puns and jokes and metaphors—and contemporary Ireland is a flowing tap of good talk. If we walk into an Irish pub, we may hear someone ask for "a ball of malt," which turns out to be a shot of whiskey. This side of our pleasure in language forms an element of most poems, but in some poems it seems to be the largest or most prominent element. Wit can be used for delight or for humor, or it can be an instrument of moral outrage and denunciation, and not cool at all. Alexander Pope (1688–1744) is angry when he denounces "Atticus" (really his old friend, the writer Joseph Addison):

> Peace to all such! but were there One whose fires
> True Genius kindles, and fair Fame inspires;
> Blest with each talent and each art to please,
> And born to write, converse, and live with ease:
> Should such a man, too fond to rule alone,
> Bear, like the Turk, no brother near the throne;
> View him with scornful, yet with jealous eyes,

And hate for arts that caus'd himself to rise;
Damn with faint praise, assent with civil leer,
And without sneering, teach the rest to sneer;
Willing to wound, and yet afraid to strike,
Just hint a fault, and hesitate dislike;
Alike reserv'd to blame, or to commend,
A tim'rous foe, and a suspicious friend;
Dreading ev'n fools, by Flatterers besieg'd,
And so obliging, that he ne'er obliged;
Like *Cato*, give his little Senate laws,
And sit attentive to his own applause. . . .

And yet, we take pleasure in the fierce delicacy of this assassination, in the pauses that almost always occur after the fourth or fifth syllable, and in the balance of phrasing on each side of the pause: "Damn with faint praise, assent with civil leer, / And without sneering, teach the rest to sneer."

There are gentler examples of wit. Take Richard Wilbur's (1921–   ) "Museum Piece":

The good grey guardians of art
Patrol the halls on spongy shoes,
Impartially protective, though
Perhaps suspicious of Toulouse.

Here dozes one against the wall,
Disposed upon a funeral chair.
A Degas dancer pirouettes
Upon the parting of his hair.

See how she spins! The grace is there,
But strain as well is plain to see.
Degas loved the two together:
Beauty joined to energy.

Edgar Degas purchased once
A fine El Greco, which he kept
Against the wall beside his bed
To hang his pants on while he slept.

This poem seems to be complete on its surface, with nothing happening under its silvery top—yet it is a considerable pleasure. *Think* of daring to rhyme "shoes" with "Toulouse." The image of the Degas ballerina dancing on the museum guard's hair part is as silly and delightful as the rhyme. The third stanza is witty with its careful use of "plain" as part of the idiom "plain to see"—Wilbur is praising and practicing the art of plain surfaces—and witty also in rhyming the monosyllabic simple verb "see" with the intellectual polysyllablic noun "energy." The final stanza, with its comic anecdote, suggests—without quite endorsing—an attitude toward the dark and mysterious pole of art as exemplified in El Greco, an attitude which may combine technical admiration ("A *fine* El Greco"; otherwise why would Degas buy it?) with absence of the half-religious awe with which many of us look at an El Greco.

Wilbur's rhymes add to his neatness and precision, as did Pope's exact couplets, but a poet can write in free verse and still achieve this degree of finish. Marianne Moore (and Pope and Wilbur, for that matter) has written poems which move toward the pole of the dark voyage, but here is a poem of Marianne Moore's (1887–   ), called "Silence," which I think is pleasurable largely because of its precision and wit:

My father used to say,
"Superior people never make long visits,
have to be shown Longfellow's grave
or the glass flowers at Harvard.
Self-reliant like the cat—
that takes its prey to privacy,
the mouse's limp tail hanging like a shoelace from its mouth—
they sometimes enjoy solitude,
and can be robbed of speech
by speech which has delighted them.
The deepest feeling always shows itself in silence;
not in silence, but restraint."
Nor was he insincere in saying, "Make my house your inn."
Inns are not residences.

Here, the cat and the mouse—that marvelous shoelace!—are evidence of something at work underneath the surface (it is difficult to find poems one likes which are perfectly polar), but the main thrust of the poem is surely the series of definitions and redefinitions at the end. We sense a search not for lively and expressive speech, but rather for a precise wording that will tell no lies. "Nor was he insincere in saying, 'Make my house your inn.' / Inns are not residences."

At the other extreme of my continuum I speak of the dark voyage—the poem as an unconscious, undirected voyage of discovery, sailing on inward seas. This poem reveals in fantastic imagery the interior continent of the self. Yet the possibility that this kind of poem can exist (poems exist only when they have the potential to reach other people) depends on the conviction that at the deepest levels of our inner selves, we resemble each other. Certainly we share more when we are one week old (hunger, fear, frustration, comfort, abandonment, bliss) than we share when we are twenty—except that when we are twenty (and thirty, and seventy) we share memories, and sometimes re-enactments, of hunger, fear, frustration, comfort, abandonment, and bliss.

Typically, poetry has exhorted us to rediscover our instinctual selves. It is obvious that the poets, who tend to be highly intelligent, are exhorting *themselves;* they are as encumbered as anyone—perhaps more so—by civilized restraints and restrictions. At one point in his rational life, Plato found it necessary to expel poets from his theoretical Republic; they represented the instinctual rather than the rational life. Romantics like Wordsworth and Shelley continually asserted the value of the imagination, and described the transport of relaxing the brain to release the feelings. Blake made the dark voyage again and again, and sometimes what he saw there was a terror the civilized world attempts to deny, as in "The Sick Rose":

O Rose, thou art sick!
The invisible worm
That flies in the night,
In the howling storm,

Has found out thy bed
Of crimson joy,
And his dark secret love
Does thy life destroy.

This is one poem I do not try to talk about.

D. H. Lawrence's (1885–1930) poetry sometimes appears careless, as if the poet were so impatient that he would not go back to change a mistaken word. The gesture is one of great hurtling emotion, unstoppable. Some of his poems are magnificent, and some are exhortations to the life of feeling, like "Song of a Man Who Has Come Through":

Not I, not I, but the wind that blows through me!
A fine wind is blowing the new direction of Time.

If only I let it bear me, carry me, if only it carry me!
If only I am sensitive, subtle, oh, delicate, a winged gift!
If only, most lovely of all, I yield myself and am borrowed
By the fine, fine wind that takes its course through the
    chaos of the world
Like a fine, an exquisite chisel, a wedge-blade inserted;
If only I am keen and hard like the sheer tip of a wedge
Driven by invisible blows,
The rock will split, we shall come at the wonder, we
    shall find the Hesperides.

Oh, for the wonder that bubbles into my soul,
I would be a good fountain, a good well-head,
Would blur no whisper, spoil no expression.

What is the knocking?
What is the knocking at the door in the night?
It is somebody wants to do us harm.

No, no, it is the three strange angels.
Admit them, admit them.

The begining is an urgent wish that the "I" be passive to the inside
and to the instinctual self, imaged as a wind. This sense of part
of oneself (the ego) being passive to another deeper part of oneself
is common in man's experience, and is even a tenet of some re-
ligions, especially Eastern ones. The directive, rational "I" is the
enemy. To "come through" is to find a way beyond the ego. Law-
rence jumps from one image to another, from wind to chisel to
fountain; as the fountain he is especially a poet, loosing "expres-
sion." Then he enacts, dramatically, the answer to his wish. He
hears a knocking—a possible response to his prayer—and he is
frightened. We are all frightened of the release of the deep self;
it is natural and appropriate to be frightened. "It is somebody
wants to do us harm." But then Lawrence recovers, loses his
fear, and submits—and therefore comes through.

Many readers connect the "three strange angels" with the
"Herperides" earlier. The Hesperides were nymphs who guarded
golden apples in Greek myth. Maybe Lawrence was thinking of
these nymphs when he wrote "the three strange angels." I cannot
say that the association is *wrong*—so little is *wrong*—but I am
skeptical. The nymphs *guard* the apples which, in "we shall find
the Hesperides," are an image of what we seek. I think that "the
three strange angels" are simply "the three strange angels" (like

Eliot's "three white leopards"). Not to question their identity is to "come through." In the final submission which is triumph, Lawrence tells himself, "Admit them. Admit them."

The typical poem of younger American poets now is a dark voyage in the underground of the psyche. Literary sources are surrealism, a literary and artistic movement that flourished in France from the mid-twenties on, and modern Spanish poetry, with its typically fantastic images. When the Chilean poet Pablo Neruda (1904–   ) receives a gift of hand-knitted socks, he tells us, in Robert Bly's translation:

I resisted
the mad impulse
to put them
in a golden
cage
and each day give them
birdseed
and pieces of pink melon.

The German Expressionist poet Georg Trakl has also been important to many young poets. Paul Celan, I suspect, learned from the Expressionists and Surrealists. The Expressionist distorts reality to convey emotion; in an Expressionist painting the lady's face may be green. The Surrealist does not distort reality so much as assume the reality of dream; in Surrealism limp watches have the same validity as stiff ones—one watch comes from Switzerland and the other comes from sleep, but who denies that sleep is as real as Switzerland?

But the young Americans do not need to look only at recent poets like Neruda and Trakl. They can look to a vast part of the tradition of the poet as seer, as the man possessed of truth, as the madman expelled from Plato's Republic. Today, the intellectual justification of the poet's prophesy tends to be Freudian or Jungian rather than Eleusinian or Taoist. Only the theology has changed.

One of the best of the younger Americans is Robert Bly (1926–   ), and I want to quote his small and simple poem about the war in Vietnam, "Counting the Small-Boned Bodies":

Let's count the bodies over again.

If only we could make the bodies smaller,
The size of skulls,
We could make a whole plain white with skulls
                    in the moonlight!

If we could only make the bodies smaller,
Maybe we could get
A whole year's kill in front of us on a desk!

If we could only make the bodies smaller,
We could fit
A body into a finger-ring, for a keepsake forever.

The wit is here—a harsh wit contrasting the civilization of desks
and "keepsakes forever" with the barbarism of the body count, a
barbarism which comes to resemble, within a conventional ad-
vertising slogan, the shrunken-head collection of a savage tribe.
But the wit of this poem depends on an act of the imagination,
an act of the magical part of our brains where, as in a dream
or as in the fantasies of a very young child—or as in *Alice in
Wonderland*, which the Surrealists claim for their own—things can
grow tiny or huge, miniscule or enormous, at the decision of om-
nipotent fantasy.

Other poems that exhort and exemplify the dark voyage are
some of Theodore Roethke's (pp. 171–179), others by Lawrence
(pp. 262–264), Blake (pp. 128–133), Keats (pp. 134–140), and Whit-
man (pp. 146–152). But most of the greatest poems have some dark
voyage in them, and some cool of wit. Look at Andrew Marvell's
"To His Coy Mistress" on page 213. It is funny, charming, delight-
ful—and dark. Even in the first witty parts, the exaggeration is so
extreme, and the fear of death so close, that wit and darkness
coexist in the same lines. Then at the end, in the sexual imagery
and in the image of the sun, the poem enters a world of total
inwardness. To represent both poles in the same poem is—I ex-
pand my metaphor out of existence—to become universal.

7
COPING WITH A POEM

People have talked a lot about explicating poems, or analyzing them. Usually they only paraphrase the poem and then talk about their paraphrase. In a perfect world, maybe we would not have to talk about poems at all. But it helps—to see if we see the same things in a poem, and to enlarge each other's perceptions of a poem—to talk about it, in the imperfect world we inhabit. But I do not want to claim to *analyze* a poem; analysis sounds finite, like something performed on white mice. A poem is not finite; there is always more to notice, more to speculate on. I prefer to use a vaguer word, and to talk about coping with a poem. I want to talk about the way the words work, the noise they make, the feelings they communicate. I would like to *notice* everything I can about a poem—always knowing that, a year from now, I will probably see other things, and will not notice some things that seem important to me now. Also, "coping" rather than "analyzing" or "explicating" allows me to speculate, to wonder if this might be a way to understand a line, and not to assert a truth as if I were certain. Some things I feel certain of; many other things are just speculations.

Here is another poem by Thomas Hardy, called "Transformations." I have chosen it because it is obviously simple, and because it is not so obvious nor so simple as it looks. The best thing for you to do now—in folowing this introduction to the pleasures of poetry—is to read the poem slowly and carefully before you read what I say about it. Take notes on it. If you can, write an extended note on it. Then later, when you feel yourself committed to a reading of the poem, let yourself look at what I have said. You do not have to agree. But it will help if you compare my coping with your own, and see if there are some things you have not been noticing. If you are a beginning reader of poetry, there will be some pleasures that you miss.

Portion of this yew
Is a man my grandsire knew,
Bosomed here at its foot:
This branch may be his wife,
A ruddy human life
Now turned to a green shoot.

These grasses must be made
Of her who often prayed,
Last century, for repose;
And the fair girl long ago
Whom I often tried to know
May be entering this rose.

So, they are not underground,
But as nerves and veins abound
In the growths of upper air,
And they feel the sun and rain,
And the energy again
That made them what they were!

Taking the poem as a whole, it is easy to name the subject—in a general way. Hardy is talking about how people endure after their deaths as their bodies (molecules from their bodies) become parts of plant life. All right. But this general sense is mere commonplace—*everybody* has talked about turning into grass or flowers after death—and the pleasures of poetry always lie in the particulars, not in the generalized content. My quick paraphrase of this poem is neither complicated nor moving, but the poem itself is another matter.

The title is "Transformations." A lot of people, first reading the poem, think that Hardy is talking about the *cycle* of life. But I suggest that to talk about a cycle, in this poem, is not to use words carefully. (One of the uses of poetry is that it teaches us to use words carefully.) A cycle is a complete circle, and implies a motion from human being back to human being. People have written such poems, with their flavor of cannibalism, and Hardy could have done so if he had meant to; the girl could have been entering a fruit tree, and he could eat the fruit, and therefore the girl would be part of human life again. But Hardy is talking about *transformation*, the motion of matter from one sort of object to another. In this case, though it would not be necessary, the people are transformed into trees, grass, and flowers.

Let us look at the first two lines of the poem, "Portion of this yew/Is a man my grandsire knew, . . ." These lines have three beats each, iambic largely but with soft syllables missing and added (they scan /$\cup$/$\cup$/ | $\cup$ $\cup$ /$\cup$/$\cup$/) and they rhyme nicely: direct rhyme of a noun and a verb that we would not normally connect, but that come together without strain, with an effect of plainness. If we read carefully, trying to be sensitive to the insides of words, we know a good deal. The sentence is simple and declarative. How does Hardy *know* that a portion (some part) of this yew is a man his grandsire knew? ("My grandsire" knew him, so presumably "I" did not. This presumption seems to put the dead man far back in time.) The answer is simple, providing we use a little common sense. Also, it helps to know that a yew tree, an evergreen, commonly grows in graveyards. Hardy (I won't call him "the speaker of the poem") is walking in a graveyard. He either sees a stone, or remembers where someone was buried. Maybe his grandsire told him—but that is not the sort of thing we *know*, or that it is even useful to speculate on. The grave is next to a yew tree; it is common sense, then, to say that, "Portion of this yew/Is a man. . . ."

The third line gives some readers trouble. Because of the word "Bosomed," and also because of the later information about the dead man's wife, they think that the line refers to a woman. But this is not sensible. Hardy's punctuation—as a glance at a few poems will tell you—is conventional, and he would never join two complete sentences with a comma, or break the second sentence with the heavy stop of a colon. Readers who make this mistake are not looking closely. They are racing through the words as if they were reading a newspaper, grabbing at whatever sense can seem approximate or immediate.

No, the "portion" of "the man" is "Bosomed here at its foot." Hardy is talking about the hump of a grave, which could be *like* a bosom, but which could also be held to the tree as a child is held at the bosom of his mother. I think either reading or both readings work in the poem. It is also true that a yew tree characteristically has little knobs or bumps on it, rather harsh facsimiles of bosoms. I think this last reading of the line is far-fetched, but maybe someone else can see more in it than I can.

The rhyme word of the third line, which is also three feet long, stands out by itself, ready to be picked up by the sixth line, which unifies the stanza. Glancing at the poem as a whole again, we can see that it has three stanzas—the third a summation or conclusion based on data collected in the first two; each of the three stanzas is divided into two parts, at the third line. This structural consistency is another, small, reason why a sensible reader will reject the thought that "Bosomed" in line three goes with "wife" in line four.

In the fourth line, the situation of the poet walking in the graveyard is reinforced. Husbands and wives tend to be buried next to each other. Noticing the hump of the husband's grave, Hardy naturally notices or remembers the grave of the wife, which is also near the yew. But the verb "is" changes to the verb "may be"; he knows, when he talks of a person becoming a green shoot—a *particular* part of the tree—that he is being fanciful, and his "may be" is his modest acknowledgment of his fancifulness. It was easy to assert, with fair certainty, that "Portion of this yew/Is a man...."

"A ruddy human life/Now turned to a green shoot." Having expressed his fancy as fancy, Hardy fleshes it out in the fifth and sixth lines as if it were fact; his imagination seizes on it and develops it. "Ruddy" means red-cheeked and healthy. The word can be slang in England, a euphemism for "bloody" or "God-awful." Anyone who, having consulted a dictionary, thinks Hardy could have meant "god-awful" is not being very sensitive. The "green" of "green shoot" heightens the red of "ruddy." Blood and chlorophyll, the two great life sustainers, stand in colorful contrast. "Human," of course, contrasts with "shoot," and "turned" is the action that creates "transformation." Having imagined a possibility, based on an original probability, Hardy's imagination takes off. Eventually we will want to wonder whether the movement toward greater and greater fancifulness is part of the inner speech of this simple poem.

The second stanza extends the fancy, though it continues the scheme of the poem by talking of two more buried people. "These grasses" (moving away from the yew, we turn to cemetery grass— perhaps the grass of a particular grave his eye moves toward) "must be made/Of her who often prayed,/Last century, for repose." First we may notice that "must be" is a different sort of verb from "is" or "may be." It could mean, "these grasses absolutely incontrovertibly have to be," but this sense of "must be" would violate the attitude of modest fancy that Hardy has set up. He is not being that extravagant. Fortunately, there is an idiomatic sense of "must be" which roughly means "stands to reason that." Returned to a built-up area we knew as a child, we say, "The baseball field must have been over there," and we are talking about a probability, not a fact.

The woman prayed, and therefore bent over as grass does in the wind, or kept low to the ground like grass—as opposed to yew trees. She prayed "Last century," which does not logically have to mean a long time ago, but otherwise why would Hardy say so? We begin to have the sense that Hardy writes as an old man. The irony of praying for repose, and getting it as grass (in the poet's fancy), is clear enough, and the verbally similar (but differently spelled) rhymes of "made" and "prayed" are satisfying.

The last half of the second stanza is the most fanciful, and I think it is probably my favorite part of the poem. "And the fair girl long ago" seems to confirm the speaker's age: He is looking at the grave of someone he "long ago" wished to court. Hardy remembers the girl "Whom I often tried to know" as fair and imagines her becoming a beautiful flower. He recalls that he failed to know her; here we have a small nostalgic romantic story.

I said that Hardy imagined her becoming a beautiful flower. What he wrote was not my prosaic paraphrase but, "May be entering this rose." Here is a rose growing in the graveyard, presumably near the grave of this remembered girl. Hardy reverts to "May be" with its acknowledgment of fantasy. But here it is part of a verb compound, and not the whole verb—she "May be entering" at this moment. The implication of the present tense (implication only, not statement) is that she has died more recently, an old lady who had long ago been a fair girl.

But for me the unforgettable, untranslatable, nearly unmentionable beauty lies in the strange verb "entering." Her molecules rise up the green stem as if they were going inside a house—or as if, most strangely, they were a man entering a woman. This brings me to a level of the poem which is tenuous, which is perhaps not even there—but it seems consistent. I refer to the way in which sexes seem to change or switch. We do not distinguish between male and female daisies, but usually with people, we think of male in male terms and female in female terms. In this poem, the first man we meet is "bosomed" at the root of the yew, and though this can mean only that he is clutched to the mother's bosom, I suggest that there is a way in which the word grants him bosoms also, changes his sex. When his wife is fancifully reincarnated, she becomes a phallic "shoot." I see no sexual change in the next woman. The young girl "May be entering this rose."

The final stanza changes tactics. Instead of talking about the individual dead it generalizes, referring to "they"—all the dead. And it moves by false logic, saying, "So," as if the generalizations followed from the particulars. Clearly they do not. Hardy knows that because of his fancies ("may be"), he has not proved that the dead, for instance, "feel" things again. Hardy is *intending* his illogic, just as Robert Bly must know that his thoughts about making bodies smaller are fantastic. Both the illogic and the fantastic image serve the same purpose: They express the poet's feeling.

In reading "Transformations," I think it is important that we keep our intelligence alert and register Hardy's illogic—in order to follow the track of his feeling. The second line of the last stanza is another brilliant mixture of real observations with (more importantly) emotional distortions. We do not think of a plant as having nerves in the same way that a human does. We do think of leaves as having veins, and of stems as having little capillaries along which chlorophyll, like blood, might travel. So "nerves" is fancy and "veins" has the reality of leaf-veins that are analogous to human veins. But there is also a visual level to the line. A tree or bush without leaves, against the sky, can look like an anatomical diagram of human nerves and veins. This distant visual background gives more weight to Hardy's fantastic assertion that these people live again, even in their feelings.

"Abound" is a lively, fruitful word, expressive in its denial of death. "In the growths of upper air" effectively removes the old corpses from claustrophobic coffins and liberates them into oxygen. "Growths," literally applied to trees, grass, and the rose-bush, carries energy like "abound." It is another denial of death.

The final three-line portion is the most unrealistic and the most ecstatic of the poem. "And they feel the sun and rain"—well, we can *imagine* plants feeling sun and rain, because we can see their reaction to drought and damp, but we only assert when we say that they feel, we do not know it. Suddenly the emotional necessity behind this poem becomes clear—if it had not become clear earlier. An old man walks in the graveyard which is populated with dead whom he knew or knew of. He begins to imagine their survival—scientifically feasible—as molecules of vegetable matter. Then suddenly he insists on their survival as sentient objects, insists on the denial of death. The old man is expressing, by means of the distortion of his illogic, his moving desire to endure, to survive death, to feel "the energy again" that makes him what he is. Notice that he does not say that the plants feel the energy that makes them what they *are;* rather, "That made them what they *were!*" It is the human state that the ·old·man wants. So Hardy makes a poem that starts with a realistic commonplace and ends with scientific falsities which represent a common and deep emotion: We wish to survive our deaths.

8
WRITING POEMS

If we love poetry, we usually try to write it. I think that an excellent way to learn to read poems is to try to write them. (Creative writing courses can be justified only on these grounds; we cannot turn out poets as if we were General Motors turning out cars.) Mostly, we learn by writing what we want to write, and then by being tough on ourselves, and crossing out, and rewriting and rewriting. Writing is extremely hard work. Practically no one has ever found it easy, or has been able to write decently on a first draft. But writing poetry is an enormous pleasure. Once a man has had the pleasure of making a metaphor. . . .

The attitude to cultivate from the start is that revision is a way of life. We must write the first time as well as we can; then stare at it until we can see holes in it, cross out, write in what we can, and then cross out some more. So what if it takes us a long time to write a poem? What are we living for anyway?

Poets learn craft by revision, but they cannot tinker with the essentially mediocre and make it great. Some poets believe in throwing away their unsuccessful drafts and starting again. A poet I know has told me that sometimes, when a poem is not coming right, he will take a nap and then write a new draft immediately on waking, without reference to the old version. We all have to find our own ways. Sometimes when I was writing formal poems I could make a form come right by switching the form, like changing pentameter quatrains into tetrameter couplets. (Rhyming "The Sleeping Giant" seemed to help the poem.) I remember the advice Auguste Rodin gave young sculptors when they were having trouble with a maquette (a model, in wax or clay or whatever, of a big scpluture). He told them not to keep poking it with tools and making minor changes, but to drop it on the floor and see what it looked like then.

Some people—deliberately or not—have learned by imitation. I think it is typical, in fact, when we are young to learn by a series of infatuations. This month I imitate Yeats, next week Marvell, next month Roethke. Each time I learn something new. Some artists have set out purposely to imitate styles and have learned to extend their own abilities. As in athletics or in acting, we can learn by mimickry. Eventually, when we are are at the right point, we assert our own identity. But there is no pushing it. It comes or it doesn't come.

Getting ideas is the hard part. It seems to me that I have to wait on them. But a lighter, or imitative, kind of poem—a practice poem—can be fabricated. We can also fabricate a wild surrealism, writing "automatically" and deliberately not knowing what we are doing. Some artists have suppressed their rationality by drugs or alcohol, others by techniques of meditation. I know a young poet who made a breakthrough by writing with earphones blasting rock music into his head.

In time we develop a nose for poems. In the beginning, I would advise against trying to write about big abstractions, like "Love" or "Racial Conflict." We should write instead about a tree or a person, and let our feelings come through the images we use. In fact, the best way to begin writing poems is to begin with descriptions. Ideas and feelings come in, as we describe. When we start from the Big Idea, we write with the substance of a cloud. "Love" is a word with no love in it. "Cool thighs," "long hair"—these are phrases that might begin to contain love, or erotic feeling.

So, as Ezra Pound said a long time ago, "Go in fear of abstractions." If we can write a poem without any of them, *just* using touch/feel/see/hear/smell words, chances are we will write more movingly.

Also, go in fear of clichés and dead metaphors. We develop a sense of tact that identifies them, and cut them out. Everybody writes them in first drafts; that is why first drafts won't do. It takes a while, and usually the eyes of other readers, to get rid of all the commonplace language our heads are stuffed with. Reading our poems literally (can a door both "yawn" and "beckon"?) will help.

With rhythm, advice gets harder. Mere meter can be counted, but to make good noises seems like an instinctive thing. If it is not instinctive, it is based on reading hundreds and thousands of poems, and on revising our own over and over again. This is the kind of knowledge which we learn in order to forget—the tennis stroke, or riding a bicycle—and it is obviously acquired knowledge, but it comes to seem instinctual. Our sense of the form of the poem—that click of the box which is a resolution of rhythm, image, and feeling—lies deep inside us, but it comes from our reading, in which we develop our changing sense of what a good poem is, and from our revising toward that goal.

One or two things, at least, can be said about rhythm. Short-lined free verse which stops the sense at the end of a line sounds prosey:

It has no interest
because the sense
is the same as the line.
There is no difference.
One can go on and on
chopping prose like this.

So short-lined free verse usually needs enjambment, and long-lined free verse does not, though it can tolerate it. One cannot generalize about iambic pentameter, except to say that counting it and having it come out right is not enough. Iambic pentameter can work well either end-stopped or enjambed. When we use a shorter line, like a dimeter or a trimeter, the same rule of thumb applies which applied to free verse: better run-on.

The language of our poems must grow from the way we talk. A student of mine once wrote in a poem that he went into "the Romance Languages Building every morn." Until the last word he was talking his own language; then he was talking book talk. The trouble with archaic language is very much like the trouble with clichés: It puts a barrier between the reader and the feeling, a barrier of old books, or, in the case of clichés, a barrier of newspapers or slovenly speech. The only true test for idiomatic diction, when we are interrogating our drafts, looking for things to cut out, is: Could I conceivably have spoken these words without irony? My student would never have said to his roommate that he was off to the Romance Language Building this morn.

Maybe one of the most important things to have, when we are writing poems, is a reader. The reader must be an embodied Muse, someone sympathetic to our endeavors, but hard on us—someone to point out clichés, dead metaphors, rhythmical ineptitude, archaisms, and other mistakes.

A final technical matter—small but important—is the adjective.

Virtually every beginning poet hurts himself by an addiction to adjectives. Verbs are by far the most important things for poems —especially wonderful tough monosyllables like "grasp" and "cry." Nouns are the next most important. Adjectives tend to be useless. The right one at the right time is perfect, but the typical amateur writes with every noun carrying its little adjective, like a puny bodyguard. "The white snow on the green grass is like. . . ." "Snow on grass" is stronger and quicker.

Compression is an important thing, and omitting adjectives can often compress and strengthen at the same time. "Grass" is a bit greener than "green grass"; it is surely shorter. Also, in a poem where three images are doing the same thing, it is stronger to omit two and keep one. Less is more. That slogan is one to bear in mind.

Most of us tend to overexplain. From a lack of confidence in our images, we add a useless line or stanza of editorial comment, usually a nudge-in-the-ribs which says, "in case you didn't get it, this is what I meant," and makes an abstract summary of content. But abstract summaries tend to weaken the real emotion of images and metaphors. Abstractions often limit the ambivalent range of feeling which concrete words are able to carry. Once I wrote a poem in which I embodied feelings of being stuck and paralyzed by describing a skeleton strapped in the cockpit of an undiscovered, crashed, World War II fighter plane. At the end I said that even if the pilot had made it back to the aircraft carrier, and was alive now, he would feel the same way:

> . . . and every
> morning takes his chair, his pale
> hands on the black arms, and sits
> upright, held
> by the firm webbing.

As it ends now, I hope everyone can recognize the feeling, which all of us undergo from time to time. But when I first wrote the poem, I overexplained: ". . . the firm webbing/of job and house and. . . ." By my overspecificity, I limited the feeling to a man with a job and a house. The feeling of being stuck belongs to everybody—high school students, old people, housewives—it is not my property alone.

Finally, of course, poetry is not a matter of slogans but of the spirit. We must learn—if we are to write well—to discover the dark parts of ourselves and be true to them. We must also learn the shapes and feelings of words in the mouth, and what feels best. We must learn to make art. Art is long and life is short.

But however long we work, and however much or little public success comes to us, we will never arrive anywhere. If we feel that we know we are good, we are already dead—like the skeleton in the cockpit. When I was young I thought that we climbed a mountain to reach a plateau. Now I know that we climb to climb, and if we ever reach a place where we can see no rocks above us, we have fallen down the mountain. Old poets give us examples of this continuing labor. The greatest influence old poets can have on contemporary ones is spiritual and not stylistic. I always think of Yeats, who revised his poems continually, and who throughout his life expressed his dissatisfaction with what he had written in the past. In poems and in letters we see him continually disappointed in what he has accomplished but determined to continue trying. Shortly before he died he wrote the poem, "The Circus Animal's Desertion," in which he dismissed his life's work, but swore at the end, "I must lie down where all the ladders start,/In the foul rag-and-bone shop of the heart." Three weeks before he died he wrote a letter saying that he was resting, "after writing much verse." He knows "for certain that my time will not be long . . ." but, "In two or three weeks . . . I will begin to write my most fundamental thoughts. . . ."

To die like that, in the midst of work, is the best death anyone could wish for. In writing poems, as in everything else, the work is the thing and not the response to the work. Though we may work for potential love or fame, applause for our old work is nothing if we are not making new poems. When we are not in the midst of working, applause is almost a curse; it is a reminder that we are no longer the person who did the old work. Whether we are Nobel prize winners or unrecognized beginners, the pleasure of writing poetry is one-fiftieth in the praise, and the rest in the act of making a metaphor.

9
QUESTION PERIOD

Usually at the end of my poetry readings there is a question period. Some questions come up again and again.

What is the difference between poetry and prose?

Poetry *tends* to be more intense, more emotional, more fantastic, more concentrated, more metaphorical, and more tightly organized in rhythm. All these things are only tendencies. We could make a list of characteristics of any length, depending on how we subdivided them, and score a piece of writing according to how many of these characteristics it represented, or what degree of these characteristics it fulfilled. Some poems would score nothing in some categories. Meter is a characteristic of many poems, but not of all. It is not a characteristic we associate with prose. Therefore poems in English *tend* to be metrical but prose seldom does. Some poems are largely without metaphor, but very few; some passages of prose have more metaphors than some passages of poetry. Most passages of poetry are more metaphorical than most passages of prose.

We must characterize the difference between poetry and prose in such a vague way because the vagueness is real. A family resemblance makes poetry different from prose. Actually, I do not think the distinction is very interesting. A friend of mine used to say that he would define a poem as anything which anybody ever called a poem. Then the hard part begins, when we decide whether it's any good.

Do you put hidden meanings in your poems?

Sure.

I have gone into this question on pages 48–60. I would like to add one thing to what I said in that earlier chapter: Poets intend a great many things in their poems *after* they have written them. The poet may write something down because it feels better—say, "yellow" instead of "gold." Later, as he looks at the poem in manuscript and interrogates it, or thinks about it as he is walking down the street, he may realize why he prefers "yellow" to "gold." He wants to suggest, perhaps, something more organic and less metallic, or he wants to pick up the "l"s from an earlier part of the line. Or he doesn't want a rhyme with the word "told" in a previous line. So he lets it stand. He is intending something, consciously, by not crossing it out. At the beginning, he did not know what he was doing. By the time he finishes the poem, he may be aware of much of what he has done. The things which were hidden from him (by himself) in the moment of composition are no longer completely hidden. But on the other hand, it is probable that there are at least some things in the poem of which he is still not aware, but which are really *there*.

How does somebody get started as a poet?

Everybody has a different story. Usually people start writing when they are young. Maybe the fact is merely that a lot of people write poetry when they are young. There is a saying in England, "To be twenty and a poet is to be twenty. To be thirty and a poet is to be a poet." Why a few people persist, and become poets, is perhaps the real question.

People often get started because they read something that they like, and then they imitate it. Or they have recently enjoyed a poem, and they have an emotion that seems to them intense or poetical, and they use lines of verse to attempt to make shape of this experience.

What is it like to be a poet when you are growing up?

People tend to think poets are weird. I don't know if that would be so true now, but it was in the forties when I began to write poems. I think it was all right to be a girl and write poems, but not to be a boy. Whenever I would express a strong conviction about anything, the standard rejoinder would be, "Go write a poem about it." Adolescents are cruel, and being a poet was a disaster that I could be taunted with, like having two heads. The taunting had its value for me. It made me feel special; it gave me the romantic self-glorification I wanted. It provided an excuse for the alienation I probably would have felt anyway. And it made me intriguing—and not just weird—at least to some people.

Why do you write poems?

Love, probably—in all sorts of ways. Probably many poets start to write poems to make girls love them. Probably it is one of the reasons they continue to write poems, even when they are old. Fame is an impersonal version of love. Yeats has written about being discouraged about his work, and then reading his poems in a small village in Ireland, and being moved by some young student who approached him with a battered copy of Yeats's poems, obviously read and reread. This is love. This is the reward.

Also, we come to write poems out of habit. Writing poetry is necessary to the poet. If I do not write from time to time, I become anxious and depressed. Sometimes I wake up in the middle of the night with phrases in my head. Writing is totally a part of one's life, one's identity. Living is writing. Writing is living. During two years when I could not write, I felt dead.

Also, a poet comes to love the art. One discovers a devotion to the art that one practices, a devotion which is not egotistical. One can try to make poems because one loves poetry so much, and yet remain aware that one may live out a lifetime without having made a good poem.

How do you get ideas?

I don't get them, they come. I feel passive to them. They aren't exactly ideas, either—not for me, at any rate. I get phrases and words, usually. Occasionally I get something like the whole shape of the poem, an image or a sequence like a dream. But usually the poem begins with words and stanzas, and I don't know what is going to come next, and I let my hand do the work. Not everyone feels this way; some people feel more in control. But I believe that most poets feel rather passive to the content of their poems. They cannot stimulate the beginnings of a poem.

I have also found that a state of mind, rather than a particular content, brings a poem on. Sometimes, it is true, I will respond to an immediate situation—a death, or love, or the death of a love—by reaching for pen and paper. But I think most of my best poems have come during periods when I simply felt loose, and a whole series of ideas would present themselves to me, a series of phrases, beginnings of poems, sometimes whole drafts, on different subjects—insofar as a poem is ever "on a subject."

Are poets different from other people?

I believe that artists must feel more openly than most people do, and must have a more active fantasy life. They must live more and they must die more. They live by extremes partly because they believe in intensity, and partly because their own art requires this from them. The poet cannot protect himself from feeling, by lies or simply by diminution of feeling (turning down the volume) or he will be no good. He must learn to live with the volume turned up, even though it is dangerous.

Are poets crazier than other people?

Maybe they are saner. Nobody has done a statistical survey, so far as I know. Not turning down the volume may lead to all sorts of troubles for poets. But on the other hand, to have an outlet for expression is therapeutic. It is not only expression, either—it is shapeliness. Robert Frost used to speak of his poems as occupational therapy, like the wallets or ashtrays which people make in insane asylums, which seem to give shape to chaotic lives.

But isn't poetry sort of crazy, in itself?

Apparently there is some relationship between the poet and the schizophrenic. The poet is able to drop back to parts of the mind which are prerational. Maybe that's the wrong way to put it. Maybe he is able to leapfrog over reason to parts of the mind which are beyond reason. Usually this action is termed "regression in the service of the ego," a psychoanalyst's formula to distinguish the poet from the schizophrenic. The schizophrenic regresses to his own disservice. The poet or the artist may use elements of primary process thinking for purposes which are expressive and shapely and therapeutic, both for himself and potentially for other people.

Then is poetry therapeutic for readers?

There is one way in which poetry is dangerous. It requires the good reader, like the poet, to turn the volume up in order to receive strong and deep feeling. This is difficult and it can be dangerous. It can involve extremities of pleasure, but equally it can involve extremities of pain. Reading poems also makes shapes out of these difficult extremes, for the sensitive reader. The reader of poetry is making wallets too.

The material the poet is bringing under control, if the poetry is great, is strong material. (Our lives, if we are open to feeling, are "strong material.") We need a strong cage—the bars are the click of the box—but a strong cage is nothing if there is no lion inside it. One kind of bad poem makes a strong cage with bars two inches thick and heavy wire between the bars, and inside the cage there is only a little bunny rabbit going hippity-hop. This bunny is an evasive lion—or a lion with the volume turned down.

Why do you like to read poems aloud?
What does it have to do with writing poems?

I suppose poets like to read poems aloud because it is the most immediate way of publishing them. But reading poems aloud is also strangely different from writing them. Writing a poem is a lonely act. Poets need solitude, poets need long periods of meditation, and many poets need to keep the poem close to themselves a long time before they even show it to anybody else. Then they go out on the reading circuit and they find themselves doing the most opposite thing in the world. They are being totally public. Somehow I think that this reversal from the internal to the external is a useful things for poets.

Poetry readings were not fashionable until a few years ago. Twenty years ago most poets read their poems only two or three times a year. Now many of us can read thirty or fifty times a year if we wish, and are likely to read at least twenty or twenty-five. I think that American poetry is in a good period right now, and I think that the poetry reading is a part of the reason. Poems are becoming more oral, more a matter of the ear and the mouth, and less a matter of the eye and the printed word on the page. Of course the quantity of readings also tends to make us better performers, because we practice so much and begin to take pride in the way we read.

What function does poetry fill in the modern world?

The same function it always filled. The modern world has nothing to do with it. This is the sort of question that panels are always being asked to answer, and it is a question that irritates me. Poetry continually changes, from generation to generation, but I think it is still the container and transmitter of feeling and wisdom, from generation to generation.

How do you choose the form of a poem?

Usually, whether a poem is in meter or in free verse, the original "given" of the poem decides the form—that is, the phrase or two, or the lines, that come to me at the beginning contain, in themselves, indications of the form. Sometimes, when a poem has not gone well, after some period of working on it, I will shake it up by trying to put it in a different form.

I have noticed a recurrent pattern like this: I think abstractly about a particular form—maybe the sonnet when I was writing in meter, or asymmetrical, end-stopped free verse now—just as a phenomenon, not in connection with anything I am writing. Two weeks later I find myself beginning a poem and it comes to me in the form that I had been thinking about earlier. Some sort of preparation has gone on, inside my head, of which I was not conscious.

How do you get published?

There is no way except to send poems out to magazines over and over again, and to keep on getting them rejected. People are always writing me letters and asking me how to get started, as if there were some magical answer. There isn't. Friends, if they are influential, can help a little, perhaps. But almost everyone I have known who has started as a poet has simply sent out four or five poems at a time to magazines that he liked. Almost everyone gets rejected at first. Poetry editors are fallible like anybody else. They see a strange name and they don't know whether to trust their reactions. After they have continued to read a man's poems for a while, they may get used to his name, and also to the way that he thinks and feels and writes, and they may feel more confident of their reactions and start to accept his work. More often, he will begin to get notes and even letters of rejection, after the first plethora of rejection slips, and then finally he receives his first acceptance, followed by more rejections. Then he gets a second acceptance and a third. Then he discovers that putting his poems in magazines is not the panacea he once imagined it to be.

When you read aloud, why do you stop at the end of lines?

Because that's the way the lines are written. Without line structure, we lose the major means of controlling the rhythm of the poem. I don't actually stop, I hope, unless the sense of the line does. But I pause a little even if the sense hurtles on to the beginning of the next line (the effect called enjambment) in order to indicate, with my voice, the line structure visible on the page. I know that many actors, doing Shakespeare for instance, never pause at the ends of lines unless the sense forces them to. I think they are mistaken. Shakespeare could have written in paragraphs if he had wanted to.

When you write, are you trying to communicate
an emotional experience?

Certainly something like communication is intended in the act of writing a poem, or at least in the act of finishing a poem—that is, my idea of a good poem includes the concept that somebody else can respond to it. Whether the reader feels what I feel, I can never know, because we can never feel what another person feels. But one does have the sense of assent or agreement, when one reads certain poems at certain times, at least. I think that I know some of what Andrew Marvell felt, when I read "To His Coy Mistress." But when I begin to write a poem—when the poem advances on me as I sit there unsuspecting—I am not consciously trying to "communicate an emotional experience." I am receiving messages from some other part of myself—I am talking to myself, perhaps. Communication comes about mostly in the polishing, the finishing, but it is there partly from the start, because potential communication is part of the definition of a poem.

For whom do you write?

A psychoanalyst once delivered a paper about writers at a conference, and distributed mimeographed copies of his talk beforehand. His secretary had typed up his notes from an illegible longhand and had made a lot of mistakes. The first correction he had to make was, "For 'autistic' read 'artistic' throughout."

At another conference I attended, a linguist presented a model of the English language, and I kept looking through it for poetry.

I found it under "austistic utterance," which he said could be later refined into lyric poetry. Autism starts with a child babbling in his crib. The child who remains autistic never gets outside himself. The poet does, and the shaping of his words is directed toward other people, but it begins with the pleasure in his own mouth. If he does not have this pleasure, he is not a poet.

I cannot say that I really write for any particular group of people. It is true that I sometimes hear the voices of my friends commenting on my poems as I write them—self-criticism by ventriloquism—but I don't really think I'm exactly writing for my friends. Richard Wilbur once said that all poems were addressed to the Muse, and that the Muse was made up to conceal the fact that poems were not addressed to anybody in particular.

Can you know too much to write? Can you be too intelligent to be a poet?

No. I used to think this was true, but now I think that this sort of excuse is just an excuse. I think that when someone thinks that his self-critical powers keep him from writing, or that he doesn't write because he knows he will not be as good as Shakespeare, or that he doesn't write because he thinks somebody else has said it all before, he is actually not writing because he is afraid. He is using the intelligence in the way it is usually used, as a means of evading feeling. Poets have to be intelligent, but intelligence is relatively common. Many people have enough intelligence to control language, but they lack the courage which allows the artist to free his imagination to create a work of art at a possible cost.

Should students start with older poetry or new poetry?

There is no question of "should." As a matter of practical fact, most students are more likely to come to poetry through new things than through old things. Once they have learned how to read, they can move backward in time and pick up the old poetry. I think it is pointless to teach an introductory poetry class chronologically, beginning with the oldest poetry first. This method might reach a few people—we are all different—but it will alienate most students. I think a better strategy, on the part of the teacher, is to start with relatively new things.

Do you write on a schedule?

I used to. And many people do at some point in their lives. I used to work from six to eight in the morning. Now I write when I feel like it—which is sometimes not at all for a couple of weeks, and then a great deal for several days. I don't think there is any right or wrong about it. To write on a schedule may be useful, especially when a person is young—it was for me. But one should do what feels right.

How much knowledge of the author's background is necessary for the reading of poetry?

Not much, I think—it can even hurt our reading. Yet when we love a poet we want to know more about him, and to read about his life, and after that we usually feel, rightly or wrongly, that we understand some of his poems in a different way. Sometimes we substitute the author's biography for the poems themselves, as people often do with Yeats, for instance. Instead of reading the poems, they seize any detail in the poem that they can relate to his life as a means of evading the serious content, the deep feeling, which lies at the center of the poem and which can be disturbing. That is the *trouble* with devoting ourselves to the author's background. Historical background is important, as I have said before, in defining vocabulary. Vocabulary has to be taken in a very wide sense—it has to include the knowledge that the Elizabethans had deer parks, for example. It definitely helps a reader to be intelligent and to know a lot. But he should beware of substituting the author's biography, or historical background, or prose philosophy, for what actually exists in the lines of his poems.

What is the best way to teach poetry?

I think that we should teach feelings, responses, images, and noise long before intellectual analysis and prosodical detail. A man cannot build a camel by starting with a hoof. He must start with a whole camel, and ride it, and smell it, and live with it. Then, he still cannot build a camel, unless he is God. But he can carry in his head the idea of a whole camel.

TEN GREAT
POETS

William Shakespeare (1564-1616)

from THE SONNETS

18

Shall I compare thee to a summer's day?
Thou art more lovely and more temperate:
Rough winds do shake the darling buds of May,
And summer's lease hath all too short a date:
Sometime too hot the eye of heaven shines,
And often is his gold complexion dimm'd;
And every fair from fair sometime declines,
By chance or nature's changing course untrimm'd:
But thy eternal summer shall not fade
Nor lose possession of that fair thou ow'st.
Nor shall Death brag thou wand'rest in his shade,
When in eternal lines to time thou grow'st;
  So long as men can breathe or eyes can see,
  So long lives this and this gives life to thee.

29

When, in disgrace with fortune and men's eyes,
I all alone beweep my outcast state
And trouble deaf heaven with my bootless cries
And look upon myself and curse my fate,
Wishing me like to one more rich in hope,
Featured like him, like him with friends possess'd,
Desiring this man's art and that man's scope,
With what I most enjoy contented least;
Yet in these thoughts myself almost despising
Haply I think on thee, and then my state,
Like to the lark at break of day arising
From sullen earth, sings hymns at heaven's gate;
  For thy sweet love remember'd such wealth brings
  That then I scorn to change my state with kings.

55

Not marble, nor the gilded monuments
Of princes, shall outlive this powerful rhyme;
But you shall shine more bright in these contents
Than unswept stone, besmeared with sluttish time.
When wasteful war shall statues overturn,
And broils root out the work of masonry,
Nor Mars his sword nor war's quick fire shall burn
The living record of your memory.
'Gainst death and all-oblivious enmity
Shall you pace forth; your praise shall still find room
Even in the eyes of all posterity
That wear this world out to the ending doom.
   So, till the judgment that yourself arise,
   You live in this, and dwell in lovers' eyes.

64

When I have seen by Time's fell hand defaced
The rich proud cost of outworn buried age;
When sometime lofty towers I see down-razed,
And brass eternal slave to mortal rage:
When I have seen the hungry ocean gain
Advantage on the kingdom of the shore,
And the firm soil win of the watery main,
Increasing store with loss and loss with store:
When I have seen such interchange of state,
Or state itself confounded to decay;
Ruin hath taught me thus to ruminate—
That Time will come and take my love away.
   This thought is as a death, which cannot choose
   But weep to have that which it fears to lose.

71

No longer mourn for me when I am dead
Than you shall hear the surly sullen bell
Give warning to the world that I am fled
From this vile world, with vilest worms to dwell;
Nay, if you read this line, remember not
The hand that writ it, for I love you so

That I in your sweet thoughts would be forgot
If thinking on me then should make you woe.
Oh, if, I say, you look upon this verse
When I perhaps compounded am with clay,
Do not so much as my poor name rehearse,
But let your love even with my life decay;
  Lest the wise world should look into your moan,
  And mock you with me after I am gone.

94

They that have power to hurt, and will do none,
That do not do the thing they most do show,
Who, moving others, are themselves as stone,
Unmoved, cold, and to temptation slow—
They rightly do inherit heaven's graces,
And husband nature's riches from expense;
They are the lords and owners of their faces,
Others, but stewards of their excellence.
The summer's flower is to the summer sweet
Though to itself it only live and die,
But if that flower with base infection meet,
The basest weed outbraves his dignity:
  For sweetest things turn sourest by their deeds;
  Lilies that fester smell far worse than weeds.

106

When in the chronicle of wasted time
I see description of the fairest wights,
And beauty making beautiful old rhyme
In praise of ladies dead, and lovely knights,
Then, in the blazon of sweet beauty's best,
Of hand, of foot, of lip, of eye, of brow,
I see their antique pen would have expressed
Even such a beauty as you master now.
So all their praises are but prophecies
Of this our time, all you prefiguring;
And, for they looked but with divining eyes,
They had not skill enough your worth to sing!
  For we, which now behold these present days,
  Have eyes to wonder, but lack tongues to praise.

107

Not mine own fears nor the prophetic soul
Of the wide world dreaming on things to come,
Can yet the lease of my true love control,
Supposed as forfeit to a confined doom.
The mortal moon hath her eclipse endured,
And the sad augurs mock their own presage;
Incertainties now crown themselves assured,
And peace proclaims olives of endless age.
Now with the drops of this most balmy time
My love looks fresh, and Death to me subscribes,
Since, spite of him, I'll live in this poor rhyme,
While he insults o'er dull and speechless tribes.
   And thou in this shalt find thy monument,
   When tyrants' crests and tombs of brass are spent.

116

Let me not to the marriage of true minds
Admit impediments. Love is not love
Which alters when it alteration finds,
Or bends with the remover to remove.
O no! it is an ever-fixed mark
That looks on tempests, and is never shaken;
It is the star to every wandering bark,
Whose worth's unknown, although his height be taken.
Love's not Time's fool, though rosy lips and cheeks
Within his bending sickle's compass come;
Love alters not with his brief hours and weeks,
But bears it out even to the edge of doom.
   If this be error and upon me proved,
   I never writ, nor no man ever loved.

129

Th' expense of spirit in a waste of shame
Is lust in action; and till action, lust
Is perjur'd, murd'rous, bloody, full of blame,
Savage, extreme, rude, cruel, not to trust;
Enjoy'd no sooner but despised straight,

Past reason hunted, and no sooner had,
Past reason hated, as a swallowed bait
On purpose laid to make the taker mad;
Mad in pursuit and in possession so;
Had, having, and in quest to have, extreme;
A bliss in proof, and prov'd, a very woe;
Before, a joy propos'd; behind a dream.
  All this the world well knows; yet none knows well
  To shun the heaven that leads men to this hell.

146

Poor soul, the center of my sinful earth,
Pressed by these rebel powers that thee array,
Why dost thou pine within and suffer dearth,
Painting thy outward walls so costly gay?
Why so large cost, having so short a lease,
Dost thou upon thy fading mansion spend?
Shall worms, inheritors of this excess,
Eat up thy charge? Is this thy body's end?
Then, soul, live thou upon thy servant's loss,
And let that pine to aggravate thy store;
Buy terms divine in selling hours of dross;
Within be fed, without be rich no more:
  So shalt thou feed on Death, that feeds on men,
  And Death once dead, there's no more dying then.

SPEECHES FROM THE PLAYS

The Barge She Sat In

The barge she sat in, like a burnished throne,
Burned on the water: the poop was beaten gold;
Purple the sails, and so perfumed that
The winds were love-sick with them; the oars were silver,
Which to the tune of flutes kept stroke, and made
The water which they beat to follow faster,
As amorous of their strokes. For her own person,
It beggared all description: she did lie
In her pavilion—cloth-of-gold of tissue—
O'er-picturing that Venus where we see

The fancy out work nature: on each side her
Stood pretty dimpled boys, like smiling Cupids,
With divers-coloured fans, whose wind did seem
To glow the delicate cheeks which they did cool,
And what they undid did.

from ANTONY AND CLEOPATRA

Once More Unto the Breach, Dear Friends

Once more unto the breach, dear friends, once more;
Or close the wall up with our English dead.
In peace there's nothing so becomes a man
As modest stillness and humility.
But when the blast of war blows in our ears,
Then imitate the action of the tiger,
Stiffen the sinews, summon up the blood,
Disguise fair nature with hard-favored rage.
Then lend the eye a terrible aspect,
Let it pry through the portage of the head
Like the brass cannon. Let the brow o'erwhelm it
As fearfully as doth a galled rock
O'erhand and jutty his confounded base,
Swilled with the wild and wasteful ocean.
Now set the teeth and stretch the nostril wide,
Hold hard the breath, and bend up every spirit
To his full height. On, on, you noblest English,
Whose blood is fet from fathers of war proof!
Fathers that, like so many Alexanders,
Have in these parts from morn till even fought,
And sheathed their swords for lack of argument.
Dishonor not your mothers. Now attest
That those whom you called fathers did beget you.
Be copy now to men of grosser blood,
And teach them how to war. And you, good yeomen,
Whose limbs were made in England, show us here
The mettle of your pasture. Let us swear
That you are worth your breeding which I doubt not,
For there is none of you so mean and base
That hath not noble lustre in your eyes.
I see you stand like greyhounds in the slips,
Straining upon the start. The game's afoot.
Follow your spirit, and upon this charge
Cry "God for Harry, England, and Saint George!"

from KING HENRY THE FIFTH

Let's Talk of Graves

Let's talk of graves, of worms, and epitaphs.
Make dust our paper, and with rainy eyes
Write sorrow on the bosom of the earth . . .
For God's sake, let us sit upon the ground,
And tell sad stories of the death of kings:
How some have been deposed; some slain in war;
Some haunted by the ghosts they have deposed;
Some poisoned by their wives; some sleeping killed;
All murdered: for within the hollow crown
That rounds the mortal temples of a king
Keeps Death his court; and there the antick sits,
Scoffing his state, and grinning at his pomp;
Allowing him a breath, a little scene,
To monarchize, be feared, and kill with looks;
Infusing him with self and vain conceit—
As if this flesh which walls about our life,
Were brass impregnable; and humoured thus,
Comes at the last, and with a little pin
Bores through his castle-wall, and—farewell king!

from KING RICHARD THE SECOND

SONGS FROM THE PLAYS

Blow, Blow, Thou Winter Wind!

Blow, blow, thou winter wind,
Thou art not so unkind
As man's ingratitude;
Thy tooth is not so keen
Because thou art not seen,
Although thy breath be rude.
Heigh ho! sing heigh ho! unto the green holly:
Most friendship is feigning, most loving mere folly:
Then, heigh ho! the holly!
This life is most jolly.
Freeze, freeze, thou bitter sky,
Thou dost not bite so nigh
As benefits forgot:
Though thou the waters warp,
Thy sting is not so sharp

WILLIAM SHAKESPEARE 🜍 97

As friend remembered not.
Heigh ho! sing heigh ho! unto the green holly:
Most friendship is feigning, most loving mere folly:
Then, heigh ho! the holly!
This life is most jolly.

from AS YOU LIKE IT

It Was a Lover and His Lass

It was a lover and his lass,
With a hey, and a ho, and a hey nonino,
That o'er the green corn-field did pass
In the spring-time, the only pretty ring-time,
When birds do sing, hey ding a ding, ding!
Sweet lovers love the spring.

Between the acres of the rye,
With a hey, and a ho, and a hey nonino,
These pretty country folks would lie,
In spring-time, the only pretty ring-time,
When birds do sing, hey ding a ding, ding!
Sweet lovers love the spring.

This carol they began that hour,
With a hey, and a ho, and a hey nonino,
How that a life was but a flower
In spring-time, the only pretty ring-time,
When birds do sing, hey ding a ding, ding!
Sweet lovers love the spring.

And therefore take the present time,
With a hey, and a ho, and a hey nonino,
For love is crowned with the prime
In spring-time, the only pretty ring-time,
When birds do sing, hey ding a ding, ding!
Sweet lovers love the spring.

from AS YOU LIKE IT

When That I Was

When that I was and a little tiny boy,
With hey, ho, the wind and the rain,

A foolish thing was but a toy,
    For the rain it raineth every day.

But when I came to man's estate
    With hey, ho, the wind and the rain,
'Gainst knaves and thieves men shut their gate,
    For the rain it raineth every day.

But when I came, alas! to wive,
    With hey, ho, the wind and the rain,
By swaggering could I never thrive,
    For the rain it raineth every day.

But when I came unto my beds,
    With hey, ho, the wind and the rain,
With toss-pots still had drunken heads,
    For the rain it raineth every day.

A great while ago the world begun,
    With hey, ho, the wind and the rain,
But that's all one, our play is done,
    And we'll strive to please you every day.

from TWELFTH NIGHT

Fear No More

Fear no more the heat o' the sun,
    Nor the furious winter's rages;
Thou thy wordly task hast done,
    Home art gone, and ta'en thy wages;
Golden lads and girls all must,
As chimney-sweepers, come to dust.

Fear no more the frown o' the great,
    Thou art past the tyrant's stroke:
Care no more to clothe and eat;
    To thee the reed is as the oak:
The sceptre, learning, physic, must
All follow this, and come to dust.

Fear no more the lightning-flash,
    Nor the all-dreaded thunder-stone;
Fear not slander, censure rash;
    Thou hast finished joy and moan;

WILLIAM SHAKESPEARE   99

All lovers young, all lovers must
Consign to thee, and come to dust.

No exorciser harm thee!
    Nor no witchcraft charm thee!
Ghost unlaid forbear thee!
    Nothing ill come near thee!
Quiet consummation have;
And renowned by thy grave!

from CYMBELINE

Full Fathom Five

Full fathom five thy father lies;
    Of his bones are coral made;
Those are pearls that were his eyes;
    Nothing of him that doth fade
But doth suffer a sea-change
Into something rich and strange.
Sea-nymphs hourly ring his knell:
    Hark! Now I hear them—
        Ding, dong, bell.

from THE TEMPEST

John Donne (1572-1631)

SONG

Go and catch a falling star,
  Get with child a mandrake root,
Tell me where all past years are,
  Or who cleft the devil's foot;
Teach me to hear mermaids singing,
Or to keep off envy's stinging,
    And find
    What wind
Serves to advance an honest mind.

If thou be'st born to strange sights,
  Things invisible to see,
Ride ten thousand days and nights
  Till age snow white hairs on thee;
Thou, when thou return'st wilt tell me
All strange wonders that befell thee,
    And swear
    No where
Lives a woman true, and fair.

If thou find'st one, let me know;
  Such a pilgrimage were sweet.
Yet do not; I would not go,
  Though at next door we might meet.
Though she were true when you met her,
And last, till you write your letter,
    Yet she
    Will be
False, ere I come, to two, or three.

THE ECSTASY

Where, like a pillow on a bed,
  A pregnant bank swelled up, to rest
The violet's reclining head,
  Sat we two, one another's best.

Our hands were firmly cemented
  With a fast balm, which thence did spring;
Our eye-beams twisted, and did thread
  Our eyes upon one double string.

So to engraft our hands, as yet
  Was all the means to make us one;
And pictures in our eyes to get
  Was all our propagation.

As, 'twixt two equal armies, Fate
  Suspends uncertain victory,
Our souls—which to advance their state,
  Were gone out—hung 'twixt her and me.

And whilst our souls negotiate there,
  We like sepulchral statues lay;
All day the same our postures were,
  And we said nothing all the day.

If any, so by love refined,
  That he soul's language understood,
And by good love were grown all mind,
  Within convenient distance stood,

He—though he knew not which soul spake,
  Because both meant, not spoke the same—
Might thence a new concoction take,
  And part far purer than he came.

This ectasy doth unperplex
  (We said) and tell us what we love;
We see by this, it was not sex;
  We see, we saw not, what did move:

But as all several souls contain
  Mixture of things they know not what,
Love these mixed souls doth mix again,
  And makes both one, each this and that.

A single violet transplant,
  The strength, the color, and the size—
All which before was poor and scant—
  Redoubles still, and multiplies.

When love with one another so
  Interinanimates two souls,
That abler soul, which thence doth flow,
  Defects of loneliness controls.

We then, who are this new soul, know,
  Of what we are composed and made,
For th' atomies of which we grow
  Are souls, whom no change can invade.

But, O alas! so long, so far,
  Our bodies why do we forbear?
They are ours, though they're not we; we are
  Th' intelligences, they the spheres.

We owe them thanks, because they thus
  Did us, to us, at first convey,
Yielded their forces, sense, to us,
  Nor are dross to us, but allay.

On man heaven's influence works not so,
  But that it first imprints the air;
So soul into the soul may flow,
  Though it to body first repair.

As our blood labors to beget
  Spirits as like souls as it can,
Because such fingers need to knit
  That subtle knot, which makes us man:

So must pure lovers' souls descend
  To affections, and to faculties,
Which sense may reach and apprehend,
  Else a great prince in prison lies.

To our bodies turn we then, that so
  Weak men on love reveal'd may look;
Love's mysteries in souls do grow,
  But yet the body is his book.

And if some lover, such as we,
  Have heard this dialogue of one,
Let him still mark us, he shall see
  Small change when we're to bodies gone.

THE CANONIZATION

For Godsake hold your tongue, and let me love,
   Or chide my palsy, or my gout,
My five grey hairs, or ruined fortune flout;
     With wealth your state, your mind with arts improve,
       Take you a course, get you a place,
       Observe his Honor, or his Grace;
Or the king's real, or his stamped face
     Contemplate; what you will, approve,
     So you will let me love.

Alas, alas, who's injured by my love?
   What merchant's ships have my sighs drowned?
Who says my tears have overflowed his ground?
     When did my colds a forward spring remove?
       When did the heats which my veins fill
       Add one more to the plaguy bill?
Soldiers find wars, and lawyers find out still
     Litigious men, which quarrels move,
     Though she and I do love.

Call us what you will, we are made such by love;
   Call her one, me another fly,
We're tapers too, and at our own cost die,
     And we in us find the eagle and the dove.
       The Phoenix riddle hath more wit
       By us; we two being one are it.
So to one neutral thing both sexes fit,
     We die and rise the same, and prove
     Mysterious by this love.

We can die by it, if not live by love,
   And if unfit for tombs and hearse
Our legend be, it will be fit for verse;
     And if no piece of chronicle we prove,
       We'll build in sonnets pretty rooms;
       As well a well-wrought urn becomes
The greatest ashes, as half-acre tombs,
     And by these hymns all shall approve
     Us canonized for love:

And thus invoke us; You, whom reverend love
   Made one another's hermitage;
You, to whom love was peace, that now is rage;

Who did the whole world's soul contract, and drove
   Into the glasses of your eyes,
    So made such mirrors, and such spies,
That they did all to you epitomize;
   Countries, towns, courts: beg from above
   A pattern of your love.

A VALEDICTION FORBIDDING MOURNING

As virtuous men pass mildly away,
   And whisper to their souls to go,
Whilst some of their sad friends do say,
   The breath goes now, and some say, No:

So let us melt, and make no noise,
   No tear-floods, nor sigh-tempests move;
'Twere profanation of our joys
   To tell the laity our love.

Moving of th' earth brings harms and fears,
   Men reckon what it did, and meant;
But trepidation of the spheres,
   Though greater far, is innocent.

Dull sublunary lovers' love
   —Whose soul is sense—cannot admit
Absence, because it doth remove
   Those things which elemented it.

But we by a love so much refined
   That ourselves know not what it is,
Inter-assured of the mind,
   Care less eyes, lips and hands to miss.

Our two souls therefore, which are one,
   Though I must go, endure not yet
A breach, but an expansion,
   Like gold to airy thinness beat.

If they be two, they are two so
   As stiff twin compasses are two;
Thy soul, the fix'd foot, makes no show
   To move, but doth, if th' other do.

And though it in the centre sit,
    Yet, when the other far doth roam,
It leans, and hearkens after it,
    And grows erect, as that comes home.

Such wilt thou be to me, who must,
    Like th' other foot, obliquely run;
Thy firmness makes my circle just,
    And makes me end where I begun.

THE FLEA

Mark but this flea, and mark in this,
How little that which thou deniest me is;
It sucked me first, and now sucks thee,
And in this flea our two bloods mingled be.
Thou know'st that this cannot be said
A sin, nor shame, nor loss of maidenhead;
    Yet this enjoys before it woo,
    And pampered swells with one blood made of two;
    And this, alas! is more than we would do.

Oh stay, three lives in one flea spare,
Where we almost, yea, more than married are.
This flea is you and I, and this
Our marriage bed, and marriage temple is.
Though parents grudge, and you, we're met,
And cloistered in these living walls of jet.
    Though use make you apt to kill me,
    Let not to that self-murder added be,
    And sacrilege, three sins in killing three.

Cruel and sudden, hast thou since
Purpled thy nail in blood of innocence?
Wherein could this flea guilty be,
Except in that drop which it sucked from thee?
Yet thou triumph'st, and sayest that thou
Find'st not thyself nor me the weaker now.
    'Tis true; then learn how false fears be;
    Just so much honor, when thou yieldest to me,
    Will waste, as this flea's death took life from thee.

from HOLY SONNETS

7

At the round earth's imagined corners, blow
Your trumpets, angels, and arise, arise
From death, you numberless infinities
Of souls, and to your scattered bodies go;
All whom the flood did, and fire shall o'erthrow;
All whom war, dearth, age, agues, tyrannies,
Despair, law, chance, hath slain, and you whose eyes
Shall behold God, and never taste death's woe.
But let them sleep, Lord, and me mourn a space,
For, if above all these, my sins abound,
'Tis late to ask abundance of Thy grace,
When we are there; here on this lowly ground,
Teach me how to repent; for that's as good
As if Thou hadst sealed my pardon with Thy blood.

10

Death, be not proud, though some have called thee
Mighty and dreadful, for thou are not so;
For those whom thou think'st thou dost overthrow
Die not, poor Death; nor yet canst thou kill me.
From rest and sleep, which but thy pictures be,
Much pleasure; then from thee much more must flow;
And soonest our best men with thee do go—
Rest of their bones and souls' delivery!
Thou'rt slave to fate, chance, kings, and desperate men,
And dost with poison, war, and sickness dwell;
And poppy or charms can make us sleep as well
And better than thy stroke. Why swell'st thou then?
One short sleep past, we wake eternally,
And Death shall be no more: Death, thou shalt die.

14

Batter my heart, three-personed God; for you
As yet but knock, breathe, shine, and seek to mend.
That I may rise and stand, o'erthrow me and bend
Your force to break, blow, burn, and make me new.
I, like an usurped town, to another due,
Labor to admit you, but, oh, to no end;
Reason, your viceroy in me, me should defend,
But is captived and proves weak or untrue.
Yet dearly I love you and would be loved fain,
But am bethrothed unto your enemy:
Divorce me, untie or break that knot again,
Take me to you, imprison me, for I,
Except you enthrall me, never shall be free,
Nor ever chaste, except you ravish me.

A HYMN TO GOD THE FATHER

Wilt Thou forgive that sin where I begun,
   Which was my sin, though it were done before?
Wilt Thou forgive that sin, through which I run,
   And do run still, though still I do deplore?
      When Thou hast done, Thou hast not done,
        For I have more.

Wilt Thou forgive that sin by which I have won
   Others to sin, and made my sin their door?
Wilt Thou forgive that sin which I did shun
   A year or two, but wallowed in a score?
      When Thou hast done, Thou hast not done,
        For I have more.

I have a sin of fear, that when I have spun
   My last thread, I shall perish on the shore;
Swear by Thyself that at my death Thy Son
   Shall shine as He shines now, and heretofore;
      And, having done that, Thou hast done;
        I fear no more.

John Milton (1608-1674)

LYCIDAS

Yet once more, O ye laurels, and once more
Ye myrtles brown, with ivy never-sere,
I come to pluck your berries harsh and crude
And, with forc'd fingers rude,
Shatter your leaves before the mellowing year.
Bitter constraint, and sad occasion dear
Compels me to disturb your season due:
For Lycidas is dead, dead ere his prime,
Young Lycidas, and hath not left his peer:
Who would not sing for Lycidas? He knew
Himself to sing, and build the lofty rhyme.
He must not float upon his watery bier
Unwept, and welter to the parching wind,
Without the mead of some melodious tear.
  Begin then, Sisters of the sacred well,
That from beneath the seat of Jove doth spring;
Begin, and somewhat loudly sweep the string.
Hence with denial vain, and coy excuse:
So may some gentle Muse
With lucky words favour my destin'd urn:
And, as he passes, turn,
And bid fair peace be to my sable shroud.
  For we were nurs'd upon the self-same hill,
Fed the same flock by fountain, shade, and rill.
Together both, ere the high lawns appear'd
Under the opening eye-lids of the morn,
We drove afield, and both together heard
What time the grey-fly winds her sultry horn,
Battening our flocks with the fresh dews of night,
Oft, till the star, that rose, at evening, bright,
Toward heaven's descent had slop'd his westering wheel.
Meanwhile the rural ditties were not mute,
Temper'd to the oaten flute;
Rough Satyrs danc'd, and Fauns with cloven heel
From the glad sound would not be absent long;
And old Damoetas lov'd to hear our song.
  But, O the heavy change, now thou art gone,

Now thou art gone and never must return!
Thee, Shepherd, thee the woods and desert caves
With wild thyme and the gadding vine o'ergrown,
And all their echoes mourn:
The willows, and the copses green,
Shall now no more be seen
Fanning their joyous leaves to thy soft lays.
As killing as the canker to the rose,
Or taint-worm to the weanling herds that graze,
Or frost to flowers, that their gay wardrobe wear,
When first the white-thorn blows;
Such, Lycidas, thy loss to shepherd's ear.
   Where were ye, Nymphs, when the remorseless deep
Clos'd o'er the head of your lov'd Lycidas?
For neither were ye playing on the steep,
Where your old Bards, the famous Druids, lie,
Nor on the shaggy top of Mona high,
Nor yet where Deva spreads her wizard stream:
Ay me! I fondly dream!
Had ye been there—for what could that have done?
What could the Muse herself that Orpheus bore,
The Muse herself, for her enchanting son,
Whom universal Nature did lament,
When, by the rout that made the hideous roar,
His gory visage down the stream was sent,
Down the swift Hebrus to the Lesbian shore?
   Alas! what boots it with incessant care
To tend the homely, slighted shepherd's trade,
And strictly meditate the thankless Muse?
Were it not better done, as others use,
To sport with Amaryllis in the shade,
Or with the tangles of Neæra's hair?
Fame is the spur that the clear spirit doth raise
(That last infirmity of noble mind)
To scorn delights, and live laborious days;
But the fair guerdon when we hope to find,
And think to burst out into sudden blaze,
Comes the blind Fury with the abhorred shears,
And slits the thin-spun life. 'But not the praise',
Phœbus replied, and touch'd my trembling ears;
'Fame is no plant that grows on mortal soil,
Nor in the glistering foil
Set off to the world, nor in broad rumour lies;
But lives and spreads aloft by those pure eyes
And perfect witness of all-judging Jove.
As he pronounces lastly on each deed,

Of so much fame in heaven expect thy meed.
 O fountain Arethuse and thou honour'd flood,
Smooth-sliding Mincius, crown'd with vocal reeds.
That strain I heard was of a higher mood:
But now my oat proceeds,
And listens to the herald of the sea
That came in Neptune's plea;
He ask'd the waves, and ask'd the felon winds,
What hard mishap hath doom'd this gentle swain?
And question'd every gust of rugged wings
That blows from off each beaked promontory:
They knew not of his story;
And sage Hippotades their answer brings,
That not a blast was from his dungeon stray'd;
The air was calm, and on the level brine
Sleek Panope with all her sisters play'd.
It was that fatal and perfidious bark,
Built in the eclipse, and rigg'd with curses dark,
That sunk so low that sacred head of thine.
 Next Camus, reverend sire, went footing slow,
His mantle hairy, and his bonnet sedge,
Inwrought with figures dim, and on the edge
Like to that sanguine flower inscrib'd with woe.
'Ah! Who hath reft (quoth he) my dearest pledge?'
Last came, and last did go,
The pilot of the Galilean lake;
Two massy keys he bore of metals twain,
(The golden opes, the iron shuts amain),
He shook his mitred locks, and stern bespake:
'How well could I have spar'd for thee, young swain,
Enow of such, as for their bellies' sake,
Creep, and intrude, and climb into the fold!
Of other care they little reckoning make,
Than how to scramble at the shearers' feast,
And shove away the worthy bidden guest;
Blind mouths! that scarce themselves know how to hold
A sheep-hook, or have learn'd aught else the least
That to the faithful herdsman's art belongs!
What recks it them? What need they? They are sped;
And when they list, their lean and flashy songs
Grate on their scrannel pipes of wretched straw;
The hungry sheep look up, and are not fed,
But, swoln with wind and the rank mist they draw,
Rot inwardly, and foul contagion spread:
Besides what the grim wolf with privy paw
Daily devours apace, and nothing said:

But that two-handed engine at the door
Stands ready to smite once, and smite no more.'
   Return Alpheus, the dread voice is past,
That shrunk thy streams, return, Sicilian Muse,
And call the vales, and bid them hither cast
Their bells, and flowerets of a thousand hues.
Ye valleys low, where the mild whispers use
Of shades, and wanton winds, and gushing brooks,
On whose fresh lap the swart star sparely looks;
Throw hither all your quaint enamell'd eyes,
That on the green turf suck the honied showers,
And purple all the ground with vernal flowers.
Bring the rathe primrose that forsaken dies,
The tufted crow-toe, and pale jessamine,
The white pink, and the pansy freak'd with jet,
The glowing violet,
The musk-rose, and the well-attir'd woodbine,
With cowslips wan that hang the pensive head,
And every flower that sad embroidery wears:
Bid Amaranthus all his beauty shed,
And daffodillies fill their cups with tears,
To strew the laureat hearse where Lycid lies.
For, so to interpose a little ease,
Let our frail thoughts dally with false surmise;
Ay me! Whilst thee the shores and sounding seas
Wash far away, where'er thy bones are hurl'd,
Whether beyond the stormy Hebrides,
Where thou perhaps, under the whelming tide,
Visit'st the bottom of the monstrous world;
Or whether thou, to our moist vows denied,
Sleep'st by the fable of Bellerus old,
Where the great Vision of the guarded Mount
Looks towards Namancos and Bayona's hold;
Look homeward, Angel, now, and melt with ruth:
And, O ye dolphins, waft the hapless youth.
   Weep no more, woeful Shepherds, weep no more,
For Lycidas your sorrow is not dead,
Sunk though he be beneath the watery floor;
So sinks the day-star in the ocean bed,
And yet anon repairs his drooping head,
And tricks his beams, and with new-spangled ore
Flames in the forehead of the morning sky:
So Lycidas sunk low, but mounted high,
Through the dear might of Him that walk'd the waves;
Where, other groves and other streams along,
With nectar pure his oozy locks he laves,

And hears the unexpressive nuptial song,
In the blest kingdoms meek of joy and love.
There entertain him all the saints above,
In solemn troops, and sweet societies,
That sing, and, singing, in their glory move,
And wipe the tears for ever from his eyes.
Now, Lycidas, the shepherds weep no more;
Henceforth thou art the Genius of the shore,
In thy large recompense, and shalt be good
To all that wander in that perilous flood.
   Thus sang the uncouth swain to the oaks and rills,
While the still morn went out with sandals grey;
He touch'd the tender stops of various quills,
With eager thought warbling his Doric lay:
And now the sun had stretch'd out all the hills,
And now was dropt into the western bay:
At last he rose, and twitch'd his mantle blue:
To-morrow to fresh woods, and pastures new.

from THE SONNETS

7: HOW SOON HATH TIME

How soon hath time, the subtle thief of youth,
   Stolen on his wing my three-and-twenti'th year!
   My hasting days fly on with full career,
   But my late spring no bud or blossom shew'th.
Perhaps my semblance might deceive the truth,
   That I to manhood am arriv'd so near;
   And inward ripeness doth much less appear,
   That some more timely-happy spirits endu'th.
Yet be it less or more, or soon or slow,
   It shall be still in strictest measure ev'n
   To that same lot, however mean, or high,
Toward which time leads me, and the will of heav'n;
   All is, if I have grace to use it so,
   As ever in my great Task-Master's eye.

18: ON THE LATE MASSACRE IN PIEDMONT

Avenge, O Lord, thy slaughtered saints, whose bones
    Lie scattered on the Alpine mountains cold;
    Ev'n them who kept thy truth so pure of old,
    When all our fathers worshipped stocks and stones,
Forget not: in thy book record their groans
    Who were thy sheep, and in their ancient fold
    Slain by the bloody Piedmontese, that rolled
    Mother with infant down the rocks. Their moans
The vales redoubled to the hills, and they
    To heav'n. Their martyred blood and ashes sow
    O'er all the' Italian fields, where still doth sway
The triple Tyrant that from these may grow
    A hundredfold, who, having learnt thy way,
    Early may fly the Babylonian woe.

19: ON HIS BLINDNESS

When I consider how my light is spent
    Ere half my days in this dark world and wide,
    And that one talent which is death to hide
    Lodged with me useless, though my soul more bent
To serve therewith my Maker, and present
    My true account, lest He returning chide,
    "Doth God exact day-labor, light denied?"
    I fondly ask. But Patience, to prevent
That murmur, soon replies, "God doth not need
    Either man's work or his own gifts. Who best
    Bear His mild yoke, they serve Him best. His state
Is kingly: thousands at His bidding speed,
    And post o'er land and ocean without rest;
    They also serve who only stand and wait."

from COMUS

The star that bids the shepherd fold
Now the top of heaven doth hold;
And the gilded car of day
His glowing axle doth allay
In the steep Atlantic stream;
And the slope sun his upward beam

Shoots against the dusky pole,
Pacing toward the other goal
Of his chamber in the east.
Meanwhile, welcome joy and feast,
Midnight shout and revelry,
Tipsy dance and jollity.
Braid your locks with rosy twine,
Dropping odors, dropping wine.
Rigor now is gone to bed;
And Advice with scrupulous head,
Strict Age, and sour Severity,
With their grave saws, in slumber lie.
We, that are of purer fire,
Imitate the starry quire,
Who, in their nightly watchful spheres,
Lead in swift round the months and years.
The sounds and seas, with all their finny drove,
Now to the moon in wavering morrice move;
And on the tawny sands and shelves
Trip the pert fairies and the dapper elves.
By dimpled brook and fountain-brim,
The wood-nymphs, decked with daisies trim,
Their merry wakes and pastimes keep:
What hath night to do with sleep?
Night hath better sweets to prove;
Venus now wakes, and wakens Love.
Come, let us our rites begin;
'Tis only daylight that makes sin. . . .
Come, knit hands, and beat the ground
In a light fantastic round.

from PARADISE LOST

                    . . . His pride
Had cast him out from Heaven, with all his host
Of rebel Angels, by whose aid, aspiring
To set himself in glory above his peers,
He trusted to have equalled the Most High,
If he opposed, and, with ambitious aim
Against the throne and monarchy of God,
Raised impious war in Heaven and battle proud,
With vain attempt. Him the Almighty Power
Hurled headlong flaming from the ethereal sky,
With hideous ruin and combustion, down
To bottomless perdition, there to dwell

In adamantine chains and penal fire,
Who durst defy the Omnipotent to arms.
   Nine times the space that measures day and night
To mortal men, he, with his horrid crew,
Lay vanquished, rolling in the fiery gulf,
Confounded, though immortal. But his doom
Reserved him to more wrath; for now the thought
Both of lost happiness and lasting pain
Torments him: round he throws his baleful eyes,
That witnessed huge affliction and dismay,
Mixed with obdurate pride and steadfast hate.
At once, as far as Angels ken, he views
The dismal situation waste and wild.
A dungeon horrible, on all sides round,
As one great furnace flamed; yet from those flames
No light; but rather darkness visible
Served only to discover sights of woe,
Regions of sorrow, doleful shades, where peace
And rest can never dwell, hope never comes
That comes to all, but torture without end
Still urges, and a fiery deluge, fed
With ever-burning sulphur unconsumed.
Such place Eternal Justice had prepared
For those rebellious; here their prison ordained
In utter darkness, and their portion set,
As far removed from God and light of Heaven
As from the centre thrice to the utmost pole.
Oh, how unlike the place from whence they fell!
   Forthwith upright he rears from off the pool
His mighty stature; on each hand the flames
Driven backward slope their pointing spires, and, rolled
In billows, leave i' the midst a horrid vale.
Then with expanded wings he steers his flight
Aloft, incumbent on the dusky air,
That felt unusual weight; till on dry land
He lights—if it were land that ever burned
With solid, as the lake with liquid fire;
And such appeared in hue as when the force
Of subterranean wind transports a hill
Torn from Pelorus, or the shattered side
Of thundering Aetna, whose combustible
And fuelled entrails, thence conceiving fire,
Sublimed with mineral fury, aid the winds,
And leave a singèd bottom all involved
With stench and smoke.

Alexander Pope (1688-1744)

ODE ON SOLITUDE

Happy the man, whose wish and care
   A few paternal acres bound,
Content to breathe his native air,
      In his own ground.

Whose herds with milk, whose fields with bread,
   Whose flocks supply him with attire,
Whose trees in summer yield him shade,
      In winter fire.

Blest, who can unconcern'dly find
   Hours, days, and years slide soft away,
In health of body, peace of mind,
      Quiet by day,

Sound sleep by night, study and ease,
   Together mixed; sweet recreation;
And innocence, which most does please
      With meditation.

Thus let me live, unseen, unknown,
   Thus unlamented let me die,
Steal from the world, and not a stone
      Tell where I lie.

AN ESSAY ON CRITICISM
PART II

    Of all the causes which conspire to blind
Man's erring judgment, and misguide the mind,
What the weak head with strongest bias rules,
Is pride, the never-failing vice of fools,
Whatever nature has in worth denied,
She gives in large recruits of needful pride;
For as in bodies, thus in souls, we find

What wants in blood and spirits, swelled with wind.
Pride, where wit fails, steps in to our defense,
And fills up all the mighty void of sense.
If once right reason drives that cloud away,
Truth breaks upon us with resistless day.
Trust not yourself; but your defects to know,
Make use of every friend—and every foe.

A little learning is a dangerous thing;
Drink deep, or taste not the Pierian spring.
There, shallow drafts intoxicate the brain,
And drinking largely sobers us again.
Fired at first sight with what the Muse imparts,
In fearless youth we tempt the heights of arts,
While from the bounded level of our mind
Short views we take, nor see the lengths behind;
But more advanced, behold with strange surprise
New distant scenes of endless science rise!
So pleased at first the towering Alps we try,
Mount o'er the vales, and seem to tread the sky,
Th' eternal snows appear already past,
And the first clouds and mountains seem the last;
But, those attained, we tremble to survey
The growing labors of the lengthened way,
Th' increasing prospect tires our wandering eyes,
Hills peep o'er hills, and Alps on Alps arise!

A perfect judge will read each work of wit
With the same spirit that its author writ;
Survey the whole, nor seek slight faults to find
Where nature moves, and rapture warms the mind;
Nor lose, for that malignant dull delight,
The generous pleasure to be charmed with wit.
But in such lays as neither ebb nor flow,
Correctly cold, and regularly low,
That shunning faults, one quiet tenor keep,
We cannot blame indeed—but we may sleep.
In wit, as nature, what affects our hearts
Is not th' exactness of peculiar parts;
'Tis not a lip, or eye, we beauty call,
But the joint force and full result of all.
Thus when we view some well-proportioned dome,
(The world's just wonder, and even thine, O Rome!)
No single parts unequally surprise,
All comes united to th' admiring eyes;
No monstrous height, or breadth, or length appear;
The whole at once is bold and regular.

Whoever thinks a faultless piece to see,

Thinks what ne'er was, nor is, nor e'er shall be.
In every work regard the writer's end,
Since none can compass more than they intend;
And if the means be just, the conduct true,
Applause, in spite of trivial faults, is due.
As men of breeding, sometimes men of wit,
T'avoid great errors, must the less commit;
Neglect the rules each verbal critic lays,
For not to know some trifles is a praise.
Most critics, fond of some subservient art,
Still make the whole depend upon a part;
They talk of principles, but notions prize,
And all to one loved folly sacrifice.
    Once on a time, La Mancha's knight, they say,
A certain bard encountering on the way,
Discoursed in terms as just, with looks as sage,
As e'er could Dennis, of the Grecian stage;
Concluding all were desperate sots and fools,
Who durst depart from Aristotle's rules.
Our author, happy in a judge so nice,
Produced his play, and begged the knight's advice;
Made him observe the subject, and the plot,
The manners, passions, unities, what not?
All which, exact to rule, were brought about,
Were but a combat in the lists left out.
"What! leave the combat out?" exclaims the knight;
Yes, or we must renounce the Stagirite.
"Not so, by heaven!" (he answers in a rage).
"Knights, squires, and steeds must enter on the stage."
So vast a throng the stage can ne'er contain.
"Then build a new, or act it in a plain."
    Thus critics, of less judgment than caprice,
Curious not knowing, not exact but nice,
Form short ideas; and offend in arts,
(As most in manners) by a love to parts.
    Some to conceit alone their taste confine,
And glittering thoughts struck out at every line;
Pleased with a work where nothing's just or fit;
One glaring chaos and wild heap of wit.
Poets like painters, thus unskilled to trace
The naked nature and the living grace,
With gold and jewels cover every part,
And hide with ornaments their want of art.
True wit is nature to advantage dressed,
What oft was thought, but ne'er so well expressed;
Something, whose truth convinced at sight we find,

That gives us back the image of our mind.
As shades more sweetly recommend the light,
So modest plainness sets off sprightly wit.
For works may have more wit than does them good,
As bodies perish through excess of blood.
    Others for language all their care express,
And value books, as women men, for dress;
Their praise is still—the style is excellent;
The Sense, they humbly take upon content.
Words are like leaves; and where they most abound,
Much fruit of sense beneath is rarely found:
False Eloquence, like the prismatic glass,
Its gaudy colours spreads on every place;
The face of Nature we no more survey,
All glares alike, without distinction gay:
But true expression, like th' unchanging Sun,
Clears and improves whate'er it shines upon,
It gilds all objects, but it alters none.
Expression is the dress of thought, and still
Appears more decent, as more suitable;
A vile conceit in pompous words expressed,
Is like a clown in regal purple dressed:
For different styles with different subjects sort,
As several garbs with country, town, and court.
Some by old words to fame have made pretence,
Ancients in phrase, mere moderns in their sense;
Such laboured nothings, in so strange a style,
Amaze th' unlearn'd, and make the learned smile.
Unlucky, as Fungoso in the play,
These sparks with awkward vanity display
What the fine gentleman wore yesterday;
And but so mimic ancient wits at best,
As apes our grandsires, in their doublets drest.
In words, as fashions, the same rule will hold;
Alike fantastic, if too new, or old:
Be not the first by whom the new are tried,
Nor yet the last to lay the old aside.
    But most by *Numbers* judge a Poet's song;
And smooth or rough, with them is right or wrong:
In the bright Muse, though thousand charms conspire,
Her voice is all these tuneful fools admire;
Who haunt Parnassus but to please their ear,
Not mend their minds; as some to Church repair,
Not for the doctrine, but the music there.
These equal syllables alone require,
Tho' oft the ear the open vowels tire;

While expletives their feeble aid do join;
And ten low words oft creep in one dull line.
While they ring round the same unvaried chimes,
With sure returns of still expected rhymes;
Where-e'er you find "the cooling western breeze,"
In the next line, it "whispers through the trees":
If crystal streams "with pleasing murmurs creep,"
The reader's threatened (not in vain) with "sleep":
Then, at the last and only couplet fraught
With some unmeaning thing they call a thought,
A needless Alexandrine ends the song,
That, like a wounded snake, drags its slow length along.
Leave such to tune their own dull rhymes, and know
What's roundly smooth or languishingly slow;
And praise the easy vigor of a line,
Where Denham's strength, and Waller's sweetness join.
True ease in writing comes from art, not chance,
As those move easiest who have learned to dance.
'Tis not enough no harshness gives offence:
The sound must seem an echo to the sense.
Soft is the strain when Zephyr gently blows,
And the smooth stream in smoother numbers flows;
But when loud surges lash the sounding shore,
The hoarse, rough verse should like the torrent roar.
When Ajax strives some rock's vast weight to throw,
The line, too, labors, and the words move slow.
Not so when swift Camilla scours the plain,
Flies o'er th' unbending corn, and skims along the main.
Hear how Timotheus' varied lays surprise,
And bid alternate passions fall and rise!
While, at each change, the son of Libyan Jove
Now burns with glory, and then melts with love;
Now his fierce eyes with sparkling fury glow,
Now sighs steal out, and tears begin to flow:
Persians and Greeks like turns of nature found,
And the world's victor stood subdued by sound!
The power of music all our hearts allow,
And what Timotheus was, is Dryden now.
    Avoid extremes; and shun the fault of such
Who still are pleased too little or too much,
At every trifle scorn to take offence;
That always shows great pride, or little sense;
Those heads, as stomachs, are not sure the best,
Which nauseate all, and nothing can digest.
Yet let not each gay turn thy rapture move;
For fools admire, but men of sense approve:

As things seem large which we through mists descry,
Dullness is ever apt to magnify.
　　Some foreign writers, some our own despise;
The Ancients only, or the Moderns prize.
Thus Wit, like Faith, by each man is applied
To one small sect, and all are damned beside.
Meanly they seek the blessing to confine,
And force that sun but on a part to shine,
Which not alone the southern wit sublimes,
But ripens spirits in cold northern climes;
Which from the first has shone on ages past,
Enlights the present, and shall warm the last;
Tho' each may feel increases and decays,
And see now clearer and now darker days.
Regard not then if Wit be old or new,
But blame the false, and value still the true.
　　Some ne'er advance a Judgment of their own,
But catch the spreading notion of the Town;
They reason and conclude by precedent,
And own stale nonsense which they ne'er invent.
Some judge of author's names, not works, and then
Nor praise nor blame the writings, but the men.
Of all this servile herd the worst is he
That in proud dullness joins with Quality:
A constant Critic at the great man's board,
To fetch and carry nonsense for my Lord.
What woful stuff this madrigal would be,
In some starved hackney sonneteer, or me?
But let a Lord once own the happy lines,
How the wit brightens! how the style refines!
Before his sacred name flies every fault,
And each exalted stanza teems with thought!
　　The Vulgar thus through Imitation err;
As oft the Learn'd by being singular;
So much they scorn the crowd, that if the throng
By chance go right, they purposely go wrong;
So Schismatics the plain believers quit,
And are but damned for having too much wit.
Some praise at morning what they blame at night;
But always think the last opinion right.
A Muse by these is like a mistress used,
This hour she's idolized, the next abused;
While their weak heads, like towns unfortified,
Twixt sense and nonsense daily change their side.
Ask them the cause; they're wiser still, they say;
And still tomorrow's wiser than today.

We think our fathers fools, so wise we grow;
Our wiser sons, no doubt, will think us so.
Once school-divines this zealous isle o'erspread;
Who knew most sentences, was deepest read;
Faith, gospel, all, seem'd made to be disputed,
And none had sense enough to be confuted:
Scotists and Thomists, now, in peace remain,
Amidst their kindred cobwebs in Duck Lane.
If faith itself has diff'rent dresses worn,
What wonder modes in wit should take their turn?
Oft, leaving what is natural and fit,
The current folly proves the ready wit;
And authors think their reputation safe,
Which lives as long as fools are pleas'd to laugh.
      Some, valuing those of their own side or mind,
Still make themselves the measure of mankind:
Fondly we think we honor merit then,
When we but praise ourselves in other men.
Parties in wit attend on those of state,
And public faction doubles private hate.
Pride, malice, folly, against Dryden rose,
In various shapes of parsons, critics, beaux;
But sense survived, when merry jests were past;
For rising merit will buoy up at last.
Might he return, and bless once more our eyes,
New Blackmores and new Milbourns must arise:
Nay should great Homer lift his awful head,
Zoilus again would start up from the dead.
Envy will merit, as its shade, pursue;
But like a shadow, proves the substance true;
For envied Wit, like Sol eclipsed, makes known
Th' opposing body's grossness, not its own,
When first that sun too powerful beams displays,
It draws up vapours which obscure its rays;
But even those clouds at last adorn its way,
Reflect new glories, and augment the day.
      Be thou the first true merit to befriend;
His praise is lost, who stays till all commend.
Short is the date, alas, of modern rhymes,
And 'tis but just to let them live betimes.
No longer now that golden age appears,
When Patriarch-wits survived a thousand years:
Now length of Fame (our second life) is lost,
And bare threescore is all even that can boast;
Our sons their fathers' failing language see;
And such as Chaucer is, shall Dryden be.

So when the faithful pencil has designed
Some bright Idea of the master's mind,
Where a new world leaps out at his command,
And ready Nature waits upon his hand;
When the ripe colours soften and unite,
And sweetly melt into just shade and light;
When mellowing years their full perfection give,
And each bold figure just begins to live,
The treacherous colours the fair art betray,
And all the bright creation fades away!
    Unhappy Wit, like most mistaken things,
Atones not for that envy which it brings.
In youth alone its empty praise we boast,
But soon the short-lived vanity is lost:
Like some fair flower the early spring supplies,
That gaily blooms, but even in blooming dies.
What is this Wit, which must our cares employ?
The owner's wife, that other men enjoy;
Then most our trouble still when most admired,
And still the more we give, the more required;
Whose fame with pains we guard, but lose with ease,
Sure some to vex, but never all to please;
'Tis what the vicious fear, the virtuous shun,
By fools 'tis hated, and by knaves undone!
    If Wit so much from Ignorance undergo,
Ah let not Learning too commence its foe!
Of old, those met rewards who could excel,
And such were praised who but endeavoured well:
Tho' triumphs were to generals only due,
Crowns were reserved to grace the soldiers too.
Now, they who reach Parnassus' lofty crown,
Employ their pains to spurn some others down;
And while self-love each jealous writer rules,
Contending wits become the sport of fools:
But still the worst with most regret commend,
For each ill Author is as bad a Friend.
To what base ends, and by what abject ways,
Are mortals urged thro' sacred lust of praise!
Ah ne'er so dire a thirst of glory boast,
Nor in the Critic let the Man be lost.
Good-nature and good-sense must ever join;
To err is human, to forgive, divine.
    But if in noble minds some dregs remain
Not yet purged off, of spleen and sour disdain;
Discharge that rage on more provoking crimes,
Nor fear a dearth in these flagitious times.

No pardon vile Obscenity should find,
Tho' wit and art conspire to move your mind;
But Dulness with Obscenity must prove
As shameful sure as Impotence in love.
In the fat age of pleasure, wealth, and ease,
Sprung the rank weed, and thrived with large increase:
When love was all an easy Monarch's care;
Seldom at council, never in a war:
Jilts ruled the state, and statesmen farces writ;
Nay Wits had pensions, and young Lords had wit:
The Fair sat panting at a Courtier's play,
And not a Mask went unimproved away:
The modest fan was lifted up no more,
And Virgins smiled at what they blushed before,
The following licence of a Foreign reign
Did all the dregs of bold Socinus drain;
Then unbelieving priests reformed the nation,
And taught more pleasant methods of salvation;
Where Heaven's free subjects might their rights dispute,
Lest God himself should seem too absolute:
Pulpits their sacred satire learned to spare,
And Vice admired to find a flatterer there!
Encouraged thus, Wit's Titans braved the skies,
And the press groaned with licensed blasphemies.
These monsters, Critics! with your darts engage,
Here point your thunder, and exhaust your rage!
Yet shun their fault, who, scandalously nice,
Will needs mistake an author into vice;
All seems infected that th' infected spy,
As all looks yellow to the jaundiced eye.

AN ESSAY ON MAN
EPISTLE II

Know then thyself, presume not God to scan:
The proper study of mankind is man.
Placed on this isthmus of a middle state,
A being darkly wise and rudely great;
With too much knowledge for the sceptic side,
With too much weakness for the stoic's pride,
He hangs between; in doubt to act, or rest;
In doubt to deem himself a god or beast;
In doubt his mind or body to prefer;

Born but to die, and reasoning but to err;
Alike in ignorance, his reason such,
Whether he thinks too little or too much:
Chaos of thought and passion, all confused;
Still by himself abused, or disabused;
Created half to rise, and half to fall;
Great lord of all things, yet a prey to all;
Sole judge of truth, in endless error hurled;
The glory, jest, and riddle of the world!
    Go, wondrous creature; mount where science guides,
Go, measure earth, weigh air, and state the tides;
Instruct the planets in what orbs to run,
Correct old Time, and regulate the sun;
Go, soar with Plato to th' empyreal sphere,
To the first good, first perfect, and first fair;
Or tread the mazy round his followers trod,
And quitting sense call imitating God;
As eastern priests in giddy circles run,
And turn their heads to imitate the sun.
Go, teach Eternal Wisdom how to rule—
Then drop into thyself, and be a fool!
    Superior beings, when of late they saw
A mortal man unfold all nature's law,
Admired such wisdom in an earthly shape,
And showed a Newton, as we show an ape.
    Could he, whose rules the rapid comet bind,
Describe or fix one movement of his mind?
Who saw its fires here rise, and there descend,
Explain his own beginning or his end?
Alas! what wonder! Man's superior part
Unchecked may rise, and climb from art to art;
But when his own great work is but begun,
What reason weaves, by passion is undone.
    Trace science, then, with modesty thy guide;
First strip off all her equipage of pride;
Deduct what is but vanity or dress,
Or learning's luxury, or idleness,
Or tricks to show the stretch of human brain,
Mere curious pleasure, or ingenious pain;
Expunge the whole, or lop th' excrescent parts
Of all our vices have created arts;
Then see how little the remaining sum,
Which served the past, and must the times to come!
    Two principles in human nature reign;
Self-love to urge, and reason to restrain;
Nor this a good, nor that a bad we call,

Each works its end to move or govern all;
And to their proper operation still
Ascribe all good; to their improper, ill.
    Self-love, the spring of motion, acts the soul;
Reason's comparing balance rules the whole.
Man, but for that, no action could attend,
And, but for this, were active to no end;
Fixed like a plant on his peculiar spot,
To draw nutrition, propagate, and rot;
Or, meteor-like, flame lawless through the void,
Destroying others, by himself destroyed.
    Most strength the moving principle requires;
Active its task, it prompts, impels, inspires;
Sedate and quiet, the comparing lies,
Formed but to check, deliberate, and advise.
Self-love still stronger, as its objects nigh,
Reason's at distance and in prospect lie;
That sees immediate good by present sense;
Reason, the future and the consequence.
Thicker than arguments, temptations throng,
At best more watchful this, but that more strong.
The action of the stronger to suspend,
Reason still use, to reason still attend.
Attention, habit and experience gains;
Each strengthens reason, and self-love restrains.
    Let subtle schoolmen teach these friends to fight,
More studious to divide than to unite;
And grace and virtue, sense and reason split,
With all the rash dexterity of wit.
Wits, just like fools, at war about a name,
Have full as oft no meaning, or the same.
Self-love and reason to one end aspire,
Pain their aversion, pleasure their desire;
But greedy that, its object would devour,
This taste the honey, and not wound the flower;
Pleasure, or wrong or rightly understood,
Our greatest evil or our greatest good.

William Blake (1757-1827)

THE CHIMNEY SWEEPER

When my mother died I was very young,
And my father sold me while yet my tongue
Could scarcely cry " 'weep! 'weep! 'weep! 'weep!"
So your chimneys I sweep, and in soot I sleep.

There's little Tom Dacre, who cried when his head,
That curled like a lamb's back, was shaved: so I said
"Hush, Tom! never mind it, for when your head's bare
You know that the soot cannot spoil your white hair."

And so he was quiet, and that very night,
As Tom was a-sleeping, he had such a sight!
That thousands of sweepers, Dick, Joe, Ned, and Jack,
Were all of them locked up in coffins of black.

And by came an Angel who had a bright key,
And he opened the coffins and set them all free;
Then down a green plain leaping, laughing, they run,
And wash in a river, and shine in the Sun.

Then naked and white, all their bags left behind,
They rise upon clouds and sport in the wind;
And the Angel told Tom, if he'd be a good boy,
He'd have God for his father, and never want joy.

And so Tom awoke; and we rose in the dark,
And got with our bags and our brushes to work.
Tho' the morning was cold, Tom was happy and warm;
So if all do their duty they need not fear harm.

from SONGS OF INNOCENCE

THE CHIMNEY SWEEPER

A little black thing among the snow,
Crying ' 'weep! 'weep!' in notes of woe!
"Where are thy father and mother? say?"
"They are both gone up to the church to pray.

"Because I was happy upon the hearth,
"And smil'd among the winter's snow,
"They clothed me in the clothes of death,
"And taught me to sing the notes of woe.

"And because I am happy and dance and sing,
"They think they have done me no injury,
"And are gone to praise God and his priest and king,
"Who make up a heaven of our misery."

from SONGS OF EXPERIENCE

THE TYGER

Tyger! Tyger! burning bright
In the forests of the night,
What immortal hand or eye
Could frame thy fearful symmetry?

In what distant deeps or skies
Burnt the fire of thine eyes?
On what wings dare he aspire?
What the hand dare seize the fire?

And what shoulder, and what art,
Could twist the sinews of thy heart?
And when thy heart began to beat,
What dread hand? and what dread feet?

What the hammer? what the chain?
In what furnace was thy brain?
What the anvil? what dread grasp
Dare its deadly terrors clasp?

When the stars threw down their spears
And watered heaven with their tears,
Did he smile his work to see?
Did he who made the Lamb make thee?

Tyger! Tyger! burning bright
In the forests of the night,
What immortal hand or eye
Dare frame thy fearful symmetry?

from SONGS OF EXPERIENCE

WILLIAM BLAKE 129

THE GARDEN OF LOVE

I went to the Garden of Love,
And saw what I never had seen:
A Chapel was built in the midst,
Where I used to play on the green.

And the gates of this Chapel were shut,
And "Thou shalt not" writ over the door;
So I turned to the Garden of Love
That so many sweet flowers bore;

And I saw it was filled with graves,
And tomb-stones where flowers should be;
And Priests in black gowns were walking their rounds,
And binding with briars my joys and desires.

from SONGS OF EXPERIENCE

A POISON TREE

I was angry with my friend:
I told my wrath, my wrath did end.
I was angry with my foe:
I told it not, my wrath did grow.

And I watered it in fears
Night and morning with my tears,
And I sunned it with smiles
And with soft deceitful wiles.

And it grew both day and night,
Till it bore an apple bright,
And my foe beheld it shine,
And he knew that it was mine—

And into my garden stole
When the night had veiled the pole;
In the morning, glad I see
My foe outstretched beneath the tree.

from SONGS OF EXPERIENCE

LOVE'S SECRET

Never seek to tell thy love,
  Love that never told can be;
For the gentle wind does move
  Silently, invisibly.

I told my love, I told my love,
  I told her all my heart;
Trembling, cold, in ghastly fears,
  Ah! she did depart!

Soon as she was gone from me,
  A traveler came by,
Silently, invisibly:
  He took her with a sigh.

MOCK ON, MOCK ON, VOLTAIRE, ROUSSEAU

Mock on, mock on, Voltaire, Rousseau,
  Mock on, mock on; 'tis all in vain;
You throw the sand against the wind
  And the wind blows it back again.

And every sand becomes a gem
  Reflected in the beams divine;
Blown back, they blind the mocking eye,
  But still in Israel's paths they shine.

The atoms of Democritus
  And Newton's particles of light
Are sands upon the Red Sea shore,
  Where Israel's tents do shine so bright.

from MILTON

PREFACE

And did those feet in ancient time
Walk upon England's mountains green?
And was the Holy Lamb of God
On England's pleasant pastures seen?

And did the countenance divine
Shine forth upon our clouded hills?
And was Jerusalem builded here
Among these dark Satanic mills?

Bring me my bow of burning gold!
Bring me my arrows of desire!
Bring me my spear! O clouds, unfold!
Bring me my chariot of fire!

I will not cease from mental fight,
Nor shall my sword sleep in my hand,
Till we have built Jerusalem
In England's green and pleasant land.

from AUGURIES OF INNOCENCE

To see a world in a grain of sand
And a Heaven in a wild flower,
Hold Infinity in the palm of your hand
And Eternity in an hour.

A robin redbreast in a cage
Puts all Heaven in a rage.
A dove-house filled with doves and pigeons
Shudders Hell through all its regions.
A dog starved at his master's gate
Predicts the ruin of the state.
A horse misused upon the road
Calls to Heaven for human blood.
Each outcry of the hunted hare
A fibre from the brain does tear.
A skylark wounded in the wing,
A cherubim does cease to sing.
The game cock clipped and armed for fight
Does the rising sun affright.
Every wolf's and lion's howl
Raises from Hell a human soul.
The wild deer wandering here and there
Keeps the human soul from care.
The lamb misused breeds public strife
And yet forgives the butcher's knife.
The bat that flits at close of eve

Has left the brain that won't believe.
The owl that calls upon the night
Speaks the unbeliever's fright.
He who shall hurt the little wren
Shall never be beloved by men.
He who the ox to wrath had moved
Shall never be by woman loved.

John Keats (1795-1821)

ON FIRST LOOKING INTO CHAPMAN'S HOMER

Much have I travell'd in the realms of gold,
And many goodly states and kingdoms seen;
Round many western islands have I been
Which bards in fealty to Apollo hold.
Oft of one wide expanse had I been told
That deep-brow'd Homer ruled as his demesne:
Yet did I never breathe its pure serene
Till I heard Chapman speak out loud and bold.
Then felt I like some watcher of the skies
When a new planet swims into his ken;
Or like stout Cortez when with eagle eyes
He stared at the Pacific—and all his men
Look'd at each other with a wild surmise—
Silent, upon a peak in Darien.

WHEN I HAVE FEARS THAT I MAY CEASE TO BE

When I have fears that I may cease to be
Before my pen has gleaned my teeming brain,
Before high-piled books in charactery,
Hold like rich garners the full ripened grain;
When I behold, upon the night's starred face,
Huge cloudy symbols of a high romance,
And think that I may never live to trace
Their shadows, with the magic hand of chance;
And when I feel, fair creature of an hour,
That I shall never look upon thee more,
Never have relish in the faery power
Of unreflecting love; then on the shore
Of the wide world I stand alone, and think
Till love and fame to nothingness do sink.

BRIGHT STAR, WOULD I WERE STEADFAST

Bright star, would I were steadfast as thou art—
Not in lone splendor hung aloft the night,
And watching, with eternal lids apart,
Like nature's patient sleepless Eremite,
The moving waters at their priestlike task
Of pure ablution round earth's human shores,
Or gazing on the new soft fallen mask
Of snow upon the mountains and the moors:
No—yet still steadfast, still unchangeable,
Pillowed upon my fair love's ripening breast
To feel for ever its soft fall and swell,
Awake for ever in a sweet unrest;
Still, still to hear her tender-taken breath,
And so live ever—or else swoon to death.

ODE TO A NIGHTINGALE

My heart aches, and a drowsy numbness pains
    My sense, as though of hemlock I had drunk,
Or emptied some dull opiate to the drains
    One minute past, and Lethe-wards had sunk:
'Tis not through envy of thy happy lot,
    But being too happy in thy happiness,
        That thou, light-winged Dryad of the trees,
        In some melodious plot
    Of beechen green, and shadows numberless,
        Singest of summer in full-throated ease.

O for a draught of vintage, that hath been
    Cooled a long age in the deep-delved earth,
Tasting of Flora and the country green,
    Dance, and Provençal song, and sun-burnt mirth!
O for a beaker full of the warm South,
    Full of the true, the blushful Hippocrene,
        With beaded bubbles winking at the brim,
        And purple-stained mouth;
That I might drink, and leave the world unseen,
    And with thee fade away into the forest dim:

Fade far away, dissolve, and quite forget
    What thou among the leaves hast never known,

The weariness, the fever, and the fret
    Here, where men sit and hear each other groan;
Where palsy shakes a few, sad, last gray hairs,
    Where youth grows pale, and spectre-thin, and dies;
        Where but to think is to be full of sorrow
            And leaden-eyed despairs;
Where beauty cannot keep her lustrous eyes,
    Or new love pine at them beyond tomorrow.

Away! away! for I will fly to thee,
    Not charioted by Bacchus and his pards,
But on the viewless wings of Poesy,
    Though the dull brain perplexes and retards:
Already with thee! tender is the night,
    And haply the Queen-Moon is on her throne,
        Clustered around by all her starry fays;
            But here there is no light,
Save what from heaven is with the breezes blown
    Through verdurous glooms and winding mossy ways.

I cannot see what flowers are at my feet,
    Nor what soft incense hangs upon the boughs,
But, in embalmed darkness, guess each sweet
    Wherewith the seasonable month endows
The grass, the thicket, and the fruit-tree wild;
    White hawthorn, and the pastoral eglantine;
        Fast-fading violets covered up in leaves;
            And mid-May's eldest child,
The coming musk-rose, full of dewy wine,
    The murmurous haunt of flies on summer eves.

Darkling I listen; and for many a time
    I have been half in love with easeful Death,
Called him soft names in many a mused rhyme,
    To take into the air my quiet breath;
Now more than ever seems it rich to die,
    To cease upon the midnight with no pain,
        While thou art pouring forth thy soul abroad
            In such an ectasy!
Still wouldst thou sing, and I have ears in vain—
    To thy high requiem become a sod.

Thou was not born for death, immortal bird!
    No hungry generations tread thee down;
The voice I hear this passing night was heard
    In ancient days by emperor and clown:

Perhaps the self-same song that found a path
    Through the sad heart of Ruth, when, sick for home,
      She stood in tears amid the alien corn;
          The same that oft-times hath
    Charmed magic casements, opening on the foam
    Of perilous seas, in faery lands forlorn.

Forlorn! the very word is like a bell
    To toll me back from thee to my sole self!
Adieu! the fancy cannot cheat so well
    As she is famed to do, deceiving elf.
Adieu! adieu! thy plaintive anthem fades
    Past the near meadows, over the still stream,
      Up the hill-side; and now 'tis buried deep
        In the next valley-glades:
    Was it a vision, or a waking dream?
      Fled is that music: do I wake or sleep?

LA BELLE DAME SANS MERCI

Ah, what can ail thee, wretched wight,
    Alone and palely loitering?
The sedge is withered from the lake,
    And no birds sing.

Ah, what can ail thee, wretched wight,
    So haggard and so woe-begone?
The squirrel's granary is full,
    And the harvest's done.

I see a lily on thy brow
    With anguish moist and fever dew,
And on thy cheek a fading rose
    Fast withereth too.

I met a lady in the meads,
    Full beautiful, a faery's child:
Her hair was long, her foot was light,
    And her eyes were wild.

I set her on my pacing steed,
    And nothing else saw all day long;
For sideways would she lean, and sing
    A faery's song.

I made a garland for her head,
    And bracelets too, and fragrant zone;
She looked at me as she did love,
    And made sweet moan.

She found me roots of relish sweet,
    And honey wild, and manna dew,
And sure in language strange she said,
    "I love thee true!"

She took me to her elfin grot,
    And there she wept and sighed full sore;
And there I shut her wild, wild eyes
    With kisses four.

And there she lulléd me asleep,
    And there I dream—Ah! woe betide!
The latest dream I ever dreamed
    On the cold hill's side.

I saw pale kings, and princes too,
    Pale warriors, death-pale were they all;
Who cried—"La Belle Dame Sans Merci
    Hath thee in thrall!"

I saw their starved lips in the gloom,
    With horrid warning gaped wide,
And I awoke and found me here,
    On the cold hill side.

And this is why I sojourn here,
    Alone and palely loitering,
Though the sedge is withered from the lake,
    And no birds sing.

ODE ON A GRECIAN URN

Thou still unravish'd bride of quietness,
    Thou foster-child of silence and slow time,
Sylvan historian, who canst thus express
    A flowery tale more sweetly than our rhyme:
What leaf-fring'd legend haunts about thy shape
    Of deities or mortals, or of both,
        In Tempe or the dales of Arcady?
    What men or gods are these? What maidens loth?

What mad pursuit? What struggle to escape?
　　What pipes and timbrels? What wild ecstasy?

Heard melodies are sweet, but those unheard
　　Are sweeter; therefore, ye soft pipes, play on;
Not to the sensual ear, but, more endear'd,
　　Pipe to the spirit ditties of no tone:
Fair youth, beneath the trees, thou canst not leave
　　Thy song, nor ever can those trees be bare;
　　　　Bold lover, never, never canst thou kiss,
Though winning near the goal—yet, do not grieve;
　　She cannot fade, though thou hast not thy bliss,
　　　　For ever wilt thou love, and she be fair!

Ah, happy, happy boughs! that cannot shed
　　Your leaves, nor ever bid the spring adieu;
And, happy melodist, unwearièd,
　　For ever piping songs for ever new;
More happy love! more happy, happy love!
　　For ever warm and still to be enjoy'd,
　　　　For ever panting, and for ever young;
All breathing human passion far above,
　　That leaves a heart high-sorrowful and cloy'd,
　　　　A burning forehead, and a parching tongue.

Who are these coming to the sacrifice?
　　To what green altar, O mysterious priest,
Lead'st thou that heifer lowing at the skies,
　　And all her silken flanks with garlands drest?
What little town by river or sea shore,
　　Or mountain-built with peaceful citadel,
　　　　Is emptied of this folk, this pious morn?
And, little town, thy streets for evermore
　　Will silent be; and not a soul to tell
　　　　Why thou art desolate, can e'er return.

O Attic shape! Fair attitude! with brede
　　Of marble men and maidens overwrought,
With forest branches and the trodden weed;
　　Thou, silent form, dost tease us out of thought
As doth eternity. Cold pastoral!
　　When old age shall this generation waste,
　　　　Thou shalt remain, in midst of other woe
Than ours, a friend to man, to whom thou say'st,
　　"Beauty is truth, truth beauty," that is all
　　　　Ye know on earth, and all ye need to know.

TO AUTUMN

Season of mists and mellow fruitfulness,
    Close bosom-friend of the maturing sun;
Conspiring with him how to load and bless
    With fruit the vines that round the thatch-eaves run;
To bend with apples the mossed cottage-trees,
    And fill all fruit with ripeness to the core;
        To swell the gourd, and plump the hazel shells
With a sweet kernel; to set budding more,
And still more, later flowers for the bees,
Until they think warm days will never cease,
        For Summer has o'er-brimmed their clammy cells.

Who hath not seen thee oft amid thy store?
    Sometimes whoever seeks abroad may find
Thee sitting careless on a granary floor,
    Thy hair soft-lifted by the winnowing wind;
Or on a half-reaped furrow sound asleep,
    Drowsed with the fume of poppies, while thy hook
        Spares the next swath and all its twined flowers;
And sometimes like a gleaner thou dost keep
    Steady thy laden head across a brook;
    Or by a cider-press, with patient look,
        Thou watchest the last oozings, hours by hours.

Where are the songs of Spring? Ay, where are they?
    Think not of them, thou has thy music too,—
While barrèd clouds bloom the soft-dying day,
    And touch the stubble-plains with rosy hue;
Then in a wailful choir, the small gnats mourn
    Among the river sallows, borne aloft
        Or sinking as the light wind lives or dies;
And full-grown lambs loud bleat from hilly bourn;
    Hedge-crickets sing; and now with treble soft
    The redbreast whistles from a garden-croft,
        And gathering swallows twitter in the skies.

Alfred, Lord Tennyson (1809-1892)

ULYSSES

It little profits that an idle king,
By this still hearth, among these barren crags,
Matched with an aged wife, I mete and dole
Unequal laws unto a savage race,
That hoard, and sleep, and feed, and know not me.
I cannot rest from travel: I will drink
Life to the lees: all times I have enjoyed
Greatly, have suffered greatly, both with those
That loved me, and alone; on shore, and when
Through scudding drifts the rainy Hyades
Vext the dim sea. I am become a name;
For always roaming with a hungry heart
Much have I seen and known: cities of men
And manners, climates, councils, governments,
Myself not least, but honored of them all,
And drunk delight of battle with my peers,
Far on the ringing plains of windy Troy.
I am a part of all that I have met;
Yet all experience is an arch wherethrough
Gleams that untraveled world, whose margin fades
For ever and for ever when I move.
How dull it is to pause, to make an end,
To rust unburnished, not to shine in use!
As though to breathe were life. Life piled on life
Were all too little, and of one to me
Little remains: but every hour is saved
From that eternal silence, something more,
A bringer of new things; and vile it were
For some three suns to store and hoard myself,
And this gray spirit yearning in desire
To follow knowledge, like a sinking star,
Beyond the utmost bound of human thought.
   This is my son, mine own Telemachus,
To whom I leave the scepter and the isle—
Well-loved of me, discerning to fulfill
This labor, by slow prudence to make mild

A rugged people, and through soft degrees
Subdue them to the useful and the good.
Most blameless is he, centered in the sphere
Of common duties, decent not to fail
In offices of tenderness, and pay
Meet adoration to my household gods,
When I am gone. He works his work, I mine.
    There lies the port: the vessel puffs her sail:
There gloom the dark broad seas. My mariners,
Souls that have toiled, and wrought, and thought with me—
That ever with a frolic welcome took
The thunder and the sunshine, and opposed
Free hearts, free foreheads—you and I are old;
Old age hath yet his honor and his toil;
Death closes all: but something ere the end,
Some work of noble note, may yet be done,
Not unbecoming men that strove with Gods.
The lights begin to twinkle from the rocks:
The long day wanes: the slow moon climbs: the deep
Moans round with many voices. Come, my friends,
'Tis not too late to seek a newer world.
Push off, and sitting well in order smite
The sounding furrows; for my purpose holds
To sail beyond the sunset, and the baths
Of all the western stars, until I die.
It may be that the gulfs will wash us down:
It may be we shall touch the Happy Isles,
And see the great Achilles, whom we knew.
Though much is taken, much abides; and though
We are not now that strength which in old days
Moved earth and heaven, that which we are, we are,
One equal temper of heroic hearts,
Made weak by time and fate, but strong in will
To strive, to seek, to find, and not to yield.

TEARS, IDLE TEARS

    Tears, idle tears, I know not what they mean,
Tears from the depth of some divine despair
Rise in the heart, and gather to the eyes,
In looking on the happy autumn-fields,
And thinking of the days that are no more.

Fresh as the first beam glittering on a sail,
That brings our friends up from the underworld,
Sad as the last which reddens over one
That sinks with all we love below the verge;
So sad, so fresh, the days that are no more.

Ah, sad and strange as in dark summer dawns
The earliest pipe of half-awakened birds
To dying ears, when unto dying eyes
The casement slowly grows a glimmering square;
So sad, so strange, the days that are no more.

Dear as remembered kisses after death,
And sweet as those by hopeless fancy feigned
On lips that are for others; deep as love,
Deep as first love, and wild with all regret;
O Death in Life, the days that are no more!

NOW SLEEPS THE CRIMSON PETAL

Now sleeps the crimson petal, now the white;
Nor waves the cypress in the palace walk;
Nor winks the gold fin in the porphyry font.
The firefly wakens. Waken thou with me.

Now droops the milk-white peacock like a ghost,
And like a ghost she glimmers on to me.

Now lies the Earth all Danaë to the stars,
And all thy heart lies open unto me.

Now slides the silent meteor on, and leaves
A shining furrow, as thy thoughts in me.

Now folds the lily all her sweetness up,
And slips into the bosom of the lake;
So fold thyself, my dearest, thou, and slip
Into my bosom and be lost in me.

ALFRED, LORD TENNYSON   ❧   143

from IN MEMORIAM

7

Dark house, by which once more I stand
    Here in the long unlovely street,
    Doors, where my heart was used to beat
So quickly, waiting for a hand,

A hand that can be clasped no more—
    Behold me, for I cannot sleep,
    And like a guilty thing I creep
At earliest morning to the door.

He is not here; but far away
    The noise of life begins again,
    And ghastly thro' the drizzling rain
On the bald street breaks the blank day.

THE EAGLE

He clasps the crag with crooked hands:
Close to the sun in lonely lands,
Ringed with the azure world, he stands.

The wrinkled sea beneath him crawls;
He watches from his mountain walls,
And like a thunderbolt he falls.

BREAK, BREAK, BREAK

Break, break, break,
    On thy cold gray stones, O Sea!
And I would that my tongue could utter
    The thoughts that arise in me.

O well for the fisherman's boy,
    That he shouts with his sister at play!
O well for the sailor lad,
    That he sings in his boat on the bay!

And the stately ships go on
  To their haven under the hill;
But O for the touch of a vanished hand,
  And the sound of a voice that is still!

Break, break, break,
  At the foot of thy crags, O Sea!
But the tender grace of a day that is dead
  Will never come back to me.

JUNE BRACKEN AND HEATHER
To—

There on the top of the down,
The wild heather round me and over me June's high blue,
When I look'd at the bracken so bright and the heather
    so brown,
I thought to myself I would offer this book to you,
This, and my love together,
To you that are seventy-seven,
With a faith as clear as the heights of the June-blue heaven,
And a fancy as summer-new
As the green of the bracken amid the gloom of the heather.

Walt Whitman (1819-1892)

OUT OF THE CRADLE ENDLESSLY ROCKING

Out of the cradle endlessly rocking,
Out of the mocking-bird's throat, the musical shuttle,
Out of the Ninth-month midnight,
Over the sterile sands and the fields beyond, where the child
    leaving his bed wander'd alone, bareheaded, barefoot,
Down from the shower'd halo,
Up from the mystic play of shadows twining and twisting
    as if they were alive,
Out from the patches of briers and blackberries,
From the memories of the bird that chanted to me,
From your memories sad brother, from the fitful risings and
    fallings I heard,
From under that yellow half-moon late-risen and swollen as if
    with tears,
From those beginning notes of yearning and love there in
    the mist,
From the thousand responses of my heart never to cease,
From the myriad thence-arous'd words,
From the word stronger and more delicious than any,
From such as now they start the scene revisiting,
As a flock, twittering, rising, or overhead passing,
Borne hither, ere all eludes me, hurriedly,
A man, yet by these tears a little boy again,
Throwing myself on the sand, confronting the waves,
I, chanter of pains and joys, uniter of here and hereafter,
Taking all hints to use them, but swiftly leaping beyond them,
A reminiscence sing.

Once Paumanok,
When the lilac-scent was in the air and Fifth-month grass
    was growing,
Up this seashore in some briers,
Two feather'd guests from Alabama, two together,
And their nest, and four light-green eggs spotted with brown,
And every day the he-bird to and fro near at hand,
And every day the she-bird crouch'd on her nest, silent, with
    bright eyes,

And every day, I, a curious boy, never too close, never
    disturbing them,
Cautiously peering, absorbing, translating.

Shine! shine! shine!
Pour down your warmth, great sun!
While we bask, we two together.

Two together!
Winds blow south, or winds blow north,
Day come white, or night come black,
Home, or rivers and mountains from home,
Singing all time, minding no time,
While we two keep together.

Till of a sudden,
May-be kill'd, unknown to her mate,
One forenoon the she-bird crouch'd not on the nest,
Nor return'd that afternoon, nor the next,
Nor ever appear'd again.

And thenceforward all summer in the sound of the sea,
And at night under the full of the moon in calmer weather,
Over the hoarse surging of the sea,
Or flitting from brier to brier by day,
I saw, I heard at intervals the remaining one, the he-bird,
The solitary guest from Alabama.

Blow! blow! blow!
Blow up sea-winds along Paumanok's shore;
I wait and I wait till you blow my mate to me.

Yes, when the stars glisten'd,
All night long on the prong of a moss-scallop'd stake,
Down almost amid the slapping waves,
Sat the lone singer wonderful causing tears.

He call'd on his mate,
He pour'd forth the meanings which I of all men know.

Yes my brother I know,
The rest might not, but I have treasur'd every note,
For more than once dimly down to the beach gliding,
Silent, avoiding the moonbeams, blending myself with the
    shadows,
Recalling now the obscure shapes, the echoes, the sounds and
    sights after their sorts,

The white arms out in the breakers tirelessly tossing,
I, with bare feet, a child, the wind wafting my hair,
Listen'd long and long.

Listen'd to keep, to sing, now translating the notes,
Following you my brother.

Soothe! soothe! soothe!
Close on its wave soothes the wave behind,
And again another behind embracing and lapping, every one
*   close,*
But my love soothes not me, not me.

Low hangs the moon, it rose late,
It is lagging—O I think it is heavy with love, with love.

O madly the sea pushes upon the land,
With love, with love.

O night! do I not see my love fluttering out among the breakers?
What is that little black thing I see there in the white?

Loud! loud! loud!
Loud I call to you, my love!

High and clear I shoot my voice over the waves,
Surely you must know who is here, is here,
You must know who I am, my love.

Low-hanging moon!
What is that dusky spot in your brown yellow?
O it is the shape, the shape of my mate!
O moon do not keep her from me any longer.

Land! land! O land!
Whichever way I turn, O I think you could give me my mate
*   back again if only you would,*
For I am almost sure I see her dimly whichever way I look.

O rising stars!
Perhaps the one I want so much will rise, will rise with
*   some of you.*

O throat! O trembling throat!
Sound clearer through the atmosphere!
Pierce the woods, the earth,
Somewhere listening to catch you must be the one I want.

Shake out carols!
Solitary here, the night's carols!
Carols of lonesome love! death's carols!
Carols under that lagging, yellow, waning moon!
O under that moon where she droops almost down into
    the sea!
O reckless despairing carols.

But soft! sink low!
Soft! let me just murmur,
And do you wait a moment you husky-nois'd sea,
For somewhere I believe I heard my mate responding to me,
So, faint, I must be still, be still to listen,
But not altogether still, for then she might not come
    immediately to me.

Hither my love!
Here I am! here!
With this just-sustain'd note I announce myself to you,
This gentle call is for you my love, for you.

Do not be decoy'd elsewhere,
That is the whistle of the wind, it is not my voice,
That is the fluttering, the fluttering of the spray,
Those are the shadows of leaves.

O darkness! O in vain!
O I am very sick and sorrowful.

O brown halo in the sky near the moon, dropping upon
    the sea!
O troubled reflection in the sea!
O throat! O throbbing heart!
And I singing uselessly, uselessly all the night.

O past! O happy life! O songs of joy!
In the air, in the woods, over fields,
Loved! loved! loved! loved! loved!
But my mate no more, no more with me!
We two together no more.

The aria sinking,
All else continuing, the stars shining,
The winds blowing, the notes of the bird continuous echoing,
With angry moans the fierce old mother incessantly moaning,

On the sands of Paumanok's shore gray and rustling,
The yellow half-moon enlarged, sagging down, drooping, the
  face of the sea almost touching,
The boy ecstatic, with his bare feet the waves, with his hair
  the atmosphere dallying,
The love in the heart long pent, now loose, now at last
  tumultuously bursting,
The aria's meaning, the ears, the soul, swiftly depositing,
The strange tears down the cheeks coursing,
The colloquy there, the trio, each uttering,
The undertone, the savage old mother incessantly crying,
To the boy's soul's questions sullenly timing, some drown'd
  secret hissing,
To the outsetting bard.

Demon or bird! (said the boy's soul,)
Is it indeed toward your mate you sing? or is it really to me?
For I, that was a child, my tongue's use sleeping, now I have
  heard you,
Now in a moment I know what I am for, I awake,
And already a thousand singers, a thousand songs, clearer,
  louder and more sorrowful than yours,
A thousand warbling echos have started to life within me,
  never to die.

O you singer solitary, singing by yourself, projecting me,
O solitary me listening, never more shall I cease perpetuating
  you,
Never more shall I escape, never more the reverberations,
Never more the cries of unsatisfied love be absent from me,
Never again leave me to be the peaceful child I was before
  what there in the night,
By the sea under the yellow and sagging moon,
The messenger there arous'd, the fire, the sweet hell within,
The unknown want, the destiny of me.

O give me the clew! (it lurks in the night here somewhere,)
O if I am to have so much, let me have more!

A word then, (for I will conquer it,)
The word final, superior to all,
Subtle, sent up—what is it? I listen;
Are you whispering it, and have been all the time, you
  sea-waves?
Is that it from your liquid rims and wet sands?

Whereto answering, the sea,
Delaying not, hurrying not,
Whisper'd me through the night, and very plainly before
  daybreak,
Lisp'd to me the low and delicious word death,
And again, death, death, death, death,
Hissing melodious, neither like the bird nor like my arous'd
  child's heart,
But edging near as privately for me rustling at my feet,
Creeping thence steadily up to my ears and laving me softly
  all over,
Death, death, death, death, death.

Which I do not forget,
But fuse the song of my dusky demon and brother,
That he sang to me in the moonlight on Paumanok's gray
  beach,
With the thousand responsive songs at random,
My own songs awaked from that hour,
And with them the key, the word up from the waves,
The word of the sweetest song and all songs,
That strong and delicious word which, creeping to my feet,
(Or like some old crone rocking the cradle, swathed in sweet
  garments, bending aside,)
The sea whisper'd me.

THE DALLIANCE OF THE EAGLES

Skirting the river road, (my forenoon walk, my rest,)
Skyward in air a sudden muffled sound, the dalliance of the
  eagles,
The rushing amorous contact high in space together,
The clinching interlocking claws, a living, fierce, gyrating wheel,
Four beating wings, two beaks, a swirling mass tight grappling,
In tumbling turning clustering loops, straight downward falling,
Till o'er the river pois'd, the twain yet one, a moment's lull,
A motionless still balance in the air, then parting, talons loosing,
Upward again on slow-firm pinions slanting, their separate
  diverse flight.
She hers, he his, pursuing.

A FARM PICTURE

Through the ample open door of the peaceful country barn,
A sunlit pasture field with cattle and horses feeding,
And haze and vista, and the far horizon fading away.

AN ARMY CORPS ON THE MARCH

With its cloud of skirmishers in advance,
With now the sound of a single shot snapping like a whip,
    and now an irregular volley,
The swarming ranks press on and on, the dense brigades
    press on,
Glittering dimly, toiling under the sun—the dust-cover'd men,
In columns rise and fall to the undulations of the ground,
With artillery interspers'd—the wheels rumble, the horses
    sweat,
As the army corps advances.

WHEN LILACS LAST IN THE
DOORYARD BLOOM'D

1

When lilacs last in the dooryard bloom'd,
And the great star early droop'd in the western sky in the night,
I mourn'd and yet shall mourn with ever-returning spring.

Ever-returning spring, trinity sure to me you bring,
Lilac blooming perennial and drooping star in the west,
And thought of him I love.

2

O powerful western fallen star!
O shades of night—O moody, tearful night!
O great star disappear'd—O the black murk that hides the star!
O cruel hands that hold me powerless—O helpless soul of me!
O harsh surrounding cloud that will not free my soul.

3

In the dooryard fronting an old farm-house near the
    white-wash'd palings,
Stands the lilac-bush tall-growing with heart-shaped leaves of
    rich green,
With many a pointed blossom rising delicate, with the perfume
    strong I love,
With every leaf a miracle—and from this bush in the dooryard,
With delicate-color'd blossoms and heart-shaped leaves of rich
    green,
A sprig with its flower I break.

4

In the swamp in secluded recesses,
A shy and hidden bird is warbling a song.

Solitary the thrush,
The hermit withdrawn to himself, avoiding the settlements,
Sings by himself a song.

Song of the bleeding throat,
Death's outlet song of life, (for well dear brother I know,
If thou wast not granted to sing thou would'st surely die.)

5

Over the breast of the spring, the land, amid cities,
Amid lanes and through old woods, where lately the violets
    peep'd from the ground, spotting the gray debris,
Amid the grass in the fields each side of the lanes, passing
    the endless grass,
Passing the yellow-spear'd wheat, every grain from its shroud
    in the dark-brown fields uprisen,
Passing the apple-tree blows of white and pink in the orchards,
Carrying a corpse to where it shall rest in the grave,
Night and day journeys a coffin.

6

Coffin that passes through lanes and streets,
Through day and night with the great cloud darkening the land,
With the pomp of the inloop'd flags with the cities draped
    in black,
With the show of the States themselves as of crape-veil'd
    women standing,

With processions long and winding and the flambeaus of the
    night,
With the countless torches lit, with the silent sea of faces and
    the unbared heads,
With the waiting depot, the arriving coffin, and the somber
    faces,
With dirges through the night, with the thousand voices rising
    strong and solemn,
With all the mournful voices of the dirges pour'd around the
    coffin,
The dim-lit churches and the shuddering organs—where amid
    these you journey,
With the tolling tolling bells' perpetual clang,
Here, coffin that slowly passes,
I give you my sprig of lilac.

7

(Nor for you, for one alone,
Blossoms and branches green to coffins all I bring,
For fresh as the morning, thus would I chant a song for you
    O sane and sacred death.

All over bouquets of roses,
O death, I cover you over with roses and early lilies,
But mostly and now the lilac that blooms the first,
Copious I break, I break the sprigs from the bushes,
With loaded arms I come, pouring for you,
For you and the coffins all of you O death.)

8

O western orb sailing the heaven,
Now I know what you must have meant as a month since I
    walk'd,
As I walk'd in silence the transparent shadowy night,
As I saw you had something to tell as you bent to me night
    after night,
As you droop'd from the sky low down as if to my side,
    (while the other stars all look'd on,)
As we wander'd together the solemn night, (for something I
    know not what kept me from sleep,)
As the night advanced, and I saw on the rim of the west how
    full you were of woe,
As I stood on the rising ground in the breeze in the cool
    transparent night,

As I watch'd where you pass'd and was lost in the netherward
  black of the night,
As my soul in its trouble dissatisfied sank, as where you sad orb,
Concluded, dropt in the night, and was gone.

9

Sing on there in the swamp,
O singer bashful and tender, I hear your notes, I hear your call,
I hear, I come presently, I understand you,
But a moment I linger, for the lustrous star has detain'd me,
The star my departing comrade holds and detains me.

10

O how shall I warble myself for the dead one there I loved?
And how shall I deck my song for the large sweet soul that
  has gone?
And what shall my perfume be for the grave of him I love?

Sea-winds blown from east and west,
Blown from the Eastern sea and blown from the Western sea,
  till there on the prairies meeting,
These and with these and the breath of my chant,
I'll perfume the grave of him I love.

11

O what shall I hang on the chamber walls?
And what shall the pictures be that I hang on the walls,
To adorn the burial-house of him I love?

Pictures of growing spring and farms and homes,
With the Fourth-month eve at sundown, and the gray smoke
  lucid and bright,
With floods of the yellow gold of the gorgeous, indolent,
  sinking sun, burning, expanding the air,
With the fresh sweet herbage under foot, and the pale green
  leaves of the trees prolific,
In the distance the flowing glaze, the breast of the river, with
  a wind-dapple here and there,
With ranging hills on the banks, with many a line against
  the sky, and shadows,
And the city at hand with dwellings so dense, and stacks of
  chimneys,
And all the scenes of life and the workshops, and the workmen
  homeward returning.

12

Lo, body and soul—this land,
My own Manhattan with spires, and the sparkling and hurrying
    tides, and the ships,
The varied and ample land, the South and the North in the
    light, Ohio's shores and flashing Missouri,
And ever the far-spreading prairies cover'd with grass and corn.

Lo, the most excellent sun so calm and haughty,
The violet and purple morn with just-felt breezes,
The gentle soft-born measureless light,
The miracle spreading bathing all, the fulfill'd noon,
The coming eve delicious, the welcome night and the stars,
Over my cities shining all, enveloping man and land.

13

Sing on, sing on you gray-brown bird,
Sing from the swamps, the recesses, pour your chant from
    the bushes,
Limitless out of the dusk, out of the cedars and pines.

Sing on dearest brother, warble your reedy song,
Loud human song, with voice of uttermost woe.

O liquid and free and tender!
O wild and loose to my soul—O wondrous singer!
You only I hear—yet the star holds me, (but will soon depart,)
Yet the lilac with mastering odor holds me.

14

Now while I sat in the day and look'd forth,
In the close of the day with its light and the fields of spring,
    and the farmers preparing their crops,
In the large unconscious scenery of my land with its lakes and
    forests,
In the heavenly aerial beauty, (after the perturb'd winds and
    the storms,)
Under the arching heavens of the afternoon swift passing, and
    the voices of children and women,
The many-moving sea-tides, and I saw the ships how they
    sail'd,
And the summer approaching with richness, and the
    fields all busy with labor,

And the infinite separate houses, how they all went on, each
    with its meals and minutia of daily usages,
And the streets how their throbbings throbb'd, and the cities
    pent—lo, then and there,
Falling upon them all and among them all, enveloping me
    with the rest,
Appear'd the cloud, appear'd the long black trail,
And I knew death, its thought, and the sacred knowledge of
    death.

Then, with the knowledge of death as walking one side of me,
And the thought of death close-walking the other side of me,
And I in the middle as with companions, and as holding the
    hands of companions,
I fled forth to the hiding receiving night that talks not,
Down to the shores of the water, the path by the swamp in
    the dimness,
To the solemn shadowy cedars and ghostly pines so still.

And the singer so shy to the rest receiv'd me,
The gray-brown bird I know receiv'd us comrades three,
And he sang the carol of death, and a verse for him I love.

From deep secluded recesses,
From the fragrant cedars and the ghostly pines so still,
Came the carol of the bird.

And the charm of the carol rapt me,
As I held as if by their hands my comrades in the night,
And the voice of my spirit tallied the song of the bird.

Come lovely and soothing death,
Undulate round the world, serenely arriving, arriving,
In the day, in the night, to all, to each,
Sooner or later delicate death.

Prais'd be the fathomless universe,
For life and joy, and for objects and knowledge curious,
And for love, sweet love—but praise! praise!
For the sure-enwinding arms of cool-enfolding death.

Dark mother always gliding near with soft feet,
Have none chanted for thee a chant of fullest welcome?
Then I chant it for thee, I glorify thee above all,
I bring thee a song that when thou must indeed come,
    come unfalteringly.

Approach strong deliveress,
When it is so, when thou hast taken them I joyously sing the
    dead,
Lost in the loving floating ocean of thee,
Laved in the flood of thy bliss O death.

From me to thee glad serenades,
Dances for thee I propose saluting thee, adornments and
    feastings for thee,
And the sights of the open landscape and the high-spread
    sky are fitting,
And life and the fields, and the huge and thoughtful night.

The night in silence under many a star,
The ocean shore and the husky whispering wave whose voice
    I know,
And the soul turning to thee O vast and well-veil'd death,
And the body gratefully nestling close to thee.

Over the tree-tops I float thee a song,
Over the rising and sinking waves, over the myriad fields and
    the prairies wide,
Over the dense-pack'd cities all and the teeming wharves and
    ways,
I float this carol with joy, with joy to thee O death.

15

To the tally of my soul,
Loud and strong kept up the gray-brown bird,
With pure deliberate notes spreading filling the night.

Loud in the pines and cedars dim,
Clear in the freshness moist and the swamp-perfume,
And I with my comrades there in the night.

While my sight that was bound in my eyes unclosed,
As to long panoramas of visions.

And I saw askant the armies,
I saw as in noiseless dreams hundreds of battle-flags,
Borne through the smoke of the battles and pierc'd with
    missiles I saw them,
And carried hither and yon through the smoke, and torn and
    bloody,
And at last but a few shreds left on the staffs (and all in
    silence,)
And the staffs all splinter'd and broken.

I saw battle-corpses, myriads of them,
And the white skeletons of young men, I saw them,
I saw the debris and debris of all the slain soldiers of the war,
But I saw they were not as was thought,
They themselves were fully at rest, they suffer'd not,
The living remain'd and suffer'd, the mother suffer'd,
And the wife and the child and the musing comrade suffer'd,
And the armies that remain'd suffer'd.

16

Passing the visions, passing the night,
Passing, unloosing the hold of my comrades' hands,
Passing the song of the hermit bird and the tallying song of
    my soul,
Victorious song, death's outlet song, yet varying ever-altering
    song,
As low and wailing, yet clear the notes, rising and falling,
    flooding the night,
Sadly sinking and fainting, as warning and warning, and yet
    again bursting with joy,
Covering the earth and filling the spread of the heaven,
As that powerful psalm in the night I heard from recesses,
Passing, I leave thee lilac with heart-shaped leaves,
I leave thee there in the door-yard, blooming, returning with
    spring.

I cease from my song for thee,
From my gaze on thee in the west, fronting the west,
    communing with thee,
O comrade lustrous with silver face in the night.

Yet each to keep and all, retrievements out of the night,
The song, the wondrous chant of the gray-brown bird,
And the tallying chant, the echo arous'd in my soul,
With the lustrous and drooping star with the countenance
    full of woe,
With the holders holding my hand nearing the call of the bird,
Comrades mine and I in the midst, and their memory ever
    to keep, for the dead I loved so well,
For the sweetest, wisest soul of all my days and lands—and
    this for his dear sake,
Lilac and star and bird twined with the chant of my soul,
There in the fragrant pines and the cedars dusk and dim.

William Butler Yeats (1865-1939)

SEPTEMBER 1913

What need you, being come to sense,
But fumble in a greasy till
And add the halfpence to the pence
And prayer to shivering prayer, until
You have dried the marrow from the bone?
For men were born to pray and save:
Romantic Ireland's dead and gone,
It's with O'Leary in the grave.

Yet they were of a different kind,
The names that stilled your childish play,
They have gone about the world like wind,
But little time had they to pray
For whom the hangman's rope was spun,
And what, God help us, could they save?
Romantic Ireland's dead and gone,
It's with O'Leary in the grave.

Was it for this the wild geese spread
The grey wing upon every tide;
For this that all that blood was shed,
For this Edward Fitzgerald died,
And Robert Emmet and Wolfe Tone,
All that delirium of the brave?
Romantic Ireland's dead and gone,
It's with O'Leary in the grave.

Yet could we turn the years again,
And call those exiles as they were
In all their loneliness and pain,
You'd cry, 'Some woman's yellow hair
Has maddened every mother's son':
They weighed so lightly what they gave.
But let them be, they're dead and gone,
They're with O'Leary in the grave.

THE MAGI

Now as at all times I can see in the mind's eye,
In their stiff, painted clothes, the pale unsatisfied ones
Appear and disappear in the blue depth of the sky
With all their ancient faces like rain-beaten stones,
And all their helms of silver hovering side by side,
And all their eyes still fixed, hoping to find once more,
Being by Calvary's turbulence unsatisfied,
The uncontrollable mystery on the bestial floor.

EASTER 1916

I have met them at close of day
Coming with vivid faces
From counter or desk among grey
Eighteenth-century houses.
I have passed with a nod of the head
Or polite meaningless words,
Or have lingered awhile and said
Polite meaningless words,
And thought before I had done
Of a mocking tale or a gibe
To please a companion
Around the fire at the club,
Being certain that they and I
But lived where motley is worn:
All changed, changed utterly:
A terrible beauty is born.

That woman's days were spent
In ignorant good-will,
Her nights in argument
Until her voice grew shrill.
What voice more sweet than hers
When, young and beautiful,
She rode to harriers?
This man had kept a school
And rode our wingèd horse;
This other his helper and friend
Was coming into his force;
He might have won fame in the end,
So sensitive his nature seemed,

So daring and sweet his thought.
This other man I had dreamed
A drunken, vainglorious lout.
He had done most bitter wrong
To some who are near my heart,
Yet I number him in the song;
He, too, has resigned his part
In the casual comedy;
He, too, has been changed in his turn,
Transformed utterly:
A terrible beauty is born.

Hearts with one purpose alone
Through summer and winter seem
Enchanted to a stone
To trouble the living stream.
The horse that comes from the road,
The rider, the birds that range
From cloud to tumbling cloud,
Minute by minute they change;
A shadow of cloud on the stream
Changes minute by minute;
A horse-hoof slides on the brim,
And a horse plashes within it;
The long-legged moor-hens dive,
And hens to moor-cocks call;
Minute by minute they live:
The stone's in the midst of all.

Too long a sacrifice
Can make a stone of the heart.
O when may it suffice?
That is Heaven's part, our part
To murmur name upon name,
As a mother names her child
When sleep at last has come
On limbs that had run wild.
What is it but nightfall?
No, no, not night but death;
Was it needless death after all?
For England may keep faith
For all that is done and said.
We know their dream; enough
To know they dreamed and are dead;
And what if excess of love
Bewildered them till they died?

I write it out in a verse—
MacDonagh and MacBride
And Connolly and Pearse
Now and in time to be,
Wherever green is worn,
Are changed, changed utterly:
A terribly beauty is born.

THE SECOND COMING

Turning and turning in the widening gyre
The falcon cannot hear the falconer;
Things fall apart; the centre cannot hold;
Mere anarchy is loosed upon the world,
The blood-dimmed tide is loosed, and everywhere
The ceremony of innocence is drowned;
The best lack all conviction, while the worst
Are full of passionate intensity.

Surely some revelation is at hand;
Surely the Second Coming is at hand.
The Second Coming! Hardly are those words out
When a vast image out of *Spiritus Mundi*
Troubles my sight: somewhere in sands of the desert.
A shape with lion body and the head of a man,
A gaze blank and pitiless as the sun,
Is moving its slow thighs, while all about it
Reel shadows of the indignant desert birds.
The darkness drops again; but now I know
That twenty centuries of stony sleep
Were vexed to nightmare by a rocking cradle,
And what rough beast, its hour come round at last,
Slouches towards Bethlehem to be born?

SAILING TO BYZANTIUM

I

That is no country for old men. The young
In one another's arms, birds in the trees
—Those dying generations—at their song,

The salmon-falls, the mackerel-crowded seas,
Fish, flesh, or fowl, commend all summer long
Whatever is begotten, born, and dies.
Caught in that sensual music all neglect
Monuments of unageing intellect.

II

An aged man is but a paltry thing,
A tattered coat upon a stick, unless
Soul clap its hands and sing, and louder sing
For every tatter in its mortal dress,
Nor is there singing school but studying
Monuments of its own magnificence;
And therefore I have sailed the seas and come
To the holy city of Byzantium.

III

O sages standing in God's holy fire
As in the gold mosaic of a wall,
Come from the holy fire, perne in a gyre,
And be the singing-masters of my soul.
Consume my heart away; sick with desire
And fastened to a dying animal
It knows not what it is; and gather me
Into the artifice of eternity.

IV

Once out of nature I shall never take
My bodily form from any natural thing,
But such a form as Grecian goldsmiths make
Of hammered gold and gold enamelling
To keep a drowsy Emperor awake;
Or set upon a golden bough to sing
To lords and ladies of Byzantium
Of what is past, or passing, or to come.

TWO SONGS FROM A PLAY

I

I saw a staring virgin stand
Where holy Dionysus died,

And tear the heart out of his side,
And lay the heart upon her hand
And bear that beating heart away;
And then did all the Muses sing
Of Magnus Annus at the spring,
As though God's death were but a play.

Another Troy must rise and set,
Another lineage feed the crow,
Another Argo's painted prow
Drive to a flashier bauble yet.
The Roman Empire stood appalled:
It dropped the reigns of peace and war
When that fierce virgin and her Star
Out of the fabulous darkness called.

II

In pity for man's darkening thought
He walked that room and issued thence
In Galilean turbulence;
The Babylonian starlight brought
A fabulous, formless darkness in;
Odour of blood when Christ was slain
Made all Platonic tolerance vain
And vain all Doric discipline.

Everything that man esteems
Endures a moment or a day.
Love's pleasure drives his love away,
The painter's brush consumes his dreams;
The herald's cry, the soldier's tread
Exhaust his glory and his might:
Whatever flames upon the night
Man's own resinous heart has fed.

LEDA AND THE SWAN

A sudden blow: the great wings beating still
Above the staggering girl, her thighs caressed
By the dark webs, her nape caught in his bill,
He holds her helpless breast upon his breast.

How can those terrified vague fingers push
The feathered glory from her loosening thighs?
And how can body, laid in that white rush,
But feel the strange heart beating where it lies?

A shudder in the loins engenders there
The broken wall, the burning roof and tower
And Agamemnon dead.
                           Being so caught up,
So mastered by the brute blood of the air,
Did she put on his knowledge with his power
Before the indifferent beak could let her drop?

AMONG SCHOOL CHILDREN

I

I walk through the long schoolroom questioning;
A kind old nun in a white hood replies;
The children learn to cipher and to sing,
To study reading-books and history,
To cut and sew, be neat in everything
In the best modern way—the children's eyes
In momentary wonder stare upon
A sixty-year-old smiling public man.

II

I dream of a Ledaean body, bent
Above a sinking fire, a tale that she
Told of a harsh reproof, or trivial event
That changed some childish day to tragedy—
Told, and it seemed that our two natures blent
Into a sphere from youthful sympathy,
Or else, to alter Plato's parable,
Into the yolk and white of the one shell.

III

And thinking of that fit of grief or rage
I look upon one child or t'other there
And wonder if she stood so at that age—
For even daughters of the swan can share
Something of every paddler's heritage—
And had that colour upon cheek or hair,

And thereupon my heart is driven wild:
She stands before me as a living child.

IV

Her present image floats into the mind—
Did Quattrocento finger fashion it
Hollow of cheek as though it drank the wind
And took a mess of shadows for its meat?
And I though never of Ledaean kind
Had pretty plumage once—enough of that,
Better to smile on all that smile, and show
There is a comfortable kind of old scarecrow.

V

What youthful mother, a shape upon her lap
Honey of generation had betrayed,
And that must sleep, shriek, struggle to escape
As recollection or the drug decide,
Would think her son, did she but see that shape
With sixty or more winters on its head,
A compensation for the pang of his birth,
Or the uncertainty of his setting forth?

VI

Plato thought nature but a spume that plays
Upon a ghostly paradigm of things;
Solider Aristotle played the taws
Upon the bottom of a king of kings;
World-famous golden-thighed Pythagoras
Fingered upon a fiddle-stick or strings
What a star sang and careless Muses heard:
Old clothes upon old sticks to scare a bird.

VII

Both nuns and mothers worship images,
But those the candles light are not as those
That animate a mother's reveries,
But keep a marble or a bronze repose.
And yet they too break hearts—O Presences
That passion, piety or affection knows,
And that all heavenly glory symbolise—
O self-born mockers of man's enterprise;

VIII

Labour is blossoming or dancing where
The body is not bruised to pleasure soul,
Nor beauty born out of its own despair,
Nor blear-eyed wisdom out of midnight oil.
O chestnut-tree, great-rooted blossomer,
Are you the leaf, the blossom or the bole?
O body swayed to music, O brightening glance,
How can we know the dancer from the dance?

LAPIS LAZULI

For Harry Clifton

I have heard that hysterical women say
They are sick of the palette and fiddle-bow,
Of poets that are always gay,
For everybody knows or else should know
That if nothing drastic is done
Aeroplane and Zeppelin will come out,
Pitch like King Billy bomb-balls in
Until the town lie beaten flat.

All perform their tragic play,
There struts Hamlet, there is Lear,
That's Ophelia, that Cordelia;
Yet they, should the last scene be there,
The great stage curtain about to drop,
If worthy their prominent part in the play,
Do not break up their lines to weep.
They know that Hamlet and Lear are gay;
Gaiety transfiguring all that dread.
All men have aimed at, found and lost;
Black out; Heaven blazing into the head:
Tragedy wrought to its uttermost.
Though Hamlet rambles and Lear rages,
And all the drop-scenes drop at once
Upon a hundred thousand stages,
It cannot grow by an inch or an ounce.

On their own feet they came, or on shipboard,
Camel-back, horse-back, ass-back, mule-back,
Old civilisations put to the sword.

Then they and their wisdom went to rack:
No handiwork of Callimachus,
Who handled marble as if it were bronze,
Made draperies that seemed to rise
When sea-wind swept the corner, stands;
His long lamp-chimney shaped like the stem
Of a slender palm, stood but a day;
All things fall and are built again,
And those that build them again are gay.

Two Chinamen, behind them a third,
Are carved in lapis lazuli,
Over them flies a long-legged bird,
A symbol of longevity;
The third, doubtless a serving-man,
Carries a musical instrument.

Every discoloration of the stone,
Every accidental crack or dent,
Seems a water-course or an avalanche,
Or lofty slope where it still snows
Though doubtless plum or cherry-branch
Sweetens the little half-way house
Those Chinamen climb towards, and I
Delight to imagine them seated there;
There, on the mountain and the sky,
On all the tragic scene they stare.
One asks for mournful melodies;
Accomplished fingers begin to play.
Their eyes mid many wrinkles, their eyes,
Their ancient, glittering eyes, are gay.

LONG-LEGGED FLY

That civilisation may not sink,
Its great battle lost,
Quiet the dog, tether the pony
To a distant post;
Our master Caesar is in the tent
Where the maps are spread,
His eyes fixed upon nothing,
A hand under his head.
Like a long-legged fly upon the stream
His mind moves upon silence.

That the topless towers be burnt
And men recall that face,
Move most gently if move you must
In this lonely place.
She thinks, part woman, three parts a child,
That nobody looks; her feet
Practise a tinker shuffle
Picked up on a street.
Like a long-legged fly upon the stream
Her mind moves upon silence.

That girls at puberty may find
The first Adam in their thought,
Shut the door of the Pope's chapel,
Keep those children out.
There on that scaffolding reclines
Michael Angelo.
With no more sound than the mice make
His hand moves to and fro.
Like a long-legged fly upon the stream
His mind moves upon silence.

Theodore Roethke (1908-1963)

CUTTINGS
(later)

This urge, wrestle, resurrection of dry sticks,
Cut stems struggling to put down feet,
What saint strained so much,
Rose on such lopped limbs to a new life?

I can hear, underground, that sucking and sobbing,
In my veins, in my bones I feel it,—
The small waters seeping upward,
The tight grains parting at last.
When sprouts break out,
Slippery as fish,
I quail, lean to beginnings, sheath-wet.

ORCHIDS

They lean over the path,
Adder-mouthed,
Swaying close to the face,
Coming out, soft and deceptive,
Limp and damp, delicate as a young bird's tongue;
Their fluttery fledgling lips
Move slowly,
Drawing in the warm air.

And at night,
The faint moon falling through whitewashed glass,
The heat going down
So their musky smell comes even stronger,
Drifting down from their mossy cradles:
So many devouring infants!
Soft luminescent fingers,
Lips neither dead nor alive,
Loose ghostly mouths
Breathing.

BIG WIND

Where were the greenhouses going,
Lunging into the lashing
Wind driving water
So far down the river
All the faucets stopped?—
So we drained the manure-machine
For the steam plant,
Pumping the stale mixture
Into the rusty boilers,
Watching the pressure gauge
Waver over to red,
As the seams hissed
And the live steam
Drove to the far
End of the rose-house,
Where the worst wind was,
Creaking the cypress window-frames,
Cracking so much thin glass
We stayed all night,
Stuffing the holes with burlap;
But she rode it out,
That old rose-house,
She hove into the teeth of it,
The core and pith of that ugly storm,
Ploughing with her stiff prow,
Bucking into the wind-waves
That broke over the whole of her,
Flailing her sides with spray,
Flinging long strings of wet across the roof-top,
Finally veering, wearing themselves out, merely
Whistling thinly under the wind-vents;
She sailed until the calm morning,
Carrying her full cargo of roses.

MY PAPA'S WALTZ

The whiskey on your breath
Could make a small boy dizzy;
But I hung on like death:
Such waltzing was not easy.

We romped until the pans
Slid from the kitchen shelf;
My mother's countenance
Could not unfrown itself.

The hand that held my wrist
Was battered on one knuckle;
At every step you missed
My right ear scraped a buckle.

You beat time on my head
With a palm caked hard by dirt,
Then waltzed me off to bed
Still clinging to your shirt.

THE VISITANT

1

A cloud moved close. The bulk of the wind shifted.
A tree swayed over water.
A voice said:
Stay. Stay by the slip-ooze. Stay.

Dearest tree, I said, may I rest here?
A ripple made a soft reply.
I waited, alert as a dog.
The leech clinging to a stone waited;
And the crab, the quiet breather.

2

Slow, slow as a fish she came,
Slow as a fish coming forward,
Swaying in a long wave;
Her skirts not touching a leaf,
Her white arms reaching towards me.

She came without sound,
Without brushing the wet stones,
In the soft dark of early evening,
She came,
The wind in her hair,
The moon beginning.

3

I woke in the first of morning.
Staring at a tree, I felt the pulse of a stone.

Where's she now, I kept saying,
Where's she now, the mountain's downy girl?

But the bright day had no answer.
A wind stirred in a web of appleworms;
The tree, the close willow, swayed.

ELEGY FOR JANE
My Student, Thrown by a Horse

I remember the neckcurls, limp and damp as tendrils;
And her quick look, a sidelong pickerel smile;
And how, once startled into talk, the light syllables leaped for her,
And she balanced in the delight of her thought,
A wren, happy, tail into the wind,
Her song trembling the twigs and small branches.
The shade sang with her;
The leaves, their whispers turned to kissing;
And the mold sang in the bleached valleys under the rose.

Oh, when she was sad, she cast herself down into such a pure depth,
Even a father could not find her:
Scraping her cheek against straw;
Stirring the clearest water.

My sparrow, you are not here,
Waiting like a fern, making a spiny shadow.
The sides of wet stones cannot console me,
Nor the moss, wound with the last light.

If only I could nudge you from this sleep,
My maimed darling, my skittery pigeon.
Over this damp grave I speak the words of my love:
I, with no rights in this matter,
Neither father nor lover.

I KNEW A WOMAN

I knew a woman, lovely in her bones,
When small birds sighed, she would sigh back at them;
Ah, when she moved, she moved more ways than one:
The shapes a bright container can contain!
Of her choice virtues only gods should speak,
Or English poets who grew up on Greek
(I'd have them sing in chorus, cheek to cheek).

How well her wishes went! She stroked my chin,
She taught me Turn, and Counter-turn, and Stand;
She taught me Touch, that undulant white skin;
I nibbled meekly from her proffered hand;
She was the sickle; I, poor I, the rake,
Coming behind her for her pretty sake
(But what prodigious mowing we did make).

Love likes a gander, and adores a goose:
Her full lips pursed, the errant note to seize;
She played it quick, she played it light and loose;
My eyes, they dazzled at her flowing knees;
Her several parts could keep a pure repose,
Or one hip quiver with a mobile nose
(She moved in circles, and those circles moved).

Let seed be grass, and grass turn into hay:
I'm martyr to a motion not my own;
What's freedom for? To know eternity.
I swear she cast a shadow white as stone.
But who would count eternity in days?
These old bones live to learn her wanton ways:
(I measure time by how a body sways).

THE ROSE

1

There are those to whom place is unimportant,
But this place, where sea and fresh water meet,
Is important—
Where the hawks sway out into the wind,
Without a single wingbeat,
And the eagles sail low over the fir trees,

And the gulls cry against the crows
In the curved harbors,
And the tide rises up against the grass
Nibbled by sheep and rabbits.

A time for watching the tide,
For the heron's hieratic fishing,
For the sleepy cries of the towhee,
The morning birds gone, the twittering finches,
But still the flash of the kingfisher, the wingbeat of the scoter,
The sun a ball of fire coming down over the water,
The last geese crossing against the reflected afterlight,
The moon retreating into a vague cloud-shape
To the cries of the owl, the eerie whooper.
The old log subsides with the lessening waves,
And there is silence.

I sway outside myself
Into the darkening currents,
Into the small spillage of driftwood,
The waters swirling past the tiny headlands.
Was it here I wore a crown of birds for a moment
While on a far point of the rocks
The light heightened,
And below, in a mist out of nowhere,
The first rain gathered?

2

As when a ship sails with a light wind—
The waves less than the ripples made by rising fish,
The lacelike wrinkles of the wake widening, thinning out,
Sliding away from the traveler's eye,
The prow pitching easily up and down,
The whole ship rolling slightly sideways,
The stern high, dipping like a child's boat in a pond—
Our motion continues.

But this rose, this rose in the sea-wind,
Stays,
Stays in its true place,
Flowering out of the dark,
Widening at high noon, face upward,
A single wild rose, struggling out of the white embrace of the
        morning-glory,
Out of the briary hedge, the tangle of matted underbrush,

Beyond the clover, the ragged hay,
Beyond the sea pine, the oak, the wind-tipped madrona,
Moving with the waves, the undulating driftwood,
Where the slow creek winds down to the black sand of the shore
With its thick grassy scum and crabs scuttling back into their
    glistening craters.

And I think of roses, roses,
White and red, in the wide six-hundred-foot greenhouses,
And my father standing astride the cement benches,
Lifting me high over the four-foot stems, the Mrs. Russells, and
    his own elaborate hybrids,
And how those flowerheads seemed to flow toward me, to
    beckon me, only a child, out of myself.

What need for heaven, then,
With that man, and those roses?

3

What do they tell us, sound and silence?
I think of American sounds in this silence:
On the banks of the Tombstone, the wind-harps having their say,
The thrush singing alone, that easy bird,
The killdeer whistling away from me,
The mimetic chortling of the catbird
Down in the corner of the garden, among the raggedy lilacs,
The bobolink skirring from a broken fencepost,
The bluebird, lover of holes in old wood, lilting its light song,
And that thin cry, like a needle piercing the ear, the insistent
    cicada,
And the ticking of snow around oil drums in the Dakotas,
The thin whine of telephone wires in the wind of a Michigan
    winter,
The shriek of nails as old shingles are ripped from the top
    of a roof,
The bulldozer backing away, the hiss of the sandblaster,
And the deep chorus of horns coming up from the streets in
    early morning.
I return to the twittering of swallows above water,
And that sound, that single sound,
When the mind remembers all,
And gently the light enters the sleeping soul,
A sound so thin it could not woo a bird,

Beautiful my desire, and the place of my desire.

I think of the rock singing, and light making its own silence,
At the edge of a ripening meadow, in early summer,
The moon lolling in the close elm, a shimmer of silver,
Or that lonely time before the breaking of morning
When the slow freight winds along the edge of the ravaged
    hillside,
And the wind tries the shape of a tree,
While the moon lingers,
And a drop of rain water hangs at the tip of a leaf
Shifting in the wakening sunlight
Like the eye of a new-caught fish.

        4

I live with the rocks, their weeds,
Their filmy fringes of green, their harsh
Edges, their holes
Cut by the sea-slime, far from the crash
Of the long swell,
The oily, tar-laden walls
Of the toppling waves,
Where the salmon ease their way into the kelp beds,
And the sea rearranges itself among the small islands.

Near this rose, in this grove of sun-parched, wind-warped
    madronas,
Among the half-dead trees, I came upon the true ease of myself,
As if another man appeared out of the depths of my being,
And I stood outside myself,
Beyond becoming and perishing,
A something wholly other,
As if I swayed out on the wildest wave alive,
And yet was still.
And I rejoiced in being what I was:
In the lilac change, the white reptilian calm,
In the bird beyond the bough, the single one
With all the air to greet him as he flies,
The dolphin rising from the darkening waves;

And in this rose, this rose in the sea-wind,
Rooted in stone, keeping the whole of light,
Gathering to itself sound and silence—
Mine and the sea-wind's.

THE MEADOW MOUSE

1

In a shoe box stuffed in an old nylon stocking
Sleeps the baby mouse I found in the meadow,
Where he trembled and shook beneath a stick
Till I caught him up by the tail and brought him in,
Cradled in my hand,
A little quaker, the whole body of him trembling,
His absurd whiskers sticking out like a cartoon-mouse,
His feet like small leaves,
Little lizard-feet,
Whitish and spread wide when he tried to struggle away,
Wriggling like a miniscule puppy.

Now he's eaten his three kinds of cheese and drunk from his
        bottle-cap watering-trough—
So much he just lies in one corner,
His tail curled under him, his belly big
As his head; his bat-like ears
Twitching, tilting toward the least sound.

Do I imagine he no longer trembles
When I come close to him?
He seems no longer to tremble.

2

But this morning the shoe-box house on the back porch is empty.
Where has he gone, my meadow mouse,
My thumb of a child that nuzzled in my palm?—
To run under the hawk's wing,
Under the eye of the great owl watching from the elm-tree,
To live by courtesy of the shrike, the snake, the tom-cat.

I think of the nestling fallen into the deep grass,
The turtle gasping in the dusty rubble of the highway,
The paralytic stunned in the tub, and the water rising,—
All things innocent, hapless, forsaken.

ONE HUNDRED POEMS

Geoffrey Chaucer (1340-1400)

from THE CANTERBURY TALES

from THE PROLOGUE

A good Wif was her of biside Bathe,
But she was somdel deef, and that was scathe.
Of clooth-makyng she hadde swich an haunt,
She passed hem of Ypres and of Gaunt.
In al the parisshe wif ne was ther noon
That to the offrynge bifore hire sholde goon;
And if ther dide, certeyn so wrooth was she,
That she was out of alle charitee.
Hir coverchiefs ful fyne were of ground;
I dorste swere they weyeden ten pound
That on a Sonday weren upon hir heed.
Hir hosen weren of fyn scarlet reed,
Ful streite yteyd, and shoes ful moyste and newe.
Boold was hir face and fair and reed of hewe.
She was a worthy womman al hir lyve:
Housebondes at chirche dore she hadde fyve,
Withouten oother compaignye in youthe—
But therof nedeth nat to speke as nowthe.
And thries hadde she been at Jerusalem;
She hadde passed many a straunge strem;
At Rome she hadde been, and at Boloigne,
In Galice at Seint Jame, and at Coloigne;
She koude much of wandrynge by the weye.
Gat-tothed was she, soothly for to seye.
Upon an amblere esily she sat,
Ywympled wel, and on hir heed an hat
As brood as is a bokeler or a targe;
A foot-mantel aboute hir hipes large,
And on hir feet a paire of spores sharpe.
In felaweshipe wel koude she laughe and carpe.
Of remedies of love she knew per chaunce,
For she koude of that art the olde daunce.

Anonymous (1300?-1500?)

ADAM LAY I-BOWNDYN

Adam lay i-bowndyn
    Bowndyn in a bond—
Fowre thousand wynter
    Thoght he not too long;
And al was for an appil,
    An appil that he tok,
As clerkes fynden,
    Written in here book.

Ne hadde the appil take ben,
    The appil taken ben,
Ne haddë never our lady
    A ben hevenë quene.
Blyssid be the tyme
    That appil takë was,
Ther fore we mown syngyn
    Deo Gracias.

WESTRON WINDE, WHEN WILL THOU BLOW

Westron winde, when will thou blow,
The smalle raine downe can raine?
Crist, if my love wer in my armis,
And I in my bed againe.

EDWARD

"Why dois your brand sae drap wi bluid,
    Edward, Edward,
Why dois your brand sae drap wi bluid,
    And why sae sad gang ye O?"
"O I hae killed my hauke sae guid,
    Mither, mither,
O I hae killed my hauke sae guid,
    And I had nae mair but hee O."

"Your haukis bluid was nevir sae reid,
    Edward, Edward,
Your haukis bluid was nevir sae reid,
    My deir son I tell thee O."
O I hae killed my reid roan steed,
    Mither, mither,
O I hae killed my reid roan steid,
    That erst was sae fair and free O."

"Your steid was auld, and ye hae gat mair,
    Edward, Edward,
Your steid was auld, and ye hae gat mair,
    Sum other dule ye drie O."
"O I hae killed my fadir deir,
    Mither, mither,
O I hae killed my fadir deir,
    Alas, and wae is mee O!"

"And whatten penance wul ye drie for that,
    Edward, Edward?
And whatten penance wul ye drie for that?
    My deir son, now tell me O."
"Ile set my feet in yonder boat,
    Mither, mither,
Ile set my feet in yonder boat,
    And Ile fare ovir the sea O."

"And what wul ye doe wi your towirs and your ha,
    Edward, Edward?
And what wul ye doe wi your towirs and your ha,
    That were sae fair to see O?"
"Ile let thame stand tul they doun fa,
    Mither, mither,
Ile let thame stand tul they doun fa,
    For here nevir mair maun I bee O."

"And what wul ye leive to your bairns and your wife,
    Edward, Edward?
And what wul ye leive to your bairns and your wife,
    Whan ye gang ovir the sea O?"
"The warldis room, let them beg thrae life,
    Mither, mither,
The warldis room, let them beg thrae life,
    For thame nevir mair wul I see O."

"And what wul ye leive to your ain mither deir?
  Edward, Edward?
And what wul ye leive to your ain mither deir?
  My deir son, now tell me O."
"The curse of hell frae me sall ye beir,
  Mither, mither,
The curse of hell frae me sall ye beir,
  Sic counseils ye gave to me O."

John Skelton (1460?-1529)

TO MISTRESS MARGARET HUSSEY

Mirry Margaret,
As midsomer flowre,
Jentill as faucoun
Or hawke of the towre;
  With solace and gladnes,
Moche mirthe and no madnes,
All good and no badnes,
So joyously,
So maidenly,
So womanly
Her demening
In every thinge,
Far, far passinge
That I can endight,
Or suffice to wright
Of mirry Margarete,
As midsomer flowre,
Jentill as facoun
Or hawke of the towre;
  As pacient and as still,
And as full of good will,
As faire Ysaphill;
Coliaunder,
Swete pomaunder,
Good Cassaunder;
Steadfast of thought,
Wele made, wele wrought;
Far may be sought
Erst that ye can finde

So corteise, so kinde
As mirry Margarete,
This midsomer flowre,
Jentill as faucoun
Or hawke of the towre.

Thomas Wyatt (1503-1542)

I FIND NO PEACE
Description of the Contrarious Passions in a Lover

I find no peace, and all my war is done;
I fear and hope, I burn, and freeze like ice;
I fly aloft, yet can I not arise;
And nought I have, and all the world I seize on,
That locks nor loseth, holdeth me in prison,
And holds me not, yet can I scape no wise:
Nor letteth me live, nor die, at my devise,
And yet of death it giveth me occasion.
Without eye I see; without tongue I plain:
I wish to perish, yet I ask for health;
I love another, and I hate myself;
I feed me in sorrow, and laugh in all my pain.
Lo, thus displeaseth me both death and life,
And my delight is causer of this strife.

Nicholas Breton (1545?-1626)

COME, LITTLE BABE

Come, little babe, come, silly soul,
Thy father's shame, thy mother's grief,
Born as I doubt to all our dole,
And to thyself unhappy chief:
    Sing lullaby, and lap it warm,
    Poor soul that thinks no creature harm.

Thou little think'st and less dost know
The cause of this thy mother's moan;
Thou want'st the wit to wail her woe,
And I myself am all alone:
    Why dost thou weep? why dost thou wail?
    And know'st not yet what thou dost ail.

Come, little wretch—ah, silly heart!
Mine only joy, what can I more?
If there be any wrong thy smart,
That may the destinies implore:
    'Twas I, I say, against my will,
    I wail the time, but be thou still.

And dost thou smile? O, thy sweet face!
Would God Himself He might thee see!
No doubt thou wouldst soon purchase grace,
I know right well, for thee and me:
    But come to mother, babe, and play,
    For father false is fled away.

Sweet boy, if it by fortune chance
Thy father home again to send,
If death do strike me with his lance,
Yet mayst thou me to him commend:
    If any ask thy mother's name,
    Tell how by love she purchased blame.

Then will his gentle heart soon yield:
I know him of a noble mind:
Although a lion in the field,
A lamb in town thou shalt him find:
    Ask blessing, babe, be not afraid,
    His sugar'd words hath me betray'd.

Then mayst thou joy and be right glad;
Although in woe I seem to moan,
Thy father is no rascal lad,
A noble youth of blood and bone:
    His glancing looks, if he once smile,
    Right honest women may beguile.

Come, little boy, and rock asleep;
Sing lullaby and be thou still;
I, that can do naught else but weep,
Will sit by thee and wail my fill:
    God bless my babe, and lullaby
    From this thy father's quality.

Edmund Spenser (1552?-1599)

PROTHALAMION

Calm was the day, and through the trembling air
Sweet-breathing Zephyrus did softly play
A gentle spirit, that lightly did delay
Hot Titan's beams, which then did glister fair;
When I (whom sullen care,
Through discontent of my long fruitless stay
In prince's court, and expectation vain
Of idle hopes, which still do fly away,
Like empty shadows, did afflict my brain,)
Walk'd forth to ease my pain
Along the shore of silver streaming Thames;
Whose rutty bank, the which his river hems,
Was painted all with variable flowers,
And all the meads adorn'd with dainty gems,
Fit to deck maidens' bowers,
And crown their paramours,
Against the bridal day, which is not long:
    Sweet Thames! run softly, till I end my song.

There, in a meadow, by the river's side,
A flock of Nymphs I chancéd to espy,
All lovely daughters of the Flood thereby,
With goodly greenish locks, all loose untied,
As each had been a bride;
And each one had a little wicker basket,
Made of fine twigs, entailéd curiously,
In which they gather'd flowers to fill their flasket,
And with fine fingers cropt full feateously
The tender stalks on high.
Of every sort, which in that meadow grew,
They gather'd some; the violet, pallid blue,
The little daisy, that at evening closes,
The virgin lily, and the primrose true,
With store of vermeil roses,
To deck their bridegrooms' posies
Against the bridal day, which was not long:
    Sweet Thames! run softly, till I end my song.

With that I saw two Swans of goodly hue
Come softly swimming down along the Lee;
Two fairer birds I yet did never see;

The snow, which doth the top of Pindus strew,
Did never whiter shew,
Nor Jove himself, when he a swan would be
For love of Leda, whiter did appear;
Yet Leda was (they say) as white as he,
Yet not so white as these, nor nothing near;
So purely white they were
That even the gentle stream, the which them bare,
Seem'd foul to them, and bade his billows spare
To wet their silken feathers, lest they might
Soil their fair plumes with water not so fair,
And mar their beauties bright,
That shone as heaven's light,
Against their bridal day, which was not long:
    Sweet Thames! run softly, till I end my song.

Eftsoons, the Nymphs, which now had flowers their fill,
Ran all in haste to see that silver brood,
As they came floating on the crystal flood;
Whom when they saw, they stood amazéd still,
Their wond'ring eyes to fill;
Them seem'd they never saw a sight so fair,
Of fowls, so lovely, that they sure did deem
Them heavenly born, or to be that same pair
Which through the sky draw Venus' silver team;
For sure they did not seem
To be begot of any earthly seed,
But rather angels, or of angels' breed;
Yet were they bred of Summer's heat, they say,
In sweetest season, when each flower and weed
The earth did fresh array;
So fresh they seem'd as day,
Ev'n as their bridal day, which was not long:
    Sweet Thames! run softly, till I end my song.

Then forth they all out of their baskets drew
Great store of flowers, the honour of the field,
That to the sense did fragrant odours yield,
All which upon those goodly birds they threw,
And all the waves did strew,
That like old Peneus' waters they did seem,
When down along by pleasant Tempe's shore,
Scattered with flowers, through Thessaly they stream,
That they appear, through lilies' plenteous store,
Like a bride's chamber floor.
Two of those Nymphs, meanwhile, two garlands bound

Of freshest flowers which in that mead they found,
The which presenting all in trim array,
Their snowy foreheads therewithal they crown'd,
Whilst one did sing this lay,
Prepar'd against that day,
Against their bridal day, which was not long:
    Sweet Thames! run softly, till I end my song.

Ye gentle Birds! the world's fair ornament,
And heaven's glory, whom this happy hour
Doth lead unto your lovers' blissful bower,
Joy may you have, and gentle heart's content
Of your love's couplement;
And let fair Venus, that is Queen of Love,
With her heart-quelling son upon you smile,
Whose smile, they say, hath virtue to remove
All love's dislike, and friendship's faulty guile
For ever to assoil.
Let endless peace your steadfast hearts accord
And blessed plenty wait upon your board;
And let your bed with pleasures chaste abound,
That fruitful issue may to you afford,
Which may your foes confound,
And make your joys redound
Upon your bridal day, which is not long:
    Sweet Thames! run softly, till I end my song.

So ended she; and all the rest around
To her redoubled that her undersong,
Which said, their bridal day should not be long:
And gentle Echo from the neighbour ground
Their accents did resound.
So forth those joyous Birds did pass along
Adown the Lee, that to them murmur'd low,
As he would speak, but that he lack'd a tongue,
Yet did by signs his glad affection show,
Making his stream run slow.
And all the fowl which in his flood did dwell
Gan flock about these twain, that did excel
The rest, so far as Cynthia doth shend
The lesser stars. So they, enrangéd well,
Did on those two attend,
And their best service lend
Against their wedding day, which was not long:
    Sweet Thames! run softly, till I end my song.

At length they all to merry London came,
To merry London, my most kindly nurse,
That to me gave this life's first native source,
Though from another place I take my name,
An house of ancient fame:
There when they came, whereas those bricky towers
The which on Thames' broad aged back do ride,
Where now the studious lawyers have their bowers,
There whilome wont the Templar Knights to bide,
Till they decay'd through pride;
Next whereunto there stands a stately place,
Where oft I gainéd gifts and goodly grace
Of that great lord, which therein wont to dwell,
Whose want too well now feels my friendless case;
But ah! here fits not well
Old woes, but joys, to tell
Against the bridal day, which is not long:
    Sweet Thames! run softly, till I end my song.

Yet therein now doth lodge a noble peer,
Great England's glory, and the world's wide wonder,
Whose dreadful name late through all Spain did thunder,
And Hercules' two pillars standing near
Did make to quake and fear:
Fair branch of honour, flower of chivalry!
That fillest England with thy triumph's fame,
Joy have thou of thy noble victory,
And endless happiness of thine own name
That promiseth the same;
That through thy prowess, and victorious arms,
Thy country may be freed from foreign harms,
And great Eliza's glorious name may ring
Through all the world, fill'd with thy wide alarms,
Which some brave Muse may sing
To ages following,
Upon the bridal day, which is not long:
    Sweet Thames! run softly, till I end my song.

From those high towers this noble lord issuing,
Like radiant Hesper, when his golden hair
In th' ocean billows he hath bathéd fair,
Descended to the river's open viewing,
With great train ensuing.
Above the rest were goodly to be seen
Two gentle Knights of lovely face and feature,
Beseeming well the bower of any queen,

With gifts of wit, and ornaments of nature,
Fit for so goodly stature,
That like the twins of Jove they seem'd in sight,
Which deck the baldric of the heavens bright;
They two, forth pacing to the river's side,
Receiv'd those two fair Brides, their love's delight;
Which at th' appointed tide,
Each one did make his bride,
Against their bridal day, which is not long:
    Sweet Thames! run softly, till I end my song.

Sir Walter Raleigh (1552?-1618)

THE LIE

Go, Soul, the body's guest,
Upon a thankless arrant:
Fear not to touch the best;
The truth shall be thy warrant:
Go, since I needs must die,
And give the world the lie.

Say to the court, it glows
And shines like rotten wood;
Say to the church, it shows
What's good, and doth no good:
If church and court reply,
Then give them both the lie.

Tell potentates, they live
Acting by others' action;
Not loved unless they give,
Not strong but by a faction:
If potentates reply,
Give potentates the lie.

Tell men of high condition,
That manage the estate,
Their purpose is ambition,
Their practice only hate:
And if they once reply,
Then give them all the lie.

Tell them that brave it most,
They beg for more by spending,
Who, in their greatest cost,
Seek nothing but commending:
And if they make reply,
Then give them all the lie.

Tell zeal it wants devotion;
Tell love it is but lust:
Tell time it is but motion;
Tell flesh it is but dust:
And wish them not reply,
For thou must give the lie.

Tell age it daily wasteth;
Tell honour how it alters;
Tell beauty how she blasteth;
Tell favour how it falters:
And as they shall reply,
Give every one the lie.

Tell wit how much it wrangles
In tickle points of niceness;
Tell wisdom she entangles
Herself in over-wiseness:
And when they do reply,
Straight give them both the lie.

Tell physic of her boldness;
Tell skill it is pretension;
Tell charity of coldness;
Tell law it is contention:
And as they do reply,
So give them still the lie.

Tell fortune of her blindness;
Tell nature of decay;
Tell friendship of unkindness;
Tell justice of delay:
And if they will reply,
Then give them all the lie.

Tell arts they have no soundness,
But vary by esteeming;
Tell schools they want profoundness,
And stand too much on seeming:

If arts and schools reply,
Give arts and schools the lie.

Tell faith it's fled the city;
Tell how the country erreth;
Tell manhood shakes off pity
And virtue least preferreth:
And if they do reply,
Spare not to give the lie.

So when thou hast, as I
Commanded thee, done blabbing
—Although to give the lie
Deserves no less than stabbing—
Stab at thee he that will,
No stab the soul can kill.

TO HIS SON

Three things there be that prosper all apace,
    And flourish while they are asunder far;
But on a day, they meet all in a place,
    And when they meet, they one another mar.

And they be these: the Wood, the Weed, the Wag.
    The Wood is that that makes the gallows tree;
The Weed is that that strings the hangman's bag;
    The Wag, my pretty knave, betokens thee.

Now mark, dear boy—while these assemble not,
    Green springs the tree, hemp grows, the wag is wild;
But when they meet, it makes the timber rot,
    It frets the halter, and it chokes the child.

      God bless the Child!

Fulke Greville (1554-1628)

from CAELICA

99

Downe in the depth of mine iniquity,
That ugly center of infernall spirits;
Where each sinne feeles her owne deformity,
In these peculiar torments she inherits,
    Depriv'd of humane graces, and divine,
    Even there appeares this *saving God* of mine.

And in this fatall mirrour of transgression,
Shewes man as fruit of his degeneration,
The errours ugly infinite impression,
Which beares the faithlesse downe to desperation;
    Depriv'd of humane graces and divine,
    Even there appeares this *saving God* of mine.

In power and truth, Almighty and eternall,
Which on the sinne reflects strange desolation,
With glory scourging all the Sprites infernall,
And uncreated hell with unprivation;
    Depriv'd of humane graces, not divine,
    Even there appeares this *saving God* of mine.

For on this sp'rituall Crosse condemned lying,
To paines infernall by eternal doome,
I see my Saviour for the same sinnes dying,
And from that hell I fear'd, to free me, come;
    Depriv'd of humane graces, not divine,
    Thus hath his death rais'd up this soule of mine.

Sir Philip Sidney (1554-1586)

from ASTROPHEL AND STELLA

31

With how sad steps, O Moon! thou climb'st the skies!
How silently, and with how wan a face!
What! may it be, that even in heavenly place
That busy archer his sharp arrows tries?
Sure, if that long-with-love-acquainted eyes
Can judge of love, thou feel'st a lover's case;
I read it in thy looks; thy languish'd grace,
To me that feel the like, thy state descries.
Then, even of fellowship, O Moon, tell me,
Is constant love deem'd there but want of wit?
Are beauties there as proud as here they be?
Do they above love to be loved, and yet
    Those lovers scorn whom that love doth possess?
    Do they call virtue there ungratefulness?

George Peele (1556?-1596)

from POLYHYMNIA

His golden locks time hath to silver turned;
O time too swift, O swiftness never ceasing!
His youth 'gainst time and age hath ever spurned,
But spurned in vain; youth waneth by increasing:
Beauty, strength, youth, are flowers but fading seen;
Duty, faith, love, are roots, and ever green.

His helmet now shall make a hive for bees;
And, lovers' sonnets turned to holy psalms,
A man-at-arms must now serve on his knees,
And feed on prayers, which are age his alms:
But though from court to cottage he depart,
His saint is sure of his unspotted heart.

And when he saddest sits in homely cell,
He'll teach his swains this carol for a song,
"Blest be the hearts that wish my sovereign well,
Curst be the souls that think her any wrong."
Goddess, allow this aged man his right,
To be your beadsman now that was your knight.

Chidiock Tichborne (1558?-1586)

HIS ELEGY
Written Before His Execution

My prime of youth is but a frost of cares;
   My feast of joy is but a dish of pain;
My crop of corn is but a field of tares;
   And all my good is but vain hope of gain:
The day is past, and yet I saw no sun;
And now I live, and now my life is done.

My tale was heard, and yet it was not told;
   My fruit is fall'n, and yet my leaves are green;
My youth is spent, and yet I am not old;
   I saw the world, and yet I was not seen:
My thread is cut, and yet it is not spun;
And now I live, and now my life is done.

I sought my death, and found it in my womb;
   I looked for life, and saw it was a shade;
I trod the earth, and knew it was my tomb;
   And now I die, and now I was but made:
My glass is full, and now my glass is run;
And now I live, and now my life is done.

Robert Southwell (1561?-1595)

THE BURNING BABE

As I in hoary winter's night stood shivering in the snow,
Surprised I was with sudden heat, which made my heart to glow;
And lifting up a fearful eye to view what fire was near,
A pretty Babe all burning bright, did in the air appear,
Who scorchéd with excessive heat, such floods of tears did shed,
As though His floods should quench His flames which with His
    tears were fed;
Alas! quoth He, but newly born, in fiery heats I fry,
Yet none approach to warm their hearts or feel my fire but I!
My faultless breast the furnace is, the fuel wounding thorns,
Love is the fire, and sighs the smoke, the ashes shame and scorns;
The fuel Justice layeth on, and Mercy blows the coals,
The metal in this furnace wrought are men's defiled souls,
For which, as now on fire I am to work them to their good,
So will I melt into a bath to wash them in My blood:
With this He vanished out of sight, and swiftly shrunk away,
And straight I calléd unto mind that it was Christmas-day.

Michael Drayton (1563-1631)

from IDEA

61

Since there's no help, come let us kiss and part;
Nay, I have done, you get no more of me;
And I am glad, yea, glad with all my heart,
That thus so cleanly I myself can free.
Shake hands for ever, cancel all our vows,
And when we meet at any time again,
Be it not seen in either of our brows
That we one jot of former love retain.
Now at the last gasp of love's latest breath,
When, his pulse failing, passion speechless lies,
When faith is kneeling by his bed of death,
And innocence is closing up his eyes,
Now if thou wouldst, when all have given him over,
From death to life thou might'st him yet recover.

Mark Alexander Boyd (1563-1601)

FRA BANK TO BANK

Fra bank to bank, fra wood to wood I rin,
    Ourhailit with my feeble fantasie;
    Like til a leaf that fallis from a tree,
Or til a reed ourblawin with the win'.
Twa gods guides me; the ane of them is blin',
    Yea and a bairn brocht up in vanitie;
    The next a wife ingenrit of the sea,
And lichter nor a dauphin with her fin.

Unhappy is the man for evermair
    That tills the sand and sawis in the air;
    But twice unhappier is he, I lairn,
That feedis in his hairt a mad desire,
And follows on a woman throw the fire,
    Led by a blind and teachit by a bairn.

Christopher Marlowe (1564-1593)

THE PASSIONATE SHEPHERD TO HIS LOVE

Come live with me and be my love,
And we will all the pleasures prove
That hills and valleys, dale and field,
And all the craggy mountains yield!

There will we sit upon the rocks
And see the shepherds feed their flocks,
By shallow rivers, to whose falls
Melodious birds sing madrigals.

There will I make thee beds of roses
With a thousand fragrant posies;
A cap of flowers, and a kirtle
Embroider'd all with leaves of myrtle;

A gown made of the finest wool
Which from our pretty lambs we pull;
Fair lined slippers for the cold,
With buckles of the purest gold;

A belt of straw and ivy buds,
With coral clasps and amber studs:
And if these pleasures may thee move,
Come live with me and be my love!

Thy silver dishes, for thy meat
As precious as the gods do eat,
Shall on an ivory table be
Prepared each day for thee and me:

The shepherd swains shall dance and sing
For thy delight each May morning.
If these delights thy mind may move,
Then live with me and be my love!

Thomas Nashe (1567-1601)

ADIEU! FAREWELL EARTH'S BLISS!

Adieu! farewell earth's bliss!
This world uncertain is:
Fond are life's lustful joys,
Death proves them all but toys.
None from his darts can fly:
I am sick, I must die.
      Lord, have mercy on us!

Rich men, trust not in wealth!
Gold cannot buy you health;
Physic himself must fade;
All things to end are made;
The plague full swift goes by;
I am sick, I must die.
      Lord, have mercy on us!

Beauty is but a flower
Which wrinkles will devour:
Brightness falls from the air;
Queens have died young and fair;
Dust hath closed Helen's eye;
I am sick, I must die.
              Lord, have mercy on us!

Strength stoops unto the grave:
Worms feed on Hector brave;
Swords may not fight with fate;
Earth still holds ope her gate;
'Come! come!' the bells do cry.
I am sick, I must die.
              Lord, have mercy on us!

Wit with his wantonness
Tasteth death's bitterness:
Hell's executioner
Hath no ears for to hear
What vain art can reply:
I am sick, I must die.
              Lord, have mercy on us!

Haste, therefore, each degree,
To welcome destiny:
Heaven is our heritage,
Earth but a player's stage:
Mount we unto the sky.
I am sick, I must die.
              Lord, have mercy on us!

Thomas Campion (1567-1620)

CHERRY-RIPE

There is a garden in her face
Where roses and white lilies grow;
A heavenly paradise is that place
Wherein all pleasant fruits do flow.
        There cherries grow which none may buy,
        Till "Cherry Ripe" themselves do cry.

Those cherries fairly do enclose
Of orient pearl a double row,
Which when her lovely laughter shows,
They look like rosebuds filled with snow;
    Yet them nor peer nor prince can buy,
    Till "Cherry Ripe" themselves do cry.

Her eyes like angels watch them still,
Her brows like bended bows do stand,
Threatening with piercing frowns to kill
All that attempt with eye or hand
    Those sacred cherries to come nigh,
    Till "Cherry Ripe" themselves do cry.

Ben Jonson (1572-1637)

ON MY FIRST SON

Farewell, thou child of my right hand, and joy;
My sin was too much hope of thee, loved boy.
Seven years thou wert lent to me, and I thee pay,
Exacted by thy fate, on the just day.
O, could I lose all father now. For why
Will man lament the state he should envy?
To have so soon 'scaped world's, and flesh's, rage,
And if no other misery, yet age?
Rest in soft peace, and, asked, say here doth lie
Ben Jonson, his best piece of poetry.
For whose sake, henceforth, all his vows be such,
As what he loves may never like too much.

TO HEAVEN

Good and great God! can I not think of Thee,
    But it must straight my melancholy be?
Is it interpreted in me disease,
    That, laden with my sins, I seek for ease?
O be Thou witness, that the reins dost know
    And hearts of all, if I be sad for show;

And judge me after, if I dare pretend
    To aught but grace, or aim at other end.
As Thou art all, so be Thou all to me,
    First, midst, and last, converted One and Three!
My faith, my hope, my love; and, in this state,
    My judge, my witness, and my advocate!
Where have I been this while exiled from Thee,
    And whither rapt, now Thou but stoop'st to me?
Dwell, dwell here still! O, being everywhere,
    How can I doubt to find Thee ever here?
I know my state, both full of shame and scorn,
    Conceived in sin, and unto labor born,
Standing with fear, and must with horror fall,
    And destined unto judgment, after all.
I feel my grief too, and there scarce is ground
    Upon my flesh t'inflict another wound;
Yet dare I not complain or wish for death
    With holy Paul, lest it be thought the breath
Of discontent; or that these prayers be
    For weariness of life, not love of Thee.

Robert Herrick (1591-1674)

DELIGHT IN DISORDER

A sweet disorder in the dress
Kindles in clothes a wantonness:
A lawn about the shoulders thrown
Into a fine distraction;
An erring lace, which here and there
Enthralls the crimson stomacher;
A cuff neglectful, and thereby
Ribands to flow confusedly;
A winning wave, deserving note,
In the tempestuous petticoat;
A careless shoe-string, in whose tie
I see a wild civility,—
Do more bewitch me, than when art
Is too precise in every part.

TO THE VIRGINS, TO MAKE MUCH OF TIME

Gather ye rosebuds while ye may:
   Old Time is still a-flying,
And this same flower that smiles to-day
   To-morrow will be dying.

The glorious lamp of heaven, the sun,
   The higher he's a-getting,
The sooner will his race be run,
   And nearer he's to setting.

That age is best which is the first,
   When youth and blood are warmer;
But, being spent, the worse, and worst
   Times, still succeed the former.

Then be not coy, but use your time,
   And while ye may, go marry:
For having lost but once your prime,
   You may for ever tarry.

Henry King (1592-1669)

THE EXEQUY

Accept, thou shrine of my dead saint,
Instead of dirges, this complaint;
And for sweet flowers to crown thy hearse,
Receive a strew of weeping verse
From thy grieved friend, whom thou might'st see
Quite melted into tears for thee.

Dear loss! since thy untimely fate
My task hath been to meditate
On thee, on thee; thou art the book,
The library whereon I look,
Though almost blind. For thee, loved clay,
I languish out, not live, the day,
Using no other exercise
But what I practise with mine eyes;

By which wet glasses I find out
How lazily time creeps about
To one that mourns; this, only this,
My exercise and business is.
So I compute the weary hours
With sighs dissolvèd into showers.

Nor wonder if my time go thus
Backward and most preposterous;
Thou hast benighted me; thy set
This eve of blackness did beget,
Who wast my day, though overcast
Before thou hadst thy noon-tide passed;
And I remember must in tears,
Thou scarce hadst seen so many years
As day tells hours. By thy clear sun
My love and fortune first did run;
But thou wilt never more appear
Folded within my hemisphere,
Since both thy light and motïon
Like a fled star is fall'n and gone;
And 'twixt me and my soul's dear wish
An earth now interposèd is,
Which such a strange eclipse doth make
As ne'er was read in almanac.

I could allow thee for a time
To darken me and my sad clime;
Were it a month, a year, or ten,
I would thy exile live till then,
And all that space my mirth adjourn,
So thou wouldst promise to return,
And putting off thy ashy shroud,
At length disperse this sorrow's cloud.

But woe is me! the longest date
Too narrow is to calculate
These empty hopes; never shall I
Be so much blest as to descry
A glimpse of thee, till that day come
Which shall the earth to cinders doom,
And a fierce fever must calcine
The body of this world like thine,
My little world. That fit of fire
Once off, our bodies shall aspire
To our souls' bliss; then we shall rise

And view ourselves with clearer eyes
In that calm region where no night
Can hide us from each other's sight.

Meantime, thou hast her, earth; much good
May my harm do thee. Since it stood
With heaven's will I might not call
Her longer mine, I give thee all
My short-lived right and interest
In her whom living I loved best;
With a most free and bounteous grief,
I give thee what I could not keep.
Be kind to her, and prithee look
Thou write into thy doomsday book
Each parcel of this rarity
Which in thy casket shrined doth lie.
See that thou make thy reck'ning straight,
And yield her back again by weight;
For thou must audit on thy trust
Each grain and atom of this dust,
As thou wilt answer Him that lent,
Not gave thee, my dear monument.

So close the ground, and 'bout her shade
Black curtains draw, my bride is laid.

Sleep on, my love, in thy cold bed,
Never to be disquieted!
My last good-night! Thou wilt not wake
Till I thy fate shall overtake;
Till age, or grief, or sickness must
Marry my body to that dust
It so much loves, and fill the room
My heart keeps empty in thy tomb.
Stay for me there, I will not fail
To meet thee in that hollow vale.
And think not much of my delay;
I am already on the way,
And follow thee with all the speed
Desire can make, or sorrows breed.
Each minute is a short degree,
And ev'ry hour a step towards thee.
At night when I betake to rest,
Next morn I rise nearer my west
Of life, almost by eight hours' sail,
Than when sleep breathed his drowsy gale.

Thus from the sun my bottom steers,
And my day's compass downward bears;
Nor labor I to stem the tide
Through which to thee I swiftly glide.

'Tis true, with shame and grief I yield,
Thou like the van first tookst the field,
And gotten hath the victory
In thus adventuring to die
Before me, whose more years might crave
A just precedence in the grave.
But hark! my pulse like a soft drum
Beats my approach, tells thee I come;
And slow howe'er my marches be,
I shall at last sit down by thee.

The thought of this bids me go on,
And wait my dissolution
With hope and comfort. Dear, forgive
The crime, I am content to live
Divided, with but half a heart,
Till we shall meet and never part.

George Herbert (1593-1633)

THE COLLAR

I struck the board, and cried, No more.
        I will abroad.
    What? shall I ever sigh and pine?
My lines and life are free; free as the road,
    Loose as the wind, as large as store.
        Shall I be still in suit?
Have I no harvest but a thorn
To let me blood, and not restore
What I have lost with cordial fruit?
        Sure there was wine
Before my sighs did dry it: there was corn
    Before my tears did drown it.
    Is the year only lost to me?
        Have I no bays to crown it?

No flowers, no garlands gay? all blasted?
      All wasted?
  Not so, my heart: but there is fruit,
    And thou hast hands.
  Recover all thy sigh-blown age
On double pleasures: leave thy cold dispute
Of what is fit and not; forsake thy cage,
     Thy rope of sands,
  Which petty thoughts have made, and made to thee
  Good cable, to enforce and draw,
    And be thy law,
While thou didst wink and wouldst not see.
     Away; take heed:
     I will abroad.
Call in thy death's-head there: tie up thy fears.
    He that forbears
  To suit and serve his need,
    Deserves his load.
But as I rav'd and grew more fierce and wild
    At every word,
  Methought I heard one calling, *Child;*
    And I replied, *My Lord.*

Thomas Carew (1595?-1640)

THE SPRING

Now that the winter's gone, the earth hath lost
Her snow-white robes; and now no more the frost
Candies the grass, or casts an icy cream
Upon the silver lake or crystal stream:
But the warm sun thaws the benumbed earth,
And makes it tender; gives a sacred birth
To the dead swallow; wakes in hollow tree
The drowsy cuckoo and the humble-bee.
Now do a choir of chirping minstrels bring,
In triumph to the world, the youthful spring:
The valleys, hills, and woods in rich array
Welcome the coming of the long'd-for May.
Now all things smile: only my love doth lower,
Nor hath the scalding noon-day sun the power

To melt that marble ice, which still doth hold
Her heart congeal'd, and makes her pity cold.
The ox, which lately did for shelter fly
Into the stall, doth now securely lie
In open fields; and love no more is made
By the fire-side, but in the cooler shade
Amyntas now doth with his Chloris sleep
Under a sycamore, and all things keep
  Time with the season: only she doth carry
  June in her eyes, in her heart January.

Edmund Waller (1606-1687)

SONG

  Go, lovely Rose!
Tell her, that wastes her time and me,
  That now she knows,
When I resemble her to thee,
How sweet and fair she seems to be.

  Tell her that's young
And shuns to have her graces spied,
  That hadst thou sprung
In deserts, where no men abide,
Thou must have uncommended died.

  Small is the worth
Of beauty from the light retired;
  Bid her come forth,
Suffer herself to be desired,
And not blush so to be admired.

  Then die! that she
The common fate of all things rare
  May read in thee:
How small a part of time they share
That are so wondrous sweet and fair!

John Suckling (1609-1642)

OUT UPON IT! I HAVE LOVED

Out upon it! I have loved
    Three whole days together;
And am like to love three more,
    If it prove fair weather!

Time shall moult away his wings,
    Ere he shall discover
In the whole wide world again
    Such a constant lover.

But the spite on't is, no praise
    Is due at all to me:
Love with me had made no stays,
    Had it any been but she.

Had it any been but she,
    And that very face,
There had been at least ere this
    A dozen dozen in her place!

Andrew Marvell (1621-1678)

THE GARDEN

How vainly men themselves amaze
To win the palm, the oak, or bays;
And their incessant labours see
Crowned from some single herb or tree,
Whose short and narrow-vergéd shade
Does prudently their toils upbraid;
While all flowers and all trees do close
To weave the garlands of repose.

    Fair Quiet, have I found thee here,
And Innocence, thy sister dear!
Mistaken long, I sought you then

In busy companies of men.
Your sacred plants, if here below,
Only among the plants will grow:
Society is all but rude
To this delicious solitude.

No white nor red was ever seen
So amorous as this lovely green.
Fond lovers, cruel as their flame,
Cut in these trees their mistress' name:
Little, alas, they know or heed,
How far these beauties hers exceed!
Fair tree! wheres'e'er your barks I wound,
No name shall but your own be found.

When we have run our passion's heat,
Love hither makes his best retreat.
The gods, that mortal beauty chase,
Still in a tree did end their race:
Apollo hunted Daphne so,
Only that she might laurel grow;
And Pan did after Syrinx speed,
Not as a nymph, but for a reed.

What wondrous life in this I lead!
Ripe apples drop about my head;
The luscious clusters of the vine
Upon my mouth do crush their wine;
The nectarine, and curious peach,
Into my hands themselves do reach;
Stumbling on melons, as I pass,
Ensnared with flowers, I fall on grass.

Meanwhile the mind, from pleasure less,
Withdraws into its happiness:
The mind, that ocean where each kind
Does straight its own resemblance find;
Yet it creates, transcending these,
Far other worlds, and other seas;
Annihilating all that's made
To a green thought in a green shade.

Here at the fountain's sliding foot,
Or at some fruit-tree's mossy root,
Casting the body's vest aside,
My soul into the boughs does glide:

There like a bird it sits and sings,
Then whets, and combs its silver wings;
And, till prepared for longer flight,
Waves in its plumes the various light.

Such was that happy garden-state,
While man there walked without a mate:
After a place so pure and sweet,
What other help could yet be meet?
But t'was beyond a mortal's share
To wander solitary there:
Two Paradises 'twere in one,
To live in Paradise alone.

How well the skilful gardener drew
Of flowers and herbs this dial new!
Where, from above, the milder sun
Does through a fragrant zodiac run;
And, as it works, the industrious bee
Computes its time as well as we.
How could such sweet and wholesome hours
Be reckoned but with herbs and flowers?

TO HIS COY MISTRESS

Had we but world enough, and time,
This coyness, Lady, were no crime.
We would sit down, and think which way
To walk, and pass our long love's day.
Thou by the Indian Ganges' side
Shouldst rubies find; I by the tide
Of Humber would complain. I would
Love you ten years before the Flood;
And you should, if you please, refuse
Till the conversion of the Jews.
My vegetable love should grow
Vaster than empires, and more slow.
An hundred years should go to praise
Thine eyes, and on thy forehead gaze;
Two hundred to adore each breast;
But thirty thousand to the rest:
An age, at least, to every part,
And the last age should show your heart.

For, Lady, you deserve this state;
Nor would I love at lower rate.
  But, at my back, I always hear
Time's winged chariot hurrying near:
And yonder, all before us lie
Deserts of vast eternity.
Thy beauty shall no more be found;
Nor, in thy marble vault, shall sound
My echoing song. Then worms shall try
That long preserved virginity:
And your quaint honour turn to dust;
And into ashes all my lust.
The grave's a fine and private place,
But none, I think, do there embrace.
  Now, therefore, while the youthful hue
Sits on thy skin like morning dew,
And while thy willing soul transpires
At every pore with instant fires,
Now let us sport us while we may;
And now, like amorous birds of prey,
Rather at once our time devour,
Than languish in his slow-chapt power.
Let us roll all our strength, and all
Our sweetness, up into one ball;
And tear our pleasures, with rough strife,
Through the iron gates of life.
  Thus, though we cannot make our sun
Stand still, yet we will make him run.

Henry Vaughan (1622-1695)

THE WORLD

I saw Eternity the other night,
Like a great ring of pure and endless light,
    All calm, as it was bright;
And round beneath it, Time in hours, days, years,
    Driven by the spheres
Like a vast shadow moved; in which the world
    And all her train were hurled.
The doting lover in his quaintest strain
    Did there complain;

Near him, his lute, his fancy, and his flights,
   Wit's sour delights;
With gloves, and knots, the silly snares of pleasure,
   Yet his dear treasure,
All scattered lay, while he his eyes did pour
   Upon a flower.

The darksome statesman, hung with weights and woe,
Like a thick midnight-fog, moved there so slow,
   He did not stay, nor go;
Condemning thoughts—like sad eclipses—scowl
   Upon his soul,
And clouds of crying witnesses without
   Pursued him with one shout.
Yet digged the mole, and lest his ways be found,
   Worked underground,
Where he did clutch his prey; but one did see
   That policy.
Churches and altars fed him; perjuries
   Were gnats and flies;
It rained about him blood and tears, but he
   Drank them as free.

The fearful miser on a heap of rust
Sat pining all his life there, did scarce trust
   His own hands with the dust,
Yet would not place one piece above, but lives
   In fear of thieves.
Thousands there were as frantic as himself,
   And hugged each one his pelf;
The downright epicure placed heav'n in sense,
   And scorned pretence;
While others, slipped into a wide excess,
   Said little less;
The weaker sort slight, trivial wares enslave,
   Who think them brave;
And poor, despised Truth sat counting by
   Their victory.

Yet some, who all this while did weep and sing,
And sing and weep, soared up into the ring;
   But most would use no wing.
Oh, fools—said I—thus to prefer dark night
   Before true light!
To live in grots and caves, and hate the day
   Because it shows the way;

The way, which from this dead and dark abode
        Leads up to God;
A way where you might tread the sun, and be
        More bright than he!
But as I did their madness so discuss,
        One whispered thus,
'This ring the Bridegroom did for none provide,
        But for His bride.'

John Dryden (1631-1700)

TO THE MEMORY OF MR. OLDHAM

Farewell, too little and too lately known,
Whom I began to think and call my own;
For sure our souls were near allied, and thine
Cast in the same poetic mould with mine.
One common note on either lyre did strike,
And knaves and fools we both abhorred alike.
To the same goal did both our studies drive:
The last set out the soonest did arrive.
Thus Nisus fell upon the slippery place,
Whilst his young friend performed and won the race.
O early ripe! to thy abundant store
What could advancing age have added more?
It might (what nature never gives the young)
Have taught the numbers of thy native tongue.
But satire needs not those, and wit will shine
Through the harsh cadence of a rugged line.
A noble error, and but seldom made,
When poets are by too much force betrayed.
Thy gen'rous fruits, though gathered ere their prime,
Still shewed a quickness; and maturing time
But mellows what we write to the dull sweets of rhyme.
Once more, hail, and farewell! farewell, thou young
But ah! too short, Marcellus of our tongue!
Thy brows with ivy and with laurels bound;
But fate and gloomy night encompass thee around.

Thomas Traherne (1637?-1674)

WONDER

How like an angel came I down!
How bright are all things here!
When first among His works I did appear,
O how their glory me did crown!
The world resembled His eternity,
In which my soul did walk;
And everything that I did see
Did with me talk.

The skies in their magnificence,
The lovely, lively air,
Oh, how divine, how soft, how sweet, how fair!
The stars did entertain my sense;
And all the works of God so bright and pure,
So rich and great did seem
As if they ever must endure
In my esteem.

A native health and innocence
Within my bones did grow;
And while my God did all his glories show,
I felt a vigor in my sense
That was all spirit: I within did flow
With seas of life like wine;
I nothing in the world did know
But 'twas divine.

Harsh, ragged objects were concealed:
Oppressions, tears, and cries,
Sins, griefs, complaints, dissensions, weeping eyes
Were hid, and only things revealed
Which heavenly spirits and the angels prize.
The state of innocence
And bliss, not trades and poverties,
Did fill my sense.

The streets were paved with golden stones;
The boys and girls were mine:
Oh, how did all their lovely faces shine!
The sons of men were holy ones;

In joy and beauty they appeared to me;
    And everything I found,
  While like an angel I did see,
    Adorned the ground.

  Rich diamond and pearl and gold
    In every place was seen;
Rare splendors, yellow, blue, red, white, and green,
  Mine eyes did everywhere behold.
Great wonders clothed with glory did appear;
    Amazement was my bliss;
  That and my wealth met everywhere;
    No joy to this!

  Cursed and devised proprieties,
    With envy, avarice,
And fraud (those fiends that spoil even Paradise)
  Flew from the splendor of mine eyes;
And so did hedges, ditches, limits, bounds:
    I dreamed not aught of those,
  But in surveying all men's grounds
    I found repose.

  For property itself was mine,
    And hedges, ornaments:
Walls, houses, coffers, and their rich contents
  To make me rich combine.
Clothes, costly jewels, laces, I esteemed
    My wealth by others worn;
  For me they all to wear them seemed
    When I was born.

Jonathan Swift (1667-1745)

THE FURNITURE OF A WOMAN'S MIND

A set of phrases learnt by rote;
A passion for a scarlet coat;
When at a play to laugh, or cry,
Yet cannot tell the reason why:
Never to hold her tongue a minute;

While all she prates has nothing in it.
Whole hours can with a coxcomb sit,
And take his nonsense all for wit:
Her learning mounts to read a song;
But half the words pronouncing wrong;
Has ev'ry repartee in store,
She spoke ten thousand times before.
Can ready compliments supply
On all occasions, cut and dry.
Such hatred to a parson's gown,
The sight will put her in a swoon.
For conversation well endu'd;
She calls it witty to be rude;
And, placing raillery in railing,
Will tell aloud your greatest failing;
Nor makes a scruple to expose
Your bandy leg, or crooked nose.
Can at her morning tea run o'er
The scandal of the day before.
Improving hourly in her skill,
To cheat and wrangle at quadrille.

    In choosing lace a critic nice,
Knows to a groat the lowest price;
Can in her female clubs dispute
What lining best the silk will suit;
What colours each complexion match:
And where with art to place a patch.

    If chance a mouse creeps in her sight,
Can finely counterfeit a fright;
So sweetly screams if it comes near her,
She ravishes all hearts to hear her.
Can dextrously her husband tease,
By taking fits whene'er she please:
By frequent practice learns the trick
At proper seasons to be sick;
Thinks nothing gives one airs so pretty;
At once creating love and pity.
If Molly happens to be careless,
And but neglects to warm her hair-lace,
She gets a cold as sure as death;
And vows she scarce can fetch her breath—
Admires how modest woman can
Be so robustious like a man.

    In party, furious to her pow'r;
A bitter Whig, or Tory sour;
Her arguments directly tend

Against the side she would defend:
Will prove herself a Tory plain,
From principles the Whigs maintain;
And, to defend the Whiggish cause,
Her topics from the Tories draws.
    Oh yes! If any man can find
More virtues in a woman's mind,
Let them be sent to Mrs. Harding;
She'll pay the charges to a farthing:
Take notice, she has my commission
To add them in the next edition;
They may outsell a better thing;
So, holla boys; God save the King.

Thomas Gray (1716-1771)

ELEGY WRITTEN IN A
COUNTRY CHURCH-YARD

The curfew tolls the knell of parting day,
    The lowing herd winds slowly o'er the lea,
The ploughman homeward plods his weary way,
    And leaves the world to darkness, and to me.

Now fades the glimmering landscape on the sight,
    And all the air a solemn stillness holds,
Save where the beetle wheels his droning flight,
    And drowsy tinklings lull the distant folds:

Save that from yonder ivy-mantled tower
    The moping owl does to the moon complain
Of such as, wandering near her secret bower,
    Molest her ancient solitary reign.

Beneath those rugged elms, that yew-tree's shade,
    Where heaves the turf in many a mouldering heap,
Each in his narrow cell for ever laid,
    The rude Forefathers of the hamlet sleep.

The breezy call of incense-breathing morn,
    The swallow twittering from the straw-built shed,

The cock's shrill clarion, or the echoing horn,
　　No more shall rouse them from their lowly bed.

For them no more the blazing hearth shall burn,
　　Or busy housewife ply her evening care:
No children run to lisp their sire's return,
　　Or climb his knees the envied kiss to share,

Oft did the harvest to their sickle yield,
　　Their furrow oft the stubborn glebe has broke;
How jocund did they drive their team afield!
　　How bow'd the woods beneath their sturdy stroke!

Let not Ambition mock their useful toil,
　　Their homely joys, and destiny obscure;
Nor Grandeur hear with a disdainful smile
　　The short and simple annals of the Poor.

The boast of heraldry, the pomp of power,
　　And all that beauty, all that wealth e'er gave,
Awaits alike th' inevitable hour:
　　The paths of glory lead but to the grave.

Nor you, ye Proud, impute to these the fault
　　If Memory o'er their tomb no trophies raise,
Where through the long-drawn aisle and fretted vault
　　The pealing anthem swells the note of praise.

Can storied urn or animated bust
　　Back to its mansion call the fleeting breath?
Can Honour's voice provoke the silent dust,
　　Or Flattery soothe the dull cold ear of Death?

Perhaps in this neglected spot is laid
　　Some heart once pregnant with celestial fire;
Hands, that the rod of empire might have sway'd,
　　Or waked to ecstasy the living lyre:

But Knowledge to their eyes her ample page,
　　Rich with the spoils of time, did ne'er unroll;
Chill Penury repress'd their noble rage,
　　And froze the genial current of the soul.

Full many a gem of purest ray serene
　　The dark unfathom'd caves of ocean bear:

Full many a flower is born to blush unseen,
And waste its sweetness on the desert air.

Some village-Hampden, that with dauntless breast
The little tyrant of his fields withstood,
Some mute inglorious Milton here may rest,
Some Cromwell, guiltless of his country's blood.

Th' applause of list'ning senates to command,
The threats of pain and ruin to despise,
To scatter plenty o'er a smiling land,
And read their history in a nation's eyes,

Their lot forbad: nor circumscribed alone
Their growing virtues, but their crimes confined;
Forbad to wade through slaughter to a throne,
And shut the gates of mercy on mankind,

The struggling pangs of conscious truth to hide,
To quench the blushes of ingenuous shame,
Or heap the shrine of Luxury and Pride
With incense kindled at the Muse's flame.

Far from the madding crowd's ignoble strife,
Their sober wishes never learn'd to stray;
Along the cool sequester'd vale of life
They kept the noiseless tenour of their way.

Yet e'en these bones from insult to protect
Some frail memorial still erected nigh,
With uncouth rhymes and shapeless sculpture deck'd,
Implores the passing tribute of a sigh.

Their name, their years, spelt by th' unletter'd Muse,
The place of fame and elegy supply:
And many a holy text around she strews,
That teach the rustic moralist to die.

For who, to dumb forgetfulness a prey,
This pleasing anxious being e'er resign'd,
Left the warm precincts of the cheerful day,
Nor cast one longing lingering look behind?

On some fond breast the parting soul relies,
Some pious drops the closing eye requires;
E'en from the tomb the voice of Nature cries,
E'en in our ashes live their wonted fires.

For thee, who, mindful of th' unhonour'd dead,
    Dost in these lines their artless tale relate;
If chance, by lonely contemplation led,
    Some kindred spirit shall inquire thy fate,

Haply some hoary-headed swain may say,
    'Oft have we seen him at the peep of dawn
Brushing with hasty steps the dews away,
    To meet the sun upon the upland lawn;

'There at the foot of yonder nodding beech
    That wreaths its old fantastic roots so high,
His listless length at noontide would he stretch,
    And pore upon the brook that babbles by.

'Hard by yon wood, now smiling as in scorn,
    Muttering his wayward fancies he would rove;
Now drooping, woeful wan, like one forlorn,
    Or crazed with care, or cross'd in hopeless love.

'One morn I miss'd him on the custom'd hill,
    Along the heath, and near his favourite tree;
Another came; nor yet beside the rill,
    Nor up the lawn, nor at the wood was he;

'The next with dirges due in sad array
    Slow through the church-way path we saw him borne,
Approach and read (for thou canst read) the lay
    Graved on the stone beneath yon aged thorn.'

The Epitaph

Here rests his head upon the lap of Earth
    A Youth, to Fortune and to Fame unknown;
Fair Science frown'd not on his humble birth,
    And Melancholy mark'd him for her own.

Large was his bounty, and his soul sincere;
    Heaven did a recompense as largely send:
He gave to Misery all he had, a tear,
    He gain'd from Heaven, 'twas all he wish'd, a friend.

No farther seek his merits to disclose,
    Or draw his frailties from their dread abode,
(There they alike in trembling hope repose,)
    The bosom of his Father and his God.

William Cowper (1731-1800)

THE CASTAWAY

Obscurest night involv'd the sky,
   Th' Atlantic billows roar'd,
When such a destin'd wretch as I,
   Wash'd headlong from on board,
Of friends, of hope, of all bereft,
His floating home forever left.

No braver chief could Albion boast
   Than he with whom he went,
Nor ever ship left Albion's coast,
   With warmer wishes sent.
He lov'd them both, but both in vain,
Nor him beheld, nor her again.

Not long beneath the whelming brine,
   Expert to swim, he lay;
Nor soon he felt his strength decline,
   Or courage die away;
But wag'd with death a lasting strife,
Supported by despair of life.

He shouted; nor his friends had fail'd
   To check the vessel's course,
But so the furious blast prevail'd
   That pitiless perforce,
They left their outcast mate behind,
And scudded still before the wind.

Some succour yet they could afford;
   And, such as storms allow,
The cask, the coop, the floated cord,
   Delay'd not to bestow.
But he (they knew) nor ship nor shore,
Whate'er they gave, should visit more.

Nor, cruel as it seem'd, could he
   Their haste himself condemn,
Aware that flight, in such a sea,
   Alone could rescue them;
Yet bitter felt it still to die
Deserted, and his friends so nigh.

He long survives, who lives an hour
  In ocean, self-upheld;
And so long he, with unspent pow'r,
  His destiny repell'd;
And ever, as the minutes flew,
Entreated help, or cried—"Adieu!"

At length, his transient respite past,
  His comrades, who before
Had heard his voice in ev'ry blast,
  Could catch the sound no more;
For then, by toil subdu'd, he drank
The stifling wave, and then he sank.

No poet wept him; but the page
  Of narrative sincere,
That tells his name, his worth, his age,
  Is wet with Anson's tear:
And tears by bards or heroes shed
Alike immortalize the dead.

I therefore purpose not, or dream,
  Descanting on his fate,
To give the melancholy theme
  A more enduring date;
But misery still delights to trace
Its semblance in another's case.

No voice divine the storm allay'd,
  No light propitious shone;
When, snatch'd from all effectual aid,
  We perish'd, each alone;
But I beneath a rougher sea,
And whelm'd in deeper gulfs than he.

Robert Burns (1759-1796)

GREEN GROW THE RASHES, O

Green grow the rashes, O,
  Green grow the rashes, O;
The sweetest hours that e'er I spend,
  Are spent amang the lasses, O!

There's nought but care on ev'ry han',
  In ev'ry hour that passes, O;
What signifies the life o' man,
  An' 'twere na for the lasses, O.

The warly race may riches chase,
  An' riches still may fly them, O;
An' tho' at last they catch them fast,
  Their hearts can ne'er enjoy them, O.

But gie me a canny hour at e'en,
  My arms about my dearie, O;
An' warly cares, an' warly men,
  May a' gae tapsalteerie, O!

For you sae douce, ye sneer at this,
  Ye're nought but senseless asses, O:
The wisest man the warl' e'er saw,
  He dearly lov'd the lasses, O.

Auld nature swears, the lovely dears
  Her noblest work she classes, O;
Her prentice han' she tried on man,
  An' then she made the lasses, O.

William Wordsworth (1770-1850)

THE WORLD IS TOO MUCH WITH US

The world is too much with us; late and soon,
Getting and spending, we lay waste our powers:
Little we see in Nature that is ours;
We have given our hearts away, a sordid boon!
This sea that bares her bosom to the moon;
The winds that will be howling at all hours,
And are up-gathered now like sleeping flowers;
For this, for everything, we art out of tune;
It moves us not.—Great God! I'd rather be
A pagan suckled in a creed outworn.
So might I, standing on this pleasant lea,
Have glimpses that would make me less forlorn;
Have sight of Proteus rising from the sea;
Or hear old Triton blow his wreathéd horn.

ODE: INTIMATIONS OF IMMORTALITY FROM RECOLLECTIONS OF EARLY CHILDHOOD

The Child is Father of the Man;
And I could wish my days to be
Bound each to each by natural piety.

1

There was a time when meadow, grove, and stream,
    The earth, and every common sight,
        To me did seem
    Appareled in celestial light,
The glory and the freshness of a dream.
It is not now as it hath been of yore;—
        Turn whereso'er I may,
          By night or day,
The things which I have seen I now can see no more.

2

        The rainbow comes and goes,
        And lovely is the rose,
        The moon doth with delight
Look round her when the heavens are bare,
        Waters on a starry night
        Are beautiful and fair;
    The sunshine is a glorious birth;
    But yet I know, where'er I go,
That there hath passed away a glory from the earth.

3

Now, while the birds thus sing a joyous song,
  And while the young lambs bound
      As to the tabor's sound,
To me alone there came a thought of grief;
A timely utterance gave that thought relief,
      And I again am strong:
The cataracts blow their trumpets from the steep;
No more shall grief of mine the season wrong;
I hear the echoes through the mountains throng,
The winds come to me from the fields of sleep,
      And all the earth is gay;
        Land and sea

Give themselves up to jollity
      And with the heart of May
Doth every beast keep holiday;—
      Thou child of joy,
Shout round me, let me hear thy shouts, thou happy shepherd boy.

4

Ye blessed Creatures, I have heard the call
      Ye to each other make; I see
The heavens laugh with you in your jubilee;
      My heart is at your festival,
      My head hath its coronal,
The fullness of your bliss, I feel—I feel it all.
      Oh evil day! if I were sullen
      While Earth herself is adorning,
         This sweet May-morning,
      And the children are culling
         On every side,
      In a thousand valleys far and wide,
      Fresh flowers; while the sun shines warm,
And the babe leaps up on his mother's arm:
      I hear, I hear, with joy I hear!
      —But there's a tree, of many, one,
A single field which I have looked upon,
Both of them speak of something that is gone:
      The pansy at my feet
      Doth the same tale repeat:
Whither is fled the visionary gleam?
Where is it now, the glory and the dream?

5

Our birth is but a sleep and a forgetting:
The soul that rises with us, our life's star,
      Hath had elsewhere its setting,
         And cometh from afar;
      Not in entire forgetfulness,
      And not in utter nakedness,
But trailing clouds of glory do we come
         From God, who is our home.
Heaven lies about us in our infancy;
Shades of the prison-house begin to close
         Upon the growing boy,
But he beholds the light, and whence it flows.
         He sees it in his joy;

The youth, who daily farther from the east
　　Must travel, still is Nature's priest,
　　　　And by the vision splendid
　　　　Is on his way attended;
At length the man perceives it die away,
And fade into the light of common day.

6

Earth fills her lap with pleasures of her own;
Yearnings she hath in her own natural kind,
And, even with something of a mother's mind,
　　　　And no unworthy aim,
　　The homely nurse doth all she can
To make her foster-child, her inmate man,
　　Forget the glories he hath known,
And that imperial palace whence he came.

7

Behold the child among his newborn blisses,
　　A six years' darling of a pygmy size!
See, where 'mid work of his own hand he lies,
Fretted by sallies of his mother's kisses,
With light upon him from his father's eyes!
See, at his feet, some little plan or chart,
Some fragment from his dream of human life,
Shaped by himself with newly learned art;
　　A wedding or a festival,
　　A mourning or a funeral;
　　　　And this hath now his heart,
　　And unto this he frames his song:
　　　　Then will he fit his tongue
To dialogues of business, love, or strife;
　　But it will not be long
　　Ere this be thrown aside,
　　And with new joy and pride
The little actor cons another part;
Filling from time to time his "humorous stage"
With all the persons, down to palsied age,
That life brings with her in her equipage;
　　As if his whole vocation
　　Were endless imitation.

8

Thou, whose exterior semblance doth belie
    Thy soul's immensity;
Thou best philosopher, who yet dost keep
Thy heritage, thou eye among the blind,
That, deaf and silent, read'st the eternal deep,
Haunted forever by the eternal mind—
    Mighty prophet! seer blest!
    On whom those truths do rest,
Which we are toiling all our lives to find,
In darkness lost, the darkness of the grave;
Thou, over whom thy immortality
Broods like the day, a master o'er a slave,
A presence which is not to be put by;
Thou little Child, yet glorious in the might
Of heaven-born freedom on thy being's height,
Why with such earnest pains dost thou provoke
The years to bring the inevitable yoke,
Thus blindly with thy blessedness at strife?
Full soon thy Soul shall have her earthly freight,
And custom lie upon thee with a weight,
Heavy as frost, and deep almost as life!

9

    O joy! that in our embers
    Is something that doth live,
    That nature yet remembers
    What was so fugitive!
The thought of our past years in me doth breed
Perpetual benediction: not indeed
For that which is most worthy to be blest—
Delight and liberty, the simple creed
Of childhood, whether busy or at rest,
With new-fledged hope still fluttering in his breast:
    Not for these I raise
    The song of thanks and praise;
    But for those obstinate questionings
    Of sense and outward things,
    Falling from us, vanishings;
    Blank misgivings of a creature
Moving about in worlds not realized,

High instincts before which our mortal nature
Did tremble like a guilty thing surprised:
    But for those first affections,
    Those shadowy recollections,
  Which, be they what they may,
Are yet the fountain-light of all our day,
Are yet a master-light of all our seeing;
  Uphold us, cherish, and have power to make
Our noisy years seem moments in the being
Of the eternal silence: truths that wake,
    To perish never;
Which neither listlessness, nor mad endeavor,
    Nor man nor boy,
Nor all that is at enmity with joy,
Can utterly abolish or destroy!
    Hence in a season of calm weather,
    Though inland far we be,
Our souls have sight of that immortal sea
    Which brought us hither,
    Can in a moment travel thither,
And see the children sport upon the shore,
And hear the mighty waters rolling evermore.

10

Then sing, ye birds! sing, sing a joyous song!
      And let the young lambs bound
      As to the tabor's sound!
  We in thought will join your throng,
    Ye that pipe and ye that play,
    Ye that through your hearts today
    Feel the gladness of the May!
What though the radiance which was once so bright
Be now forever taken from my sight,
    Though nothing can bring back the hour
Of splendor in the grass, of glory in the flower;
    We will grieve not, rather find
    Strength in what remains behind;
    In the primal sympathy
    Which having been must ever be;
    In the soothing thoughts that spring
    Out of human suffering;
    In the faith that looks through death,
In years that bring the philosophic mind.

11

And oh, ye fountains, meadows, hills, and groves,
Forebode not any severing of our loves!
Yet in my heart of hearts I feel your might;
I only have relinquished one delight
To live beneath your more habitual sway.
I love the brooks which down their channels fret,
Even more than when I tripped lightly as they;
The innocent brightness of a new-born day
      Is lovely yet;
The clouds that gather round the setting sun
Do take a sober coloring from an eye
That hath kept watch o'er man's mortality;
Another race hath been, and other palms are won.
Thanks to the human heart by which we live,
Thanks to its tenderness, its joys, and fears,
To me the meanest flower that blows can give
Thoughts that do often lie too deep for tears.

Samuel Taylor Coleridge (1772-1834)

KUBLA KHAN

In Xanadu did Kubla Khan
    A stately pleasure-dome decree;
Where Alph, the sacred river, ran
Through caverns measureless to man
    Down to a sunless sea.
So twice five miles of fertile ground
With walls and towers were girdled round:
And there were gardens bright with sinuous rills,
Where blossomed many an incense-bearing tree,
And here were forests ancient as the hills,
Enfolding sunny spots of greenery.

But oh! that deep romantic chasm which slanted
Down the green hill athwart a cedarn cover!
A savage place; as holy and enchanted
As e'er beneath a waning moon was haunted
By woman wailing for her demon-lover!

And from this chasm, with ceaseless turmoil seething,
As if this earth in fast thick pants were breathing,
A mighty fountain momently was forced:
Amid whose swift half-intermitted burst
Huge fragments vaulted like rebounding hail,
Or chaffy grain beneath the thresher's flail:
And 'mid these dancing rocks at once and ever
It flung up momently the sacred river.
Five miles meandering with a mazy motion
Through wood and dale the sacred river ran,
Then reached the caverns measureless to man,
And sank in tumult to a lifeless ocean:
And 'mid this tumult Kubla heard from far
Ancestral voices prophesying war!

      The shadow of the dome of pleasure
      Floated midway on the waves;
      Where was heard the mingled measure
      From the fountain and the caves.
It was a miracle of rare device,
A sunny pleasure-dome with caves of ice!

      A damsel with a dulcimer
      In a vision once I saw:
      It was an Abyssinian maid,
      And on her dulcimer she played,
      Singing of Mount Abora.
      Could I revive within me
      Her symphony and song,
      To such a deep delight 'twould win me,
That with music loud and long,
I would build that dome in air,
That sunny dome! those caves of ice!
And all who heard should see them there,
And all should cry, Beware! Beware!
His flashing eyes, his floating hair!
Weave a circle round him thrice,
And close your eyes with holy dread,
For he on honey-dew hath fed,
And drunk the milk of Paradise.

George Gordon, Lord Byron (1788-1824)

WHEN A MAN HATH NO FREEDOM
TO FIGHT FOR AT HOME

When a man hath no freedom to fight for at home,
    Let him combat for that of his neighbors;
Let him think of the glories of Greece and of Rome,
    And get knocked on the head for his labors.

To do good to Mankind is the chivalrous plan,
    And is always as nobly requited;
Then battle for Freedom wherever you can,
    And, if not shot or hanged, you'll get knighted.

from DON JUAN

Bob Southey! You're a poet—Poet laureate,
    And representative of all the race;
Although 'tis true that you turned out a Tory at
    Last—yours has lately been a common case;
And now, my Epic Renegade! what are ye at?
    With all the Lakers, in and out of place?
A nest of tuneful persons, to my eye
Like "four and twenty Blackbirds in a pye;

"Which pye being opened they began to sing"
    (This old song and new simile holds good),
"A dainty dish to set before the King,"
    Or Regent, who admires such kind of food;
And Coleridge, too, has lately taken wing,
    But like a hawk encumbered with his hood—
Explaining metaphysics to the nation—
I wish he would explain his Explanation.

You, Boy! are rather insolent, you know,
    At being disappointed in your wish
To supersede all warblers here below,
    And be the only Blackbird in the dish;
And then you overstrain yourself, or so,
    And tumble downward like the flying fish

Gasping on deck, because you soar too high, Bob,
And fall for lack of moisture quite a-dry, Bob!

And Wordsworth, in a rather long "Excursion"
    (I think the quarto holds five hundred pages),
Has given a sample from the vasty version
    Of his new system to perplex the sages;
'Tis poetry—at least by his assertion,
    And may appear so when the dog-star rages—
And he who understands it would be able
To add a story to the Tower of Babel.

You—Gentlemen! by dint of long seclusion
    From better company, have kept your own
At Keswick, and through still continued fusion
    Of one another's minds, at last have grown
To deem as a most logical conclusion,
    That poesy has wreaths for you alone;
There is a narrowness in such a notion,
Which makes me wish you'd change your lakes for ocean.

I would not imitate the petty thought,
    Nor coin my self-love to so base a vice,
For all the glory your conversion brought,
    Since gold alone should not have been its price,
You have your slavery; was't for that you wrought?
    And Wordsworth has his place in the Excise.
You're shabby fellows—true—but poets still,
And duly seated on the Immortal Hill.

Percy Bysshe Shelley (1792-1822)

ODE TO THE WEST WIND

1

O wild West Wind, thou breath of Autumn's being,
Thou, from whose unseen presence the leaves dead
Are driven, like ghosts from an enchanter fleeing,

Yellow, and black, and pale, and hectic red,
Pestilence-stricken multitudes: O thou,
Who chariotest to their dark wintry bed

The wingéd seeds, where they lie cold and low,
Each like a corpse within its grave, until
Thine azure sister of the spring shall blow

Her clarion o'er the dreaming earth, and fill
(Driving sweet buds like flocks to feed in air)
With living hues and odours plain and hill;

Wild Spirit, which art moving everywhere;
Destroyer and preserver; hear, oh hear!

2

Thou on whose stream, 'mid the steep sky's commotion,
Loose clouds like earth's decaying leaves are shed,
Shook from the tangled boughs of Heaven and Ocean,

Angels of rain and lightning: there are spread
On the blue surface of thine aëry surge,
Like the bright hair uplifted from the head

Of some fierce Mænad, even from the dim verge
Of the horizon to the zenith's height
The locks of the approaching storm. Thou dirge

Of the dying year, to which this closing night
Will be the dome of a vast sepulchre,
Vaulted with all thy congregated might

Of vapours, from whose solid atmosphere
Black rain, and fire, and hail will burst: oh hear!

3

Thou who didst waken from his summer dreams
The blue Mediterranean, where he lay,
Lulled by the coil of his crystalline streams.

Beside a pumice isle in Baiæ's bay,
And saw in sleep old palaces and towers
Quivering within the wave's intenser day,

All overgrown with azure moss and flowers
So sweet, the sense faints picturing them! Thou
For whose path the Atlantic's level powers

Cleave themselves into chasms, while far below
The sea-blooms and the oozy woods which wear
The sapless foliage of the ocean, know

Thy voice, and suddenly grow gray with fear,
And tremble and despoil themselves: oh hear!

4

If I were a dead leaf thou mightest bear;
If I were a swift cloud to fly with thee;
A wave to pant beneath thy power, and share

The impulse of thy strength, only less free
Than thou, O uncontrollable! If even
I were as in my boyhood, and could be

The comrade of thy wanderings over heaven,
As then, when to outstrip thy skiey speed
Scarce seemed a vision; I would ne'er have striven

As thus with thee in prayer in my sore need.
Oh lift me as a wave, a leaf, a cloud!
I fall upon the thorns of life! I bleed!

A heavy weight of hours has chained and bowed
One too like thee: tameless, and swift, and proud.

5

Make me thy lyre, even as the forest is:
What if my leaves are falling like its own!
The tumult of thy mighty harmonies

Will take from both a deep, autumnal tone,
Sweet though in sadness. Be thou, spirit fierce,
My spirit! Be thou me, impetuous one!

Drive my dead thoughts over the universe
Like withered leaves to quicken a new birth!
And, by the incantation of this verse,

Scatter, as from an unextinguished hearth
Ashes and sparks, my words among mankind!
Be through my lips to unawakened earth

The trumpet of a prophecy! O, wind,
If Winter comes, can Spring be far behind?

Robert Browning (1812-1889)

THE BISHOP ORDERS HIS TOMB AT SAINT PRAXED'S CHURCH
Rome, 15—

Vanity, saith the preacher, vanity!
Draw round my bed: is Anselm keeping back?
Nephews—sons mine . . . ah God, I know not! Well—
She, men would have to be your mother once,
Old Gandolf envied me, so fair she was!
What's done is done, and she is dead beside,
Dead long ago, and I am Bishop since,
And as she died so must we die ourselves,
And thence ye may perceive the world's a dream.
Life, how and what is it? As here I lie
In this state-chamber, dying by degrees,
Hours and long hours in the dead night, I ask
"Do I live, am I dead?" Peace, peace seems all.
Saint Praxed's ever was the church for peace;
And so, about this tomb of mine. I fought
With tooth and nail to save my niche, ye know:
—Old Gandolf cozened me, despite my care;
Shrewd was that snatch from out the corner South
He graced his carrion with, God curse the same!
Yet still my niche is not so cramped but thence
One sees the pulpit o' the epistle-side,
And somewhat of the choir, those silent seats,
And up into the aery dome where live
The angels, and a sunbeam's sure to lurk:
And I shall fill my slab of basalt there,
And 'neath my tabernacle take my rest,
With those nine columns round me, two and two,
The odd one at my feet where Anselm stands:
Peach-blossom marble all, the rare, the ripe
As fresh-poured red wine of a mighty pulse
—Old Gandolf with his paltry onion-stone,
Put me where I may look at him! True peach,
Rosy and flawless: how I earned the prize!
Draw close: that conflagration of my church
—What then? So much was saved if aught were missed!
My sons, ye would not be my death? Go dig
The white-grape vineyard where the oil-press stood,
Drop water gently till the surface sink,

And if ye find . . . ah God, I know not, I! . . .
Bedded in store of rotten fig-leaves soft,
And corded up in a tight olive-frail,
Some lump, ah God, of *lapis lazuli*,
Big as a Jew's head cut off at the nape,
Blue as a vein o'er the Madonna's breast—
Sons, all have I bequeathed you, villas, all,
That brave Frascati villa with its bath—
So, let the blue lump poise between my knees,
Like God the Father's globe on both his hands
Ye worship in the Jesu Church so gay,
For Gandolf shall not choose but see and burst!
Swift as a weaver's shuttle fleet our years;
Man goeth to the grave, and where is he?
Did I say basalt for my slab, sons? Black—
'Twas ever antique-black I meant! How else
Shall ye contrast my frieze to come beneath?
The bas-relief in bronze ye promised me,
Those Pans and Nymphs ye wot of, and perchance
Some tripod, thyrsus, with a vase or so,
The Saviour at his sermon on the mount,
St. Praxed in a glory, and one Pan
Ready to twitch the Nymph's last garment off,
And Moses with the tables . . . but I know
Ye mark me not! What do they whisper thee,
Child of my bowels, Anselm? Ah, ye hope
To revel down my villas while I gasp
Bricked o'er with beggar's moldy travertine
Which Gandolf from his tomb-top chuckles at!
Nay, boys, ye love me—all of jasper, then!
'Tis jasper ye stand pledged to, lest I grieve
My bath must needs be left behind, alas!
One block, pure green as a pistachio-nut,
There's plenty jasper somewhere in the world—
And have I not St. Praxed's ear to pray
Horses for ye, and brown Greek manuscripts,
And mistresses with great smooth marbly limbs?
—That's if ye carve my epitaph aright,
Choice Latin, picked phrase, Tully's every word,
No gaudy ware like Gandolf's second line—
Tully, my masters? Ulpian serves his need!
And then how I shall lie through centuries,
And hear the blessèd mutter of the mass,
And see God made and eaten all day long,
And feel the steady candle-flame, and taste
Good strong thick stupefying incense-smoke!

For as I lie here, hours of the dead night,
Dying in state and by such slow degrees,
I fold my arms as if they clasped a crook,
And stretch my feet forth straight as stone can point
And let the bedclothes for a mortcloth drop
Into great laps and folds of sculptor's-work:
And as yon tapers dwindle, and strange thoughts
Grow, with a certain humming in my ears,
About the life before I lived this life,
And this life too, popes, cardinals and priests,
Saint Praxed at his sermon on the mount,
Your tall pale mother with her talking eyes,
And new-found agate urns as fresh as day,
And marble's language, Latin pure, discreet,
—Aha, ELUCESCEBAT quoth our friend?
No Tully, said I, Ulpian at the best!
Evil and brief hath been my pilgrimage.
All lapis, all, sons! Else I give the Pope
My villas: will ye ever eat my heart?
Ever your eyes were as a lizard's quick,
They glitter like your mother's for my soul,
Or ye would heighten my impoverished frieze,
Piece out its starved design, and fill my vase
With grapes, and add a vizor and a Term,
And to the tripod ye would tie a lynx
That in his struggle throws the thyrsus down,
To comfort me on my entablature
Whereon I am to lie till I must ask
"Do I live, am I dead?" There, leave me, there!
For ye have stabbed me with ingratitude
To death—ye wish it—God, ye wish it! Stone—
Gritstone, a-crumble! Clammy squares which sweat
As if the corpse they keep were oozing through—
And no more lapis to delight the world!
Well, go! I bless ye. Fewer tapers there,
But in a row: and, going, turn your backs
—Ay, like departing altar-ministrants,
And leave me in my church, the church for peace,
That I may watch at leisure if he leers—
Old Gandolf, at me, from his onion-stone,
As still he envied me, so fair she was!

Matthew Arnold (1822-1888)

DOVER BEACH

The sea is calm tonight,
The tide is full, the moon lies fair
Upon the straits;—on the French coast the light
Gleams and is gone; the cliffs of England stand,
Glimmering and vast, out in the tranquil bay.
Come to the window, sweet is the night-air!

Only, from the long line of spray
Where the sea meets the moon-blanched land,
Listen! you hear the grating roar
Of pebbles which the waves draw back, and fling,
At their return, up the high strand,
Begin, and cease, and then again begin,
With tremulous cadence slow, and bring
The eternal note of sadness in.

Sophocles long ago
Heard it on the Aegean, and it brought
Into his mind the turbid ebb and flow
Of human misery; we
Find also in the sound a thought,
Hearing it by this distant northern sea.

The Sea of Faith
Was once, too, at the full, and round earth's shore
Lay like the folds of a bright girdle furled.
But now I only hear
Its melancholy, long withdrawing roar,
Retreating, to the breath
Of the night-wind, down the vast edges drear
And naked shingles of the world.

Ah, love, let us be true
To one another! for the world, which seems
To lie before us like a land of dreams,
So various, so beautiful, so new,
Hath really neither joy, nor love, nor light,
Nor certitude, nor peace, nor help for pain;
And we are here as on a darkling plain
Swept with confused alarms of struggle and flight,
Where ignorant armies clash by night.

George Meredith (1828-1909)

LUCIFER IN STARLIGHT

On a starred night Prince Lucifer uprose.
Tired of his dark dominion swung the fiend
Above the rolling ball in cloud part screened,
Where sinners hugged their specter of repose.
Poor prey to his hot fit of pride were those.
And now upon his western wing he leaned,
Now his huge bulk o'er Afric's sands careened,
Now the black planet shadowed Arctic snows.
Soaring through wider zones that pricked his scars
With memory of the old revolt from Awe,
He reached a middle height, and at the stars,
Which are the brain of heaven, he looked, and sank.
Around the ancient track marched, rank on rank,
The army of unalterable law.

Emily Dickinson (1830-1886)

AFTER GREAT PAIN

After great pain, a formal feeling comes—
The Nerves sit ceremonious, like Tombs—
The stiff Heart questions was it He, that bore,
And Yesterday, or Centuries before?

The Feet, mechanical, go round—
Of Ground, or Air, or Ought—
A Wooden way
Regardless grown,
A Quartz contentment, like a stone—

This is the Hour of Lead—
Remembered, if outlived,
As Freezing persons, recollect the Snow—
First—Chill—then Stupor—then the letting go—

I CANNOT LIVE WITH YOU

I cannot live with You—
It would be Life—
And Life is over there—
Behind the Shelf

The Sexton keeps the Key to—
Putting up
Our Life—His Porcelain—
Like a Cup—

Discarded of the Housewife—
Quaint—or Broke—
A newer Sevres pleases—
Old Ones crack—

I could not die—with You—
For One must wait
To shut the Other's Gaze down—
You—could not—

And I—Could I stand by
And see You—freeze—
Without my Right of Frost—
Death's privilege?

Nor could I rise—with You—
Because Your Face
Would put out Jesus'—
That New Grace

Glow plain—and foreign
On my homesick Eye—
Except that You than He
Shone closer by—

They'd judge Us—How—
For You—served Heaven—You know,
Or sought to—
I could not—

Because You saturated Sight—
And I had no more Eyes
For sordid excellence
As Paradise

And were You lost, I would be—
Though My Name
Rang loudest
On the Heavenly fame—

And were You—saved—
And I—condemned to be
Where You were not—
That self—were Hell to Me—

So We must meet apart—
You there—I—here—
With just the Door ajar
That Oceans are—and Prayer—
And that White Sustenance—
Despair—

A NARROW FELLOW IN THE GRASS

A narrow Fellow in the Grass
Occasionally rides—
You may have met Him—did you not
His notice sudden is—

The Grass divides as with a Comb—
A spotted shaft is seen—
And then it closes at your feet
And opens further on—

He likes a Boggy Acre
A Floor too cool for Corn—
Yet when a Boy, and Barefoot—
I more than once at Noon
Have passed, I thought, a Whip lash
Unbraiding in the Sun
When stooping to secure it
It wrinkled, and was gone—

Several of Nature's People
I know, and they know me—
I feel for them a transport
Of cordiality—

But never met this Fellow
Attended, or alone
Without a tighter breathing
And Zero at the Bone—

Lewis Carroll (1832-1898)

JABBERWOCKY

'Twas brillig, and the slithy toves
    Did gyre and gimble in the wabe:
All mimsy were the borogoves,
    And the mome raths outgrabe.

"Beware the Jabberwock, my son!
    The jaws that bite, the claws that catch!
Beware the Jubjub bird, and shun
    The frumious Bandersnatch!"

He took his vorpal sword in hand;
    Long time the manxome foe he sought—
So rested he by the Tumtum tree,
    And stood awhile in thought.

And, as in uffish thought he stood,
    The Jabberwock, with eyes of flame,
Came whiffling through the tulgey wood,
    And burbled as it came!

One, two! One, two! And through and through
    The vorpal blade went snicker-snack!
He left it dead, and with its head
  He went galumphing back.

"And hast thou slain the Jabberwock?
    Come to my arms, my beamish boy!
O frabjous day! Callooh, Callay!"
    He chortled in his joy.

'Twas brillig, and the slithy toves
    Did gyre and gimble in the wabe:
All mimsy were the borogoves,
    And the mome raths outgrabe.

Thomas Hardy (1840-1928)

THE OXEN

Christmas Eve, and twelve of the clock.
   "Now they are all on their knees,"
An elder said as we sat in a flock
   By the embers in hearthside ease.

We pictured the meek mild creatures where
   They dwelt in their strawy pen,
Nor did it occur to one of us there
   To doubt they were kneeling then.

So fair a fancy few would weave
   In these years! Yet, I feel,
If someone said on Christmas Eve,
   "Come; see the oxen kneel,

"In the lonely barton by yonder coomb
   Our childhood used to know,"
I should go with him in the gloom,
   Hoping it might be so.

THE RUINED MAID

"O 'melia, my dear, this does everything crown!
Who could have supposed I should meet you in Town?
And whence such fair garments, such prosperi-ty?"—
"O didn't you know I'd been ruined?" said she.

—"You left us in tatters, without shoes or socks,
Tired of digging potatoes, and spudding up docks;
And now you've gay bracelets and bright feathers three!"—
"Yes: that's how we dress when we're ruined," said she.

—"At home in the barton you said 'thee' and 'thou,'
And 'thik oon,' and 'theäs oon,' and 't'other'; but now
Your talking quite fits 'ee for high compa-ny!"—
"Some polish is gained with one's ruin," said she.

—"Your hands were like paws then, your face blue and bleak
But now I'm bewitched by your delicate cheek,

And your little gloves fit as on any la-dy!"—
"We never do work when we're ruined," said she.

—"You used to call home-life a hag-ridden dream,
And you'd sigh, and you'd sock; but at present you seem
To know not of megrims or melancho-ly!"—
"True. One's pretty lively when ruined," said she.

—"I wish I had feathers, a fine sweeping gown,
And a delicate face, and could strut about Town!"—
"My dear—a raw country girl, such as you be,
Cannot quite expect that. You ain't ruined," said she.

Gerard Manley Hopkins (1844-1889)

SPRING AND FALL
To a Young Child

Márgarét, are you gríeving
Over Goldengrove unleaving?
Leáves, líke the things of man, you
With your fresh thoughts care for, can you?
Áh! ás the heart grows older
It will come to such sights colder
By and by, nor spare a sigh
Though worlds of wanwood leafmeal lie;
And yet you wíll weep and know why.
Now no matter, child, the name:
Sórrows's spríngs áre the same.
Nor mouth had, no nor mind, expressed
What heart heard of, ghost guessed:
It ís the blight man was born for.
It is Margaret you mourn for.

THE WINDHOVER
To Christ Our Lord

I caught this morning morning's minion, kingdom of daylight's
        dauphin, dapple-dawn-drawn Falcon, in his riding
    Of the rolling level underneath him steady air, and striding
High there, how he rung upon the rein of a wimpling wing

In his ecstasy! then off, off forth on swing,
 As a skate's heel sweeps smooth on a bow-bend; the hurl and
  gliding
 Rebuffed the big wind. My heart in hiding
Stirred for a bird,—the achieve of, the mastery of the thing!

Brute beauty and valor and act, oh, air, pride, plume, here
 Buckle! And the fire that breaks from thee then, a billion
Times told lovelier, more dangerous, O my chevalier!

No wonder of it: shéer plód makes plough down sillon
Shine, and blue-bleak embers, ah my dear,
Fall, gall themselves, and gash gold-vermilion.

I WAKE AND FEEL THE FELL OF DARK

I wake and feel the fell of dark, not day.
What hours, O what black hoürs we have spent
This night! what sights you, heart, saw; ways you went!
And more must, in yet longer light's delay.
 With witness I speak this. But where I say
Hours I mean years, mean life. And my lament
Is cries countless, cries like dead letters sent
To dearest him that lives alas! away.
 I am gall, I am heartburn. God's most deep decree
Bitter would have me taste: my taste was me;
Bones built in me, flesh filled, blood brimmed the curse.
 Selfyeast of spirit a dull dough sours. I see
The lost are like this, and their scourge to be
As I am mine, their sweating selves; but worse.

A. E. Housman (1859-1936)

TO AN ATHLETE DYING YOUNG

The time you won your town the race
We chaired you through the market-place;
Man and boy stood cheering by,
And home we brought you shoulder-high.

To-day, the road all runners come,
Shoulder-high we bring you home,
And set you at your threshold down,
Townsman of a stiller town.

Smart lad, to slip betimes away
From fields where glory does not stay
And early though the laurel grows
It withers quicker than the rose.

Eyes the shady night has shut
Cannot see the record cut,
And silence sounds no worse than cheers
After earth has stopped the ears:

Now you will not swell the rout
Of lads that wore their honors out,
Runners whom renown outran
And the name died before the man.

So set, before its echoes fade,
The fleet foot on the sill of shade,
And hold to the low lintel up
The still-defended challenge-cup.

And round that early-laurelled head
Will flock to gaze the strengthless dead,
And find unwithered on its curls
The garland briefer than a girl's.

E. A. Robinson (1869-1935)

EROS TURANNOS

She fears him, and will always ask
   What fated her to choose him;
She meets in his engaging mask
   All reasons to refuse him;
But what she meets and what she fears
Are less than are the downward years,
Drawn slowly to the foamless weirs
   Of age, were she to lose him.

Between a blurred sagacity
  That once had power to sound him,
And Love, that will not let him be
  The Judas that she found him,
Her pride assuages her almost,
As if it were alone the cost.—
He sees that he will not be lost,
  And waits and looks around him.

A sense of ocean and old trees
  Envelops and allures him;
Tradition, touching all he sees,
  Beguiles and reassures him;
And all her doubts of what he says
Are dimmed with what she knows of days—
Till even prejudice delays
  And fades, and she secures him.

The falling leaf inaugurates
  The reign of her confusion:
The pounding wave reverberates
  The dirge of her illusion;
And home, where passion lived and died,
Becomes a place where she can hide,
While all the town and harbor side
  Vibrate with her seclusion.

We tell you, tapping on our brows,
  The story as it should be,—
As if the story of a house
  Were told, or ever could be;
We'll have no kindly veil between
Her visions and those we have seen,—
As if we guessed what hers have been,
  Or what they are or would be.

Meanwhile we do no harm; for they
  That with a god have striven,
Not hearing much of what we say,
  Take what the god has given;
Though like waves breaking it may be,
Or like a changed familiar tree,
Or like a stairway to the sea
  Where down the blind are driven.

HILLCREST

To Mrs. Edward MacDowell

No sound of any storm that shakes
Old island walls with older seas
Comes here where now September makes
An island in a sea of trees.

Between the sunlight and the shade
A man may learn till he forgets
The roaring of a world remade,
And all his ruins and regrets;

And if he still remembers here
Poor fights he may have won or lost,—
If he be ridden with the fear
Of what some other fight may cost,—

If, eager to confuse too soon,
What he has known with what may be,
He reads a planet out of tune
For cause of his jarred harmony,—

If here he venture to unroll
His index of adagios,
And he be given to console
Humanity with what he knows,—

He may by contemplation learn
A little more than what he knew,
And even see great oaks return
To acorns out of which they grew.

He may, if he but listen well,
Through twilight and the silence here,
Be told what there are none may tell
To vanity's impatient ear;

And he may never dare again
Say what awaits him, or be sure
What sunlit labyrinth of pain
He may not enter and endure.

Who knows to-day from yesterday
May learn to count no thing too strange:

Love builds of what Time takes away,
Till Death itself is less than Change.

Who sees enough in his duress
May go as far as dreams have gone;
Who sees a little may do less
Than many who are blind have done;

Who sees unchastened here the soul
Triumphant has no other sight
Than has a child who sees the whole
World radiant with his own delight.

Far journeys and hard wandering
Await him in whose crude surmise
Peace, like a mask, hides everything
That is and has been from his eyes;

And all his wisdom is unfound,
Or like a web that error weaves
On airy looms that have a sound
No louder now than falling leaves.

MR. FLOOD'S PARTY

Old Eben Flood, climbing alone one night
Over the hill between the town below
And the forsaken upland hermitage
That held as much as he should ever know
On earth again of home, paused warily.
The road was his with not a native near;
And Eben, having leisure, said aloud,
For no man else in Tilbury Town to hear:

"Well, Mr. Flood, we have the harvest moon
Again, and we may not have many more;
The bird is on the wing, the poet says,
And you and I have said it here before.
Drink to the bird." He raised up to the light
The jug that he had gone so far to fill,
And answered huskily: "Well, Mr. Flood,
Since you propose it, I believe I will."

Alone, as if enduring to the end
A valiant armor of scarred hopes outworn,
He stood there in the middle of the road
Like Roland's ghost winding a silent horn.
Below him, in the town among the trees,
Where friends of other days had honored him,
A phantom salutation of the dead
Rang thinly till old Eben's eyes were dim.

Then, as a mother lays her sleeping child
Down tenderly, fearing it may awake,
He set the jug down slowly at his feet
With trembling care, knowing that most things break;
And only when assured that on firm earth
It stood, as the uncertain lives of men
Assuredly did not, he paced away,
And with his hand extended paused again:

"Well, Mr. Flood, we have not met like this
In a long time; and many a change has come
To both of us, I fear, since last it was
We had a drop together. Welcome home!"
Convivially returning with himself,
Again he raised the jug up to the light;
And with an acquiescent quaver said:
"Well, Mr. Flood, if you insist, I might.

"Only a very little, Mr. Flood—
For auld lang syne. No more, sir; that will do."
So, for the time, apparently it did,
And Eben evidently thought so too;
For soon amid the silver loneliness
Of night he lifted up his voice and sang,
Secure, with only two moons listening,
Until the whole harmonious landscape rang—

"For auld lang syne." The weary throat gave out;
The last word wavered, and the song was done.
He raised again the jug regretfully
And shook his head, and was again alone.
There was not much that was ahead of him,
And there was nothing in the town below—
Where strangers would have shut the many doors
That many friends had opened long ago.

Robert Frost (1874-1963)

'OUT, OUT—'

The buzz-saw snarled and rattled in the yard
And made dust and dropped stove-length sticks of wood,
Sweet-scented stuff when the breeze drew across it.
And from there those that lifted eyes could count
Five mountain ranges one behind the other
Under the sunset far into Vermont.
And the saw snarled and rattled, snarled and rattled,
As it ran light, or had to bear a load.
And nothing happened: day was all but done.
Call it a day, I wish they might have said
To please the boy by giving him the half hour
That a boy counts so much when saved from work.
His sister stood beside them in her apron
To tell them 'Supper.' At the word, the saw,
As if to prove saws knew what supper meant,
Leaped out at the boy's hand, or seemed to leap—
He must have given the hand. However it was,
Neither refused the meeting. But the hand!
The boy's first outcry was a rueful laugh,
As he swung toward them holding up the hand
Half in appeal, but half as if to keep
The life from spilling. Then the boy saw all—
Since he was old enough to know, big boy
Doing a man's work, though a child at heart—
He saw all spoiled. 'Don't let him cut my hand off—
The doctor, when he comes. Don't let him, sister!'
So. But the hand was gone already.
The doctor put him in the dark of ether.
He lay and puffed his lips out with his breath.
And then—the watcher at his pulse took fright.
No one believed. They listened at his heart.
Little—less—nothing!—and that ended it.
No more to build on there. And they, since they
Were not the one dead, turned to their affairs.

TO EARTHWARD

Love at the lips was touch
As sweet as I could bear;
And once that seemed too much;
I lived on air

That crossed me from sweet things,
The flow of—was it musk
From hidden grapevine springs
Down hill at dusk?

I had the swirl and ache
From sprays of honeysuckle
That when they're gathered shake
Dew on the knuckle.

I craved strong sweets, but those
Seemed strong when I was young;
The petal of the rose
It was that stung.

Now no joy but lacks salt
That is not dashed with pain
And weariness and fault;
I crave the stain

Of tears, the aftermark
Of almost too much love,
The sweet of bitter bark
And burning clove.

When stiff and sore and scarred
I take away my hand
From leaning on it hard
In grass and sand,

The hurt is not enough:
I long for weight and strength
To feel the earth as rough
To all my length.

THE MOST OF IT

He thought he kept the universe alone;
For all the voice in answer he could wake
Was but the mocking echo of his own
From some tree-hidden cliff across the lake.
Some morning from the boulder-broken beach
He would cry out on life, that what it wants
Is not its own love back in copy speech,
But counter-love, original response.
And nothing ever came of what he cried
Unless it was the embodiment that crashed
In the cliff's talus on the other side,
And then in the far distant water splashed,
But after a time allowed for it to swim,
Instead of proving human when it neared
And someone else additional to him,
As a great buck it powerfully apeared,
Pushing the crumpled water up ahead,
And landed pouring like a waterfall,
And stumbled through the rocks with horny tread,
And forced the underbrush—and that was all.

Edward Thomas (1878-1917)

THE OWL

Downhill I came, hungry, and yet not starved;
Cold, yet had heat within me that was proof
Against the North wind; tired, yet so that rest
Had seemed the sweetest thing under a roof.

Then at the inn I had food, fire, and rest,
Knowing how hungry, cold, and tired was I.
All of the night was quite barred out except
An owl's cry, a most melancholy cry

Shaken out long and clear upon the hill,
No merry note, nor cause of merriment,
But one telling me plain what I escaped
And others could not, that night, as in I went.

And salted was my food, and my repose,
Salted and sobered, too, by the bird's voice
Speaking for all who lay under the stars,
Soldiers and poor, unable to rejoice.

Wallace Stevens (1879-1955)

DISILLUSIONMENT OF TEN O'CLOCK

The houses are haunted
By white night-gowns.
None are green,
Or purple with green rings,
Or green with yellow rings,
Or yellow with blue rings.
None of them are strange,
With socks of lace
And beaded ceintures.
People are not going
To dream of baboons and periwinkles.
Only, here and there, an old sailor,
Drunk and asleep in his boots,
Catches tigers
In red weather.

SUNDAY MORNING

1

Complacencies of the peignoir, and late
Coffee and oranges in a sunny chair,
And the green freedom of a cockatoo
Upon a rug mingle to dissipate
The holy hush of ancient sacrifice.
She dreams a little, and she feels the dark
Encroachment of that old catastrophe,
As a calm darkens among water-lights.
The pungent oranges and bright, green wings
Seem things in some procession of the dead,
Winding across wide water, without sound.

The day is like wide water, without sound,
Stilled for the passing of her dreaming feet
Over the seas, to silent Palestine,
Dominion of the blood and sepulchre.

2

Why should she give her bounty to the dead?
What is divinity if it can come
Only in silent shadows and in dreams?
Shall she not find in comforts of the sun,
In pungent fruit and bright, green wings, or else
In any balm or beauty of the earth,
Things to be cherished like the thought of heaven?
Divinity must live within herself:
Passions of rain, or moods in falling snow;
Grievings in loneliness, or unsubdued
Elations when the forest blooms; gusty
Emotions on wet roads on autumn nights;
All pleasures and all pains, remembering
The bough of summer and the winter branch.
These are the measures destined for her soul.

3

Jove in the clouds had his inhuman birth.
No mother suckled him, no sweet land gave
Large-mannered motions to his mythy mind
He moved among us, as a muttering king,
Magnificent, would move among his hinds,
Until our blood, commingling, virginal,
With heaven, brought such requital to desire
The very hinds discerned it, in a star.
Shall our blood fail? Or shall it come to be
The blood of paradise? And shall the earth
Seem all of paradise that we shall know?
The sky will be much friendlier then than now,
A part of labor and a part of pain,
And next in glory to enduring love,
Not this dividing and indifferent blue.

4

She says, "I am content when wakened birds,
Before they fly, test the reality
Of misty fields, by their sweet questionings;
But when the birds are gone, and their warm fields

Return no more, where, then, is paradise?"
There is not any haunt of prophecy,
Nor any old chimera of the grave,
Neither the golden underground, nor isle
Melodious, where spirits gat them home,
Nor visionary south, nor cloudy palm
Remote on heaven's hill, that has endured
As April's green endures; or will endure
Like her remembrance of awakened birds,
Or her desire for June and evening, tipped
By the consummation of the swallow's wings.

5

She says, "But in contentment I still feel
The need of some imperishable bliss."
Death is the mother of beauty; hence from her,
Alone, shall come fulfilment to our dreams
And our desires. Although she strews the leaves
Of sure obliteration on our paths,
The path sick sorrow took, the many paths
Where triumph rang its brassy phrase, or love
Whispered a little out of tenderness,
She makes the willow shiver in the sun
For maidens who were wont to sit and gaze
Upon the grass, relinquished to their feet.
She causes boys to pile new plums and pears
On disregarded plate. The maidens taste
And stray impassioned in the littering leaves.

6

Is there no change of death in paradise?
Does ripe fruit never fall? Or do the boughs
Hang always heavy in that perfect sky,
Unchanging, yet so like our perishing earth,
With rivers like our own that seek for seas
They never find, the same receding shores
That never touch with inarticulate pang?
Why set the pear upon those river-banks
Or spice the shores with odors of the plum?
Alas, that they should wear our colors there,
The silken weavings of our afternoons,
And pick the strings of our insipid lutes!
Death is the mother of beauty, mystical,
Within whose burning bosom we devise
Our earthly mothers waiting, sleeplessly.

7

Supple and turbulent, a ring of men
Shall chant in orgy on a summer morn
Their boisterous devotion to the sun,
Not as a god, but as a god might be,
Naked among them, like a savage source.
Their chant shall be a chant of paradise,
Out of their blood, returning to the sky;
And in their chant shall enter, voice by voice,
The windy lake wherein their lord delights,
The trees, like serafin, and echoing hills,
That choir among themselves long afterward.
They shall know well the heavenly fellowship
Of men that perish and of summer morn.
And whence they came and whither they shall go
The dew upon their feet shall manifest.

8

She hears, upon that water without sound,
A voice that cries, "The tomb in Palestine
Is not the porch of spirits lingering.
It is the grave of Jesus, where he lay."
We live in an old chaos of the sun,
Or old dependency of day and night,
Or island solitude, unsponsored, free,
Of that wide water, inescapable.
Deer walk upon our mountains, and the quail
Whistle about us their spontaneous cries;
Sweet berries ripen in the wilderness;
And, in the isolation of the sky,
At evening, casual flocks of pigeons make
Ambiguous undulations as they sink,
Downward to darkness, on extended wings.

THE COURSE OF A PARTICULAR

Today the leaves cry, hanging on branches swept by wind,
Yet the nothingness of winter becomes a little less.
It is still full of icy shades and shapen snow.

The leaves cry . . . One holds off and merely hears the cry.
It is a busy cry, concerning someone else.
And though one says that one is part of everything,

There is a conflict, there is a resistance involved;
And being part is an exertion that declines:
One feels the life of that which gives life as it is.

The leaves cry. It is not a cry of divine attention,
Nor the smoke-drift of puffed-out heroes, nor human cry.
It is the cry of leaves that do not transcend themselves,

In the absence of fantasia, without meaning more
Than they are in the final finding of the air, in the thing
Itself, until, at last, the cry concerns no one at all.

William Carlos Williams (1883-1963)

SPRING AND ALL

By the road to the contagious hospital
under the surge of the blue
mottled clouds driven from the
northeast—a cold wind. Beyond, the
waste of broad, muddy fields
brown with dried weeds, standing and fallen

patches of standing water
the scattering of tall trees

All along the road the reddish
purplish, forked, upstanding, twiggy
stuff of bushes and small trees
with dead, brown leaves under them
leafless vines—

Lifeless in appearance, sluggish
dazed spring approaches—

They enter the new world naked,
cold, uncertain of all
save that they enter. All about them
the cold, familiar wind—

Now the grass, tomorrow
the stiff curl of wildcarrot leaf

One by one objects are defined—
It quickens: clarity, outline of leaf

But now the stark dignity of
entrance—Still, the profound change
has come upon them: rooted they
grip down and begin to awaken

D. H. Lawrence (1885-1930)

WHALES WEEP NOT!

They say the sea is cold, but the sea contains
the hottest blood of all, and the wildest, the most urgent.

All the whales in the wider deeps, hot are they, as they urge
on and on, and dive beneath the icebergs.
The right whales, the sperm-whales, the hammer-heads, the killers
there they blow, there they blow, hot wild white breath out of the
    sea!

And they rock, and they rock, through the sensual ageless ages
on the depths of the seven seas,
and through the salt they reel with drunk delight
and in the tropics tremble they with love
and roll with massive, strong desire, like gods.
Then the great bull lies up against his bride
in the blue deep of the sea.
as mountain pressing on mountain, in the zest of life:
and out of the inward roaring of the inner red ocean of whale blood
the long tip reaches strong, intense, like the maelstrom-tip, and
    comes to rest
in the clasp and the soft, wild clutch of a she-whale's fathomless
    body.

And over the bridge of the whale's strong phallus, linking the
    wonder of whales
the burning archangels under the sea keep passing, back and forth,
keep passing archangels of bliss

from him to her, from her to him, great Cherubim
that wait on whales in mid-ocean, suspended in the waves of the sea
great heaven of whales in the waters, old hierarchies.

And enormous mother whales lie dreaming suckling their whale-
    tender young
and dreaming with strange whale eyes wide open in the waters of
    the beginning and the end.

And bull-whales gather their women and whale-calves in a ring
when danger threatens, on the surface of the ceaseless flood
and range themselves like great fierce Seraphim facing the threat
encircling their huddled monsters of love.
and all this happiness in the sea, in the salt
where God is also love, but without words:
and Aphrodite is the wife of whales
most happy, happy she!

and Venus among the fishes skips and is a she-dolphin
she is the gay, delighted porpoise sporting with love and the sea
she is the female tunny-fish, round and happy among the males
and dense with happy blood, dark rainbow bliss in the sea.

BAVARIAN GENTIANS

Not every man has gentians in his house
In soft September, at slow, sad Michaelmas.

Bavarian gentians, tall and dark, but dark
Darkening the day-time torch-like with the smoking blueness of
    Pluto's gloom,
ribbed hellish flowers erect, with their blaze of darkness spread
    blue
blown into points, by the heavy white draught of the day.

Torch-flowers of the blue-smoking darkness, Pluto's dark blue blaze
black lamps from the halls of Dis, smoking dark blue
giving off darkness, blue darkness, upon Demeter's yellow-pale day
whom have you come for, here in the white-cast day?

Reach me a gentian, give me a torch!
let me guide myself with the blue, forked torch of a flower
down the darker and darker stairs, where blue is darkened on
    blueness

down the way Persephone goes, just now, in first-frosted Sep-
   tember.
to the sightless realm where darkness is married to dark
and Persephone herself is but a voice, as a bride
a gloom invisible enfolded in the deeper dark
of the arms of Pluto as he ravishes her once again
and pierces her once more with his passion of the utter dark
among the splendor of black-blue torches, shedding fathomless
   darkness on the nuptials.

Give me a flower on a tall stem, and three dark flames,
for I will go to the wedding, and be wedding-guest
at the marriage of the living dark.

Ezra Pound (1885-   )

THE RIVER-MERCHANT'S WIFE: A LETTER

While my hair was still cut straight across my forehead
I played about the front gate, pulling flowers.
You came by on bamboo stilts, playing horse,
You walked about my seat, playing with blue plums.
And we went on living in the village of Chokan:
Two small people, without dislike or suspicion.

At fourteen I married My Lord you.
I never laughed, being bashful.
Lowering my head, I looked at the wall.
Called to, a thousand times, I never looked back.

At fifteen I stopped scowling,
I desired my dust to be mingled with yours
Forever and forever and forever.
Why should I climb the look out?

At sixteen you departed,
You went into far Ku-to-yen, by the river of swirling eddies,
And you have been gone five months.
The monkeys make sorrowful noise overhead.

You dragged your feet when you went out.
By the gate now, the moss is grown, the different mosses,
Too deep to clear them away!
The leaves fall early this autumn, in wind.
The paired butterflies are already yellow with August
Over the grass in the West garden;
They hurt me. I grow older.
If you are coming down through the narrows of the river Kiang,
Please let me know beforehand,
And I will come out to meet you
        As far as Cho-fu-Sa.   (*By Rihaku*[1])

[1] a Japanese name for the Chinese poet Li Po

THE RETURN

See, they return; ah, see the tentative
      Movements, and the slow feet,
      The trouble in the pace and the uncertain
      Wavering!

See, they return, one, and by one,
With fear, as half-awakened;
As if the snow should hesitate
And murmur in the wind,
          and half turn back;
These were the "Wing'd-with-Awe,"
      Inviolable.

Gods of the wingèd shoe!
With them the silver hounds,
        sniffing the trace of air!

Haie! Haie!
      These were the swift to harry;
These the keen-scented;
These were the souls of blood.

Slow on the leash,
        pallid the leash-men!

from HUGH SELWYN MAUBERLEY

4

These fought in any case,
and some believing,
    pro domo, in any case . . .

Some quick to arm,
some for adventure,
some from fear of weakness,
some from fear of censure,
some for love of slaughter, in imagination,
learning later . . .
some in fear, learning love of slaughter;

Died some, pro patria,
    non 'dulce' non 'et decor' . . .
walked eye-deep in hell
believing in old men's lies, then unbelieving
came home, home to a lie,
home to many deceits,
home to old lies and new infamy;
usury age-old and age-thick
and liars in public places.

Daring as never before, wastage as never before.
Young blood and high blood,
fair cheeks, and fine bodies;

fortitude as never before

frankness as never before,
disillusions as never told in the old days,
hysterias, trench confessions,
laughter out of dead bellies.

Marianne Moore (1887-   )

A GRAVE

Man looking into the sea,
taking the view from those who have as much right to it as you
    have to it yourself,
it is human nature to stand in the middle of a thing,
but you cannot stand in the middle of this;
the sea has nothing to give but a well excavated grave.
The firs stand in a procession, each with an emerald turkey-foot
    at the top,
reserved as their contours, saying nothing;
repression, however, is not the most obvious characteristic of the
    sea;
the sea is a collector, quick to return a rapacious look.
There are others besides you who have worn that look—
whose expression is no longer a protest; the fish no longer in-
    vestigate them
for their bones have not lasted:
men lower nets, unconscious of the fact that they are desecrating
    a grave,
and row quickly away—the blades of the oars
moving together like the feet of water-spiders as if there were no
    such thing as death.
The wrinkles progress among themselves in a phalanx—beautiful
    under networks of foam,
and fade breathlessly while the sea rustles in and out of the sea-
    weed;
the birds swim through the air at top speed, emitting catcalls as
    heretofore—
the tortoise-shell scourges about the feet of the cliffs, in motion
    beneath them;
and the ocean, under the pulsation of lighthouses and noise of bell-
    buoys,
advances as usual, looking as if it were not that ocean in which
    dropped things are bound to sink—
in which if they turn and twist, it is neither with volition nor
consciousness.

Edwin Muir (1887-1959)

THE HORSES

Barely a twelvemonth after
The seven days war that put the world to sleep,
Late in the evening the strange horses came.
By then we had made our covenant with silence,
But in the first few days it was so still
We listened to our breathing and were afraid.
On the second day
The radios failed; we turned the knobs; no answer.
On the third day a warship passed us, heading north,
Dead bodies piled on the deck. On the sixth day
A plane plunged over us into the sea. Thereafter
Nothing. The radios dumb;
And still they stand in corners of our kitchens,
And stand, perhaps, turned on, in a million rooms
All over the world. But now if they should speak,
If on a sudden they should speak again,
If on the stroke of noon a voice should speak,
We would not listen, we would not let it bring
That old bad world that swallowed its children quick
At one great gulp. We would not have it again.
Sometimes we think of the nations lying asleep,
Curled blindly in impenetrable sorrow,
And then the thought confounds us with its strangeness.
The tractors lie about our fields; at evening
They look like dank sea-monsters couched and waiting.
We leave them where they are and let them rust:
'They'll moulder away and be like other loam.'
We make our oxen drag our rusty ploughs,
Long laid aside. We have gone back
Far past our fathers' land.
                                    And then, that evening
Late in the summer the strange horses came.
We heard a distant tapping on the road,
A deepening drumming; it stopped, went on again
And at the corner changed to hollow thunder.
We saw the heads
Like a wild wave charging and were afraid.
We had sold our horses in our fathers' time
To buy new tractors. Now they were strange to us
As fabulous steeds set on an ancient shield

Or illustrations in a book of knights.
We did not dare go near them. Yet they waited,
Stubborn and shy, as if they had been sent
By an old command to find our whereabouts
And that long-lost archaic companionship.
In the first movement we had never a thought
That they were creatures to be owned and used.
Among them were some half-a-dozen colts
Dropped in some wilderness of the broken world,
Yet new as if they had come from their own Eden.
Since then they have pulled our ploughs and borne our loads
But that free servitude still can pierce our hearts.
Our life is changed; their coming our beginning.

T. S. Eliot (1888-1965)

THE WASTE LAND

"Nam Sibyllan quidem Cumis ego ipse oculis meis vidi in
ampulla pendere, et cum illi pueri dicerent: Σίβυλλα τί θέλεις;
respondebat illa: ἀποθανεῖν θέλω."

For Ezra Pound
il miglior fabbro.

I. THE BURIAL OF THE DEAD

April is the cruellest month, breeding
Lilacs out of the dead land, mixing
Memory and desire, stirring
Dull roots with spring rain.
Winter kept us warm, covering
Earth in forgetful snow, feeding
A little life with dried tubers.
Summer surprised us, coming over the Starnbergersee
With a shower of rain; we stopped in the colonnade,
And went on in sunlight, into the Hofgarten,
And drank coffee, and talked for an hour.
Bin gar keine Russin, stamm' aus Litauen, echt deutsch.
And when we were children, staying at the archduke's,
My cousin's, he took me out on a sled,
And I was frightened. He said, Marie,

Marie, hold on tight. And down we went.
In the mountains, there you feel free.
I read, much of the night, and go south in the winter.

What are the roots that clutch, what branches grow
Out of this stony rubbish? Son of man,
You cannot say, or guess, for your know only
A heap of broken images, where the sun beats,
And the dead tree gives no shelter, the cricket no relief,
And the dry stone no sound of water. Only
There is shadow under this red rock,
(Come in under the shadow of this red rock),
And I will show you something different from either
Your shadow at morning striding behind you
Or your shadow at evening rising to meet you;
I will show you fear in a handful of dust.
            Frisch weht der Wind
            Der Heimat zu
            Mein Irisch Kind,
            Wo weilest du?
"You gave me hyacinths first a year ago;
"They called me the hyacinth girl."
—Yet when we came back, late, from the Hyacinth garden,
Your arms full, and your hair wet, I could not
Speak, and my eyes failed, I was neither
Living nor dead, and I knew nothing,
Looking into the heart of light, the silence.
Oed' und leer das Meer.

Madame Sosostris, famous clairvoyante,
Had a bad cold, nevertheless
Is known to be the wisest woman in Europe,
With a wicked pack of cards. Here, said she,
Is your card, the drowned Phoenician Sailor,
(Those are pearls that were his eyes Look!)
Here is Belladonna, the Lady of the Rocks,
The lady of situations.
Here is the man with three staves, and here the Wheel,
And here is the one-eyed merchant, and this card,
Which is blank, is something he carries on his back,
Which I am forbidden to see. I do not find
The Hanged Man. Fear death by water.
I see crowds of people, walking round in a ring.
Thank you. If you see dear Mrs. Equitone,
Tell her I bring the horoscope myself:
One must be so careful these days.

Unreal City,
Under the brown fog of a winter dawn,
A crowd flowed over London Bridge, so many,
I had not thought death had undone so many.
Sighs, short and infrequent, were exhaled,
And each man fixed his eyes before his feet.
Flowed up the hill and down King William Street,
To where Saint Mary Woolnoth kept the hours
With a dead sound on the final stroke of nine.
There I saw one I knew, and stopped him, crying: "Stetson!
"You who were with me in the ships at Mylae!
"That corpse you planted last year in your garden,
"Has it begun to sprout? Will it bloom this year?
"Or has the sudden frost disturbed its bed?
"Oh keep the Dog far hence, that's friend to men,
"Or with his nails he'll dig it up again!
"You hypocrite lecteur!—mon semblable—mon frere!"

II. A GAME OF CHESS

The Chair she sat in, like a burnished throne,
Glowed on the marble, where the glass
Held up by standards wrought with fruited vines
From which a golden Cupidon peeped out
(Another hid his eyes behind his wing)
Doubled the flames of sevenbranched candelabra
Reflecting light upon the table as
The glitter of her jewels rose to meet it,
From satin cases poured in rich profusion;
In vials of ivory and coloured glass
Unstoppered, lurked her strange synthetic perfumes,
Unguent, powdered, or liquid—troubled, confused
And drowned the sense in odours; stirred by the air
That freshened from the window, these ascended
In fattening the prolonged candle-flames,
Flung their smoke into the laquearia,
Stirring the pattern on the coffered ceiling.
Huge sea-wood fed with copper
Burned green and orange, framed by the coloured stone,
In which sad light a carvèd dolphin swam.
Above the antique mantel was displayed
As though a window gave upon the sylvan scene
The change of Philomel, by the barbarous king
So rudely forced; yet there the nightingale

Filled all the desert with inviolable voice
And still she cried, and still the world pursues,
"Jug Jug" to dirty ears.
And other withered stumps of time
Were told upon the walls; staring forms
Leaned out, leaning, hushing the room enclosed.
Footsteps shuffled on the stair.
Under the firelight, under the brush, her hair
Spread out in fiery points
Glowed into words, then would be savagely still.

"My nerves are bad to-night. Yes, bad. Stay with me.
"Speak to me. Why do you never speak. Speak.
"What are you thinking of? What thinking? What?
"I never know what you are thinking. Think."

I think we are in rats' alley
Where the dead men lost their bones.

"What is that noise?"
                    The wind under the door.
"What is that noise now? What is the wind doing?"
                    Nothing again nothing.
                                        "Do
"You know nothing? Do you see nothing? Do you remember
"Nothing?"

    I remember
Those are pearls that were his eyes.
"Are you alive, or not? Is there nothing in your head?"
                                        But
O O O O that Shakespeherian Rag—
It's so elegant
So intelligent
"What shall I do now? What shall I do?"
"I shall rush out as I am, and walk the street
"With my hair down, so. What shall we do to-morrow?
"What shall we ever do?"
                    The hot water at ten.
And if it rains, a closed car at four.
And we shall play a game of chess,
Pressing lidless eyes and waiting for a knock upon the door.

    When Lil's husband got demobbed, I said—
I didn't mince my words, I said to her myself,
HURRY UP PLEASE ITS TIME

Now Albert's coming back, make yourself a bit smart.
He'll want to know what you done with that money he gave you
To get yourself some teeth. He did, I was there.
You have them all out, Lil, and get a nice set,
He said, I swear, I can't bear to look at you.
And no more can't I, I said, and think of poor Albert,
He's been in the army four years, he wants a good time,
And if you don't give it him, there's others will, I said.
Oh is there, she said. Something o' that, I said.
Then I'll know who to thank, she said, and gave me a
    straight look.
HURRY UP PLEASE ITS TIME
If you don't like it you can get on with it, I said.
Others can pick and choose if you can't.
But if Albert makes off, it won't be for the lack of telling.
You ought to be ashamed, I said, to look so antique.
(And her only thirty-one.)
I can't help it, she said, pulling a long face,
It's them pills I took, to bring it off, she said.
(She's had five already, and nearly died of young George.)
The chemist said it would be all right, but I've never been
    the same.
You are a proper fool, I said.
Well, if Albert won't leave you alone, there it is, I said,
What you get married for if you don't want children?
HURRY UP PLEASE ITS TIME
Well, that Sunday Albert was home, they had a hot gammon,
And they asked me in to dinner, to get the beauty of it hot—
HURRY UP PLEASE ITS TIME
HURRY UP PLEASE ITS TIME
Goodnight Bill. Goodnight Lou. Goodnight May. Goodnight.
Ta ta. Goodnight. Goodnight.
Good night, ladies, good night, sweet ladies, good night,
    good night.

III. THE FIRE SERMON

The river's tent is broken: the last fingers of leaf
Clutch and sink into the wet bank. The wind
Crosses the brown land, unheard. The nymphs are departed.
Sweet Thames, run softly, till I end my song.
The river bears no empty bottles, sandwich papers,
Silk handkerchiefs, cardboard boxes, cigarette ends

Or other testimony of summer nights. The nymphs are
    departed.
And their friends, the loitering heirs of city directors;
Departed, have left no addresses.
By the waters of Leman I sat down and wept . . .
Sweet Thames, run softly till I end my song,
Sweet Thames, run softly, for I speak not loud or long.
But at my back in a cold blast I hear
The rattle of the bones, and chuckle spread from ear to ear.
A rat crept softly through the vegetation
Dragging its slimy belly on the bank
While I was fishing in the dull canal
On a winter evening round behind the gashouse
Musing upon the king my brother's wreck
And on the king my father's death before him.
White bodies naked on the low damp ground
And bones cast in a little low dry garret,
Rattled by the rat's foot only, year to year.
But at my back from time to time I hear
The sound of horns and motors, which shall bring
Sweeney to Mrs. Porter in the spring.
O the moon shone bright on Mrs. Porter
And on her daughter
They wash their feet in soda water
Et O ces voix d'enfants, chantant dans la coupole!

    Twit twit twit
Jug jug jug jug jug jug
So rudely forc'd.
Tereu

    Unreal City
Under the brown fog of a winter noon
Mr. Eugenides, the Smyrna merchant
Unshaven, with a pocket full of currants
C.i.f. London: documents at sight,
Asked me in demotic French
To luncheon at the Cannon Street Hotel
Followed by a weekend at the Metropole.

    At the violet hour, when the eyes and back
Turn upward from the desk, when the human engine waits
Like a taxi throbbing waiting,
I Tiresias, though blind, throbbing between two lives,
Old man with wrinkled female breasts, can see
At the violet hour the evening hour that strives

Homeward, and brings the sailor home from sea,
The typist home at teatime, clears her breakfast, lights
Her stove, and lays out food in tins.
Out of the window perilously spread
Her drying combinations touched by the sun's last rays,
On the divan are piled (at night her bed)
Stockings, slippers, camisoles, and stays.
I Tiresias, old man with wrinkled dugs
Perceived the scene, and foretold the rest—
I too awaited the expected guest,
He, the young man carbuncular, arrives,
A small house agent's clerk, with one bold stare,
One of the low on whom assurance sits
As a silk hat on a Bradford millionaire.
The time is now propitious, as he guesses,
The meal is ended. she is bored and tired,
Endeavours to engage her in caresses
Which still are unreproved, if undesired.
Flushed and decided, he assaults at once;
Exploring hands encounter no defence;
His vanity requires no response,
And makes a welcome of indifference.
(And I Tiresias have foresuffered all
Enacted on this same divan or bed;
I who have sat by Thebes below the wall
And walked among the lowest of the dead.)
Bestows one final patronising kiss,
And gropes his way, finding the stairs unlit . . .

    She turns and looks a moment in the glass,
Hardly aware of her departed lover;
Her brain allows one half-formed thought to pass:
"Well now that's done: and I'm glad it's over."
When lovely woman stoops to folly and
Paces about her room again, alone,
She smoothes her hair with automatic hand,
And puts a record on the gramophone.

    "This music crept by me upon the waters"
And along the Strand, up Queen Victoria Street.
O City city, I can sometimes hear
Beside a public bar in Lower Thames Street,
The pleasant whining of a mandoline
And a clatter and a chatter from within
Where fishmen lounge at noon: where the walls
Of Magnus Martyr hold

Inexplicable splendour of Ionian white and gold.

> The river sweats
> Oil and tar
> The barges drift
> With the turning tide
> Red sails
> Wide
> To leeward, swing on the heavy spar.
> The barges wash
> Drifting logs
> Down Greenwich reach
> Past the Isle of Dogs.
>> Weialala leia
>> Wallala leialala

> Elizabeth and Leicester
> Beating oars
> The stern was formed
> A gilded shell
> Red and gold
> The brisk swell
> Rippled both shores
> Southwest wind
> Carried down stream
> The peal of bells
> White towers
>> Weialala leia
>> Wallala leialala

"Trams and dusty trees.
Highbury bore me. Richmond and Kew
Undid me. By Richmond I raised my knees
Supine on the floor of a narrow canoe."

"My feet are at Moorgate, and my heart
Under my feet. After the event
He wept. He promised 'a new start.'
I made no comment. What should I resent?"

"On Margate Sands.
I can connect
Nothing with nothing.
The broken fingernails of dirty hands.
My people humble people who expect
Nothing."
> la la

To Carthage then I came

Burning burning burning burning
O Lord Thou pluckest me out
O Lord Thou pluckest

burning

IV. DEATH BY WATER

Phlebas the Phoenician, a fortnight dead,
Forgot the cry of gulls, and the deep sea swell
And the profit and loss.
                              A current under sea
Picked his bones in whispers. As he rose and fell
He passed the stages of his age and youth
Entering the whirpool.
                         Gentile or Jew
O you who turn the wheel and look to windward,
Consider Phlebas, who was once handsome and tall as you.

V. WHAT THE THUNDER SAID

After the torchlight red on sweaty faces
After the frosty silence in the gardens
After the agony in stony places
The shouting and the crying
Prison and palace and reverberation
Of thunder of spring over distant mountains
He who was living is now dead
We who were living are now dying
With a little patience

Here is no water but only rock
Rock and no water and the sandy road
The road winding above among the mountains
Which are mountains of rock without water
If there were water we should stop and drink
Amongst the rock one cannot stop or think
Sweat is dry and feet are in the sand
If there were only water amongst the rock

Dead mountain mouth of carious teeth that cannot spit
Here one can neither stand nor lie nor sit
There is not even silence in the mountains
But dry sterile thunder without rain
There is not even solitude in the mountains
But red sullen faces sneer and snarl
From doors of mudcracked houses
                    If there were water

    And no rock
    If there were rock
    And also water
    And water
    A spring
    A pool among the rock
    If there were the sound of water only
    Not the cicada
    And dry grass singing
    But sound of water over a rock
    Where the hermit-thrush sings in the pine trees
    Drip drop drip drop drop drop drop
    But there is no water

    Who is the third who walks always beside you?
When I count, there are only you and I together
But when I look ahead up the white road
There is always another one walking beside you
Gliding wrapt in a brown mantle, hooded
I do not know whether a man or a woman
—But who is that on the other side of you?

    What is the sound high in the air
Murmur of maternal lamentation
Who are those hooded hordes swarming
Over endless plains, stumbling in cracked earth
Ringed by the flat horizon only
What is the city over the mountains
Cracks and reforms and bursts in the violet air
Falling towers
Jerusalem Athens Alexandria
Vienna London
Unreal

    A woman drew her long black hair out tight
And fiddled whisper music on those strings

And bats with baby faces in the violet light
Whistled, and beat their wings
And crawled head downward down a blackened wall
And upside down in air were towers
Tolling reminiscent bells, that kept the hours
And voices singing out of empty cisterns and exhausted wells.

In this decayed hole among the mountains
In the faint moonlight, the grass is singing
Over the tumbled graves, about the chapel
There is the empty chapel, only the wind's home.
It has no windows, and the door swings,
Dry bones can harm no one.
Only a cock stood on the rooftree
Co co rico co co rico
In a flash of lightning. Then a damp gust
Bringing rain

Ganga was sunken, and the limp leaves
Waited for rain, while the black clouds
Gathered far distant, over Himavant.
The jungle crouched, humped in silence.
Then spoke the thunder
DA
Datta: what have we given?
My friend, blood shaking my heart
The awful daring of a moment's surrender
Which an age of prudence can never retract
By this, and this only, we have existed
Which is not to be found in our obituaries
Or in memories draped by the beneficent spider
Or under seals broken by the lean solicitor
In our empty rooms
DA
Dayadhvam: I have heard the key
Turn in the door once and turn once only
We think of the key, each in his prison
Thinking of the key, each confirms a prison
Only at nightfall, aethereal rumours
Revive for a moment a broken Coriolanus
DA
Damyata: The boat responded
Gaily, to the hand expert with sail and oar
The sea was calm, your heart would have responded
Gaily, when invited, beating obedient
To controlling hands

I sat upon the shore

Fishing, with the arid plain behind me
Shall I at least set my lands in order?
London Bridge is falling down falling down falling down
Poi s'ascose nel foco che gli affina
Quando fiam uti chelidon—O swallow swallow
Le Prince d'Aquitaine a la tour abolie
These fragments I have shored against my ruins
Why then Ile fit you. Hieronymo's mad againe.
Datta. Dayadhvam. Damyata.

Shantih   shantih   shantih

NOTES ON "THE WASTE LAND"

Not only the title, but the plan and a good deal of the incidental symbolism of the poem were suggested by Miss Jessie L. Weston's book on the Grail legend: *From Ritual to Romance* (Cambridge). Indeed, so deeply am I indebted, Miss Weston's book will elucidate the difficulties of the poem much better than my notes can do; and I recommend it (apart from the great interest of the book itself) to any who think such elucidation of the poem worth the trouble. To another work of anthropology I am indebted in general, one which has influenced our generation profoundly; I mean *The Golden Bough;* I have used especially the two volumes *Adonis, Attis, Osiris.* Anyone who is acquainted with these works will immediately recognize in the poem certain references to vegetation ceremonies.

I. *The Burial of the Dead*

Line 20. Cf. Ezekiel II, i.

23. Cf Ecclesiastes XII, v.

31. V. Tristan und Isolde, I, verses 5–8.

42. Id. III, verse 24.

46. I am not familiar with the exact constitution of the Tarot pack of cards, from which I have obviously departed to suit my own convenience. The Hanged Man, a member of the traditional pack, fits my purpose in two ways: because he is associated in my mind with the Hanged God of Frazer, and because I associate him with the hooded figure in the passage of the disciples to Emmaus in Part V. The Phoenician Sailor and the Merchant appear later; also the "crowds of people," and Death by Water is executed in Part IV. The Man with Three Staves (an authentic member of the Tarot pack) I associate, quite arbitrarily, with the Fisher King himself.

60. Cf. Baudelaire:
"Fourmillante cité, cité pleine de rèves,
"Où le spectre en plein jour raccroche le passant."
63. Cf. Inferno III, 55–57:
"si lunga tratta
di gente, ch'io non avrei mai creduto
che morte tanta n'avesse disfatta."
64. Cf. Inferno IV, 25–27:
"Quivi, secondo che per ascoltare,
"non avea pianto, ma' che di sospiri,
"che l'aura eterna facevan tremare."
68. A phenomenon which I have often noticed.
74. Cf. the Dirge in Webster's *White Devil*.
76. V. Baudelaire, Preface to *Fleurs du Mal*.

II. *A Game of Chess*
77. Cf. *Anthony and Cleopatra*, II, ii, l. 190.
92. Laquearia. V. *Aeneid*, I. 726:
dependent lychni laquearibus aureis incensi, et noctem flammis funalia vincunt.
98. Sylvan scene. V. Milton, *Paradise Lost*, IV, 140.
99. V. Ovid, *Metamorphoses*, VI, Philomela.
100. Cf. Part III, l. 204.
115. Cf. Part III, l. 195.
118. Cf. Webster: "Is the wind in that door still?"
126. Cf. Part I, l. 37, 48.
138. Cf. the game of chess in Middleton's *Women beware Women*.

III. *The Fire Sermon*
176. V. Spenser, *Prothalamion*.
192. Cf. *The Tempest*, I, ii.
196. Cf. Marvell, *To His Coy Mistress*.
197. Cf. Day, *Parliament of Bees:*
"When of the sudden, listening, you shall hear,
"A noise of horns and hunting, which shall bring
"Actaeon to Diana in the spring,
"Where all shall see her naked skin . . ."
199. I do not know the origin of the ballad from which these lines are taken: it was reported to me from Sydney, Australia.
202. V. Verlaine, *Parsifal*.
210. The currants were quoted at a price "carriage and insurance free to London"; and the Bill of Lading etc. were to be handed to the buyer upon payment of the sight draft.
218. Tiresias, although a mere spectator and not indeed a "character," is yet the most important personage in the poem, uniting

all the rest. Just as the one-eyed merchant, seller of currants, melts into the Phoenician Sailor, and the latter is not wholly distinct from Ferdinand Prince of Naples, so all the women are one woman, and the two sexes meet in Tiresias. What Tiresias *sees*, in fact, is the substance of the poem. The whole passage from Ovid is of great anthropological interest:

'. . . Cum Iunone iocos et maior vestra profecto est
Quam, quae contingit maribus,' dixisse, 'voluptas.'
Illa negat; placuit quae sit sententia docti
Quaerere Tiresiae: venus huic erat utraque nota.
Nam duo magnorum viridi coeuntia silva
Corpora serpentum baculi violaverat ictu
Deque viro factus, mirabile, femina septem
Egerat autumnos; octavo rursus eosdem
Vidit et 'est vestrae si tanta potentia plagae,'
Dixit 'ut auctoris sortem in contraria mutet,
Nunc quoque vos feriam!' percussis anguibus isdem
Forma prior rediit genetivaque venit imago.
Arbiter hic igitur sumptus de lite iocosa
Dicta Iovis firmat; gravius Saturnia iusto
Nec pro materia fertur doluisse suique
Iudicis aeterna damnavit lumina nocte,
At pater omnipotens (neque enim licet inrita cuiquam
Facta dei fecisse deo) pro lumine adempto
Scire futura dedit poenamque levavit honore.

221. This may not appear as exact as Sappho's lines, but I had in mind the "longshore" or "dory" fisherman, who returns at nightfall.

253. V. Goldsmith, the song in *The Vicar of Wakefield*.

257. V. *The Tempest*, as above.

264. The interior of St. Magnus Martyr is to my mind one of the finest among Wren's interiors. See *The Proposed Demolition of Nineteen City Churches*: (P. S. King & Son, Ltd.).

266. The Song of the (three) Thames-daughters begins here. From line 292 to 306 inclusive they speak in turn. V. *Götter-dämmerung*, III, i: the Rhine-daughters.

279. V. Froude, *Elizabeth*, Vol. I, ch. iv, letter of De Quadra to Philip of Spain:

"In the afternoon we were in a barge, watching the games on the river. (The queen) was alone with Lord Robert and myself on the poop, when they began to talk nonsense, and went so far that Lord Robert at last said, as I was on the spot there was no reason why they should not be married if the queen pleased."

293. Cf. *Purgatorio*, V, 133:

"Ricorditi di me, che son la Pia;
"Siena mi fe', disfecemi Maremma."

307. V. St. Augustine's *Confessions:* "to Carthage then I came, where a cauldron of unholy loves sang all about mine ears."

308. The complete text of the Buddha's Fire Sermon (which corresponds in importance to the Sermon on the Mount) from which these words are taken, will be found translated in the late Henry Clarke Warren's *Buddhism in Translation* (Harvard Oriental Series). Mr. Warren was one of the great pioneers of Buddhist studies in the Occident.

309. From St. Augustine's *Confessions* again. The collocation of these two representatives of eastern and western asceticism, as the culmination of this part of the poem, is not an accident.

V. *What the Thunder Said*

In the first part of Part V three themes are employed: the journey to Emmaus, the approach to the Chapel Perilous (see Miss Weston's book) and the present decay of eastern Europe.

357. This is *Turdus aonalaschkae pallasii,* the hermit-thrush which I have heard in Quebec Province. Chapman says (*Handbook of Birds of Eastern North America*) "it is most at home in secluded woodland and thickety retreats. . . . Its notes are not remarkable for variety or volume, but in purity and sweetness of tone and exquisite modulation they are unequalled." Its "water-dripping song" is justly celebrated.

360. The following lines were stimulated by the account of one of the Antarctic expeditions (I forget which, but I think one of Shackleton's): it was related that the party of explorers, at the extremity of their strength, had the constant delusion that there was *one more member* than could actually be counted.

367-77. Cf. Hermann Hesse, *Blick ins Chaos:* "Schon ist halb Europa, schon ist zumindest der halbe Osten Europas auf dem Wege zum Chaos, fährt betrunken im heiligem Wahn am Abgrund entlang und singt dazu, singt betrunken und hymnisch wie Dmitri Karamasoff sang. Ueber diese Lieder lacht der Bürger beleidigt, der Heilige und Seher hört sie mit Tranen."

402. "Datta, dayadhvam, damyata" (Give, sympathise, control). The fable of the meaning of the Thunder is found in the *Briha-daranyaka—Upanishad,* 5, 1. A translation is found in Deussen's *Sechzig Upanishads des Veda,* p. 489.

408. Cf. Webster, *The White Devil,* V. vi:
". . . they'll remarry
Ere the worm pierce your winding-sheet, ere the spider
Make a thin curtain for your epitaphs."

412. Cf. *Inferno,* XXXIII, 46:
"ed io sentii chiavar l'uscio di sotto
all'orribile torre."
Also F. H. Bradley, *Appearance and Reality,* p. 346.

"My external sensations are no less private to myself than are my thoughts or my feelings. In either case my experience falls within my own circle, a circle closed on the outside; and, with all its elements alike, every sphere is opaque to the others which surround it. . . . In brief, regarded as an existence which appears in a soul, the whole world for each is peculiar and private to that soul."

425. V. Weston: *From Ritual to Romance;* chapter on the Fisher King.

428. V. *Purgatorio,* XXVI, 148.

> " 'Ara vos prec per aquella valor
> 'que vos guida al som de l'escalina,
> 'sovegna vos a temps de ma dolor.'
> Poi s'ascose nel foco che gli affina."

429. V. *Pervigilium Veneris.* Cf. Philomela in Parts II and III.

430. V. Gerard de Nerval, Sonnet *El Desdichado.*

432. V. Kyd's *Spanish Tragedy.*

434. Shantih. Repeated as here, a formal ending to an Upanishad. "The Peace which passeth understanding" is our equivalent to this word.

JOURNEY OF THE MAGI

'A cold coming we had of it,
Just the worst time of the year
For a journey, and such a long journey:
The ways deep and the weather sharp,
The very dead of winter.'
And the camels galled, sore-footed, refractory,
Lying down in the melting snow.
There were times we regretted
The summer palaces on slopes, the terraces,
And the silken girls bringing sherbet.
Then the camel men cursing and grumbling
And running away, and wanting their liquor and women,
And the night-fires going out, and the lack of shelters,
And the cities hostile and the towns unfriendly
And the villages dirty and charging high prices:
A hard time we had of it.
At the end we preferred to travel all night,
Sleeping in snatches,
With the voices singing in our ears, saying
That this was all folly.

Then at dawn we came down to a temperate valley,
Wet, below the snow line, smelling of vegetation;
With a running stream and a water-mill beating the darkness,
And three trees on the low sky,
And an old white horse galloped away in the meadow.
Then we came to a tavern with vine-leaves over the lintel,
Six hands at an open door dicing for pieces of silver,
And feet kicking the empty wine-skins.
But there was no information, and so we continued
And arrived at evening, not a moment too soon
Finding the place; it was (you may say) satisfactory.

All this was a long time ago, I remember,
And I would do it again, but set down
This set down
This: were we led all that way for
Birth or Death? There was a Birth, certainly,
We had evidence and no doubt. I had seen birth and death,
But had thought they were different; this Birth was
Hard and bitter agony for us, like Death, our death.
We returned to our places, these Kingdoms,
But no longer at ease here, in the old dispensation,
With an alien people clutching their gods.
I should be glad of another death.

John Crowe Ransom (1888-   )

CAPTAIN CARPENTER

Captain Carpenter rose up in his prime
Put on his pistols and went riding out
But had got wellnigh nowhere at that time
Till he fell in with ladies in a rout.

It was a pretty lady and all her train
That played with him so sweetly but before
An hour she'd taken a sword with all her main
And twined him of his nose for evermore.

Captain Carpenter mounted up one day
And rode straightway into a stranger rogue
That looked unchristian but be that as it may
The Captain did not wait upon prologue.

But drew upon him out of his great heart
The other swung against him with a club
And cracked his two legs at the shinny part
And let him roll and stick like any tub.

Captain Carpenter rode many a time
From male and female took he sundry harms
He met the wife of Satan crying "I'm
The she-wolf bids you shall bear no more arms."

Their strokes and counters whistled in the wind
I wish he had delivered half his blows
But where she should have made off like a hind
The bitch bit off his arms at the elbows.

And Captain Carpenter parted with his ears
To a black devil that used him in this wise
O jesus ere his threescore and ten years
Another had plucked out his sweet blue eyes.

Captain Carpenter got up on his roan
And sallied from the gate in hell's despite
I heard him asking in the grimmest tone
If any enemy yet there was to fight?

"To any adversary it is fame
If he risk to be wounded by my tongue
Or burnt in two beneath my red heart's flame
Such are the perils he is cast among.

"But if he can he has a pretty choice
From an anatomy with little to lose
Whether he cut my tongue and take my voice
Or whether it be my round red heart he choose."

It was the neatest knave that ever was seen
Stepping in perfume from his lady's bower
Who at this word put in his merry mien
And fell on Captain Carpenter like a tower.

I would not knock old fellows in the dust
But there lay Captain Carpenter on his back
His weapons were the old heart in his bust
And a blade shook between rotten teeth alack.

The rouge in scarlet and grey soon knew his mind
He wished to get his trophy and depart
With gentle apology and touch refined
He pierced him and produced the Captain's heart.

God's mercy rest on Captain Carpenter now
I thought him Sirs an honest gentleman
Citizen husband soldier and scholar enow
Let jangling kites eat of him if they can.

But God's deep curses follow after those
That shore him of his goodly nose and ears
His legs and strong arms at the two elbows
And eyes that had not watered seventy years.

The curse of hell upon the sleek upstart
That got the Captain finally on his back
And took the red red vitals of his heart
And made the kites to whet their beaks clack clack.

E. E. Cummings (1894-1962)

POEM, OR BEAUTY HURTS MR. VINAL

take it from me kiddo
believe me
my country, 'tis of

you, land of the Cluett
Shirt Boston Garter and Spearmint
Girl With the Wrigley Eyes(of you
land of the Arrow Ide
and Earl &
Wilson
Collars) of you i
sing:land of Abraham Lincoln and Lydia E. Pinkham,
land above all of Just Add Hot Water and Serve—
from every B. V. D.

let freedom ring

amen. i do however protest, anent the un
-spontaneous and otherwise scented merde which
greets one (Everywhere Why) as divine poesy per
that and this radically defunct periodical. i would
suggest that certain ideas gestures
rhymes, like Gillette Razor Blades
having been used and reused
to the mystical moment of dullness emphatically are
Not To Be Resharpened. (Case in point

if we are to believe these gently O sweetly
melancholy trillers amid the thrillers
these crepuscular violinists among my and your
skyscrapers—Helen & Cleopatra were Just Too Lovely,
The Snail's On The Thorn enter Morn and God's
In His andsoforth

do you get me?)according
to such supposedly indigenous
throstles Art is O World O Life
a formula:example, Turn Your Shirttails Into
Drawers and If It Isn't An Eastman It Isn't A
Kodak therefore my friends let
us now sing each and all fortissimo A-
mer
i

ca, I
love,
You. And there're a
hun-dred-mil-lion-oth-ers, like
all of you successfully if
delicately gelded(or spaded)
gentlemen(and ladies)—pretty

littleliverpill-
hearted-Nujolneeding-There's-A-Reason
americans(who tensetendoned and with
upward vacant eyes, painfully
perpetually crouched, quivering, upon the
sternly allotted sandpile
—how silently
emit a tiny violetflavored nuisance:Odor?

ono.
comes out like a ribbon lies flat on the brush

Robert Graves (1895-   )

IN BROKEN IMAGES

He is quick, thinking in clear images;
I am slow, thinking in broken images.

He becomes dull, trusting to his clear images;
I become sharp, mistrusting my broken images.

Trusting his images, he assumes their relevance;
Mistrusting my images, I question their relevance.

Assuming their relevance, he assumes the fact;
Questioning their relevance, I question the fact.

When the fact fails him, he questions his senses;
When the fact fails me, I approve my senses.

He continues quick and dull in his clear images;
I continue slow and sharp in my broken images.

He in a new confusion of his understanding;
I in a new understanding of my confusion.

Hart Crane (1899-1932)

from VOYAGES

2

And yet this great wink of eternity,
Of rimless floods, unfettered leewardings,
Samite sheeted and processioned where
Her undinal vast belly moonward bends,
Laughing the wrapt inflections of our love;

Take this Sea, whose diapason knells
On scrolls of silver snowy sentences,

The sceptred terror of whose sessions rends
As her demeanors motion well or ill,
All but the pieties of lovers' hands.

And onward, as bells off San Salvador
Salute the crocus lustres of the stars,
In these poinsettia meadows of her tides,—
Adagios of islands, O my Prodigal,
Complete the dark confessions her veins spell.

Mark how her turning shoulders wind the hours,
And hasten while her penniless rich palms
Pass superscription of bent foam and wave,—
Hasten, while they are true,—sleep, death, desire,
Close round one instant in one floating flower.

Bind us in time, O Seasons clear, and awe.
O minstrel galleons of Carib fire,
Bequeath us to no earthly shore until
Is answered in the vortex of our grave
The seal's wide spindrift gaze toward paradise.

Richard Eberhart (1904-   )

THE GROUNDHOG

In June, amid the golden fields,
I saw a groundhog lying dead.
Dead lay he; my senses shook,
And mind outshot our naked frailty.
There lowly in the vigorous summer
His form began its senseless change,
And made my senses waver dim
Seeing nature ferocious in him.
Inspecting close his maggots' might
And seething cauldron of his being,
Half with loathing, half with a strange love,
I poked him with an angry stick.
The fever arose, became a flame
And Vigour circumscribed the skies,
Immense energy in the sun,
And through my frame a sunless trembling.

My stick had done nor good nor harm.
Then stood I silent in the day
Watching the object, as before;
And kept my reverence for knowledge
Trying for control, to be still,
To quell the passion of the blood;
Until I had bent down on my knees
Praying for joy in the sight of decay.
And so I left; and I returned
In Autumn strict of eye, to see
The sap gone out of the groundhog,
But the bony sodden hulk remained.
But the year had lost its meaning,
And in intellectual chains
I lost both love and loathing,
Mured up in the wall of wisdom.
Another summer took the fields again
Massive and burning, full of life,
But when I chanced upon the spot
There was only a little hair left,
And bones bleaching in the sunlight
Beautiful as architecture;
I watched them like a geometer,
And cut a walking stick from a birch.
It has been three years, now.
There is no sign of the groundhog,
I stood there in the whirling summer,
My hand capped a withered heart,
And thought of China and of Greece,
Of Alexander in his tent;
Of Montaigne in his tower,
Of Saint Theresa in her wild lament.

W. H. Auden (1907-   )

IN MEMORY OF W. B. YEATS
(d. Jan. 1939)

1

He disappeared in the dead of winter:
The brooks were frozen, the airports almost deserted,
And snow disfigured the public statues;

The mercury sank in the mouth of the dying day.
O all the instruments agree
The day of his death was a dark cold day.

Far from his illness
The wolves ran on through the evergreen forests,
The peasant river was untempted by the fashionable quays;
By mourning tongues
The death of the poet was kept from his poems.

But for him it was his last afternoon as himself,
An afternoon of nurses and rumors;
The provinces of his body revolted,
The squares of his mind were empty,
Silence invaded the suburbs,
The current of his feeling failed: he became his admirers.

Now he is scattered among a hundred cities
And wholly given over to unfamiliar affections;
To find his happiness in another kind of wood
And be punished under a foreign code of conscience.
The words of a dead man
Are modified in the guts of the living.

But in the importance and noise of tomorrow
When the brokers are roaring like beasts on the floor of the
        Bourse,
And the poor have the sufferings to which they are fairly
        accustomed,
And each in the cell of himself is almost convinced of his
        freedom;
A few thousand will think of this day
As one thinks of a day when one did something slightly unusual.

O all the instruments agree
The day of his death was a dark cold day.

    2

    You were silly like us: your gift survived it all;
    The parish of rich women, physical decay,
    Yourself; mad Ireland hurt you into poetry.
    Now Ireland has her madness and her weather still,
    For poetry makes nothing happen: it survives
    In the valley of its saying where executives
    Would never want to tamper; it flows south

From ranches of isolation and the busy griefs,
Raw towns that we believe and die in; it survives,
A way of happening, a mouth.

3

Earth, receive an honored guest;
William Yeats is laid to rest:
Let the Irish vessel lie
Emptied of its poetry.

Time that is intolerant
Of the brave and innocent,
And indifferent in a week
To a beautiful physique,

Worships language and forgives
Everyone by whom it lives;
Pardons cowardice, conceit,
Lays its honors at their feet.

Time that with this strange excuse
Pardoned Kipling and his views,
And will pardon Paul Claudel,
Pardons him for writing well.

In the nightmare of the dark
All the dogs of Europe bark,
And the living nations wait,
Each sequestered in its hate;

Intellectual disgrace
Stares from every human face,
And the seas of pity lie
Locked and frozen in each eye.

Follow, poet, follow right
To the bottom of the night,
With your unconstraining voice
Still persuade us to rejoice;

With the farming of a verse
Make a vineyard of the curse,
Sing of human unsuccess
In a rapture of distress;

In the deserts of the heart
Let the healing fountain start,
In the prison of his days
Teach the free man how to praise.

Louis MacNeice (1907-1963)

THE SUNLIGHT ON THE GARDEN

The sunlight on the garden
Hardens and grows cold,
We cannot cage the minute
Within its nets of gold,
When all is told
We cannot beg for pardon.

Our freedom as free lances
Advances towards its end;
The earth compels, upon it
Sonnets and birds descend;
And soon, my friend,
We shall have no time for dances.

The sky was good for flying
Defying the church bells
And every evil iron
Siren and what it tells:
The earth compels,
We are dying, Egypt, dying

And not expecting pardon,
Hardened in heart anew,
But glad to have sat under
Thunder and rain with you,
And grateful too
For sunlight on the garden.

Elizabeth Bishop (1911-   )

THE MONUMENT

Now can you see the monument? It is of wood
built somewhat like a box. No. Built
like several boxes in descending sizes
one above the other.
Each is turned half-way round so that
its corners point toward the sides
of the one below and the angles alternate.
Then on the topmost cube is set
a sort of fleur-de-lys of weathered wood,
long petals of board, pierced with odd holes,
four-sided, stiff, ecclesiastical.
From it four thin, warped poles spring out,
(slanted like fishing-poles or flag-poles)
and from them jig-saw work hangs down,
four lines of vaguely whittled ornament
over the edges of the boxes
to the ground.
The monument is one-third set against
a sea; two-thirds against a sky.
The view is geared
(that is, the view's perspective)
so low there is no "far away,"
and we are far away within the view.
A sea of narrow, horizontal boards
lies out behind our lonely monument,
its long grains alternating right and left
like floor-boards—spotted, swarming-still,
and motionless. A sky runs parallel,
and it is palings, coarser than the sea's:
splintery sunlight and long-fibred clouds.
"Why does that strange sea make no sound?
Is it because we're far away?
Where are we? Are we in Asia Minor,
or in Mongolia?"

                An ancient promontory,
an ancient principality whose artist-prince
might have wanted to build a monument
to mark a tomb or boundary, or make
a melancholy or romantic scene of it . . .

"But that queer sea looks made of wood,
half-shining, like a driftwood sea.
And the sky looks wooden, grained with cloud.
It's like a stage-set; it is all so flat!
Those clouds are full of glistening splinters!
What is that?"
                          It is the monument.
"It's piled-up boxes,
outlined with shoddy fret-work, half-fallen off,
cracked and unpainted. It looks old."
—The strong sunlight, the wind from the sea,
all the conditions of its existence,
may have flaked off the paint, if ever it was painted,
and made it homelier than it was.
"Why did you bring me here to see it?
A temple of crates in cramped and crated scenery,
what can it prove?
I am tired of breathing this eroded air,
this dryness in which the monument is cracking."

It is an artifact
of wood. Wood holds together better
than sea or cloud or sand could by itself,
much better than real sea or sand or cloud.
It chose that way to grow and not to move.
The monument's an object, yet those decorations,
carelessly nailed, looking like nothing at all,
give it away as having life, and wishing;
wanting to be a monument, to cherish something.
The crudest scroll-work says "commemorate,"
while once each day the light goes around it
like a prowling animal,
or the rain falls on it, or the wind blows into it.
It may be solid, may be hollow.
The bones of the artist-prince may be inside
or far away on even dryer soil.
But roughly but adequately it can shelter
what is within (which after all
cannot have been intended to be seen).
It is the beginning of a painting,
a piece of sculpture, or poem, or monument,
and all of wood. Watch it closely.

Dylan Thomas (1914-1953)

AND DEATH SHALL HAVE NO DOMINION

And death shall have no dominion.
Dead men naked they shall be one
With the man in the wind and the west moon;
When their bones are picked clean and the clean bones gone,
They shall have stars at elbow and foot;
Though they go mad they shall be sane,
Though they sink through the sea they shall rise again;
Though lovers be lost love shall not;
And death shall have no dominion.

And death shall have no dominion.
Under the windings of the sea
They lying long shall not die windily;
Twisting on racks when sinews give way,
Strapped to a wheel, yet they shall not break;
Faith in their hands shall snap in two,
And the unicorn evils run them through;
Split all ends up they shan't crack;
And death shall have no dominion.

And death shall have no dominion.
No more may gulls cry at their ears
Or waves break loud on the seashores;
Where blew a flower may a flower no more
Lift its head to the blows of the rain;
Though they be mad and dead as nails,
Heads of the characters hammer through daisies;
Break in the sun till the sun breaks down,
And death shall have no dominion.

FERN HILL

Now as I was young and easy under the apple boughs
About the lilting house and happy as the grass was green,
    The night above the dingle starry,
       Time let me hail and climb
     Golden in the heydays of his eyes,

And honoured among wagons I was prince of the apple towns
And once below a time I lordly had the trees and leaves
      Trail with daisies and barley
    Down the rivers of the windfall light.

And as I was green and carefree, famous among the barns
About the happy yard and singing as the farm was home,
      In the sun that is young once only,
        Time let me play and be
    Golden in the mercy of his means,
And green and golden I was huntsman and herdsman, the calves
Sang to my horn, the foxes on the hills barked clear and cold,
      And the sabbath rang slowly
    In the pebbles of the holy streams.

All the sun long it was running, it was lovely, the hay
Fields high as the house, the tunes from the chimneys, it was air
      And playing, lovely and watery
        And fire green as grass.
    And nightly under the simple stars
As I rode to sleep the owls were bearing the farm away,
All the moon long I heard, blessed among stables, the night jars
      Flying with the ricks, and the horses
        Flashing into the dark.

And then to awake, and the farm, like a wanderer white
With the dew, come back, the cock on his shoulder: it was all
      Shining, it was Adam and maiden,
        The sky gathered again
    And the sun grew round that very day.
So it must have been after the birth of the simple light
In the first, spinning place, the spellbound horses walking warm
      Out of the whinnying green stable
        On to the fields of praise.

And honoured among foxes and pheasants by the gay house
Under the new made clouds and happy as the heart was long,
      In the sun born over and over,
        I ran my heedless ways,
    My wishes raced through the house high hay
And nothing I cared, at my sky blue trades, that time allows
In all his tuneful turning so few and such morning songs
      Before the children green and golden
        Follow him out of grace,

Nothing I cared, in the lamb white days, that time would take me
Up to the swallow thronged loft by the shadow of my hand,
      In the moon that is always rising,
            Nor that riding to sleep
      I should hear him fly with the high fields
And wake to the farm forever fled from the childless land.
Oh as I was young and easy in the mercy of his means,
            Time held me green and dying
      Though I sang in my chains like the sea.

Robert Lowell (1917-   )

NEW YEAR'S DAY

Again and then again . . . the year is born
To ice and death, and it will never do
To skulk behind storm-windows by the stove
To hear the postgirl sounding her French horn
When the thin tidal ice is wearing through.
Here is the understanding not to love
Each other, or tomorrow that will sieve
Our resolutions. While we live, we live

To snuff the smoke of victims. In the snow
The kitten heaved its hindlegs, as if fouled,
And died. We bent it in a Christmas box
And scattered blazing weeds to scare the crow
Until the snake-tailed sea-winds coughed and howled
For alms outside the church whose double locks
Wait for St. Peter, the distorted key.
Under St. Peter's bell the parish sea

Swells with its smelt into the burlap shack
Where Joseph plucks his hand-lines like a harp,
And hears the fearful *Puer natus est*
Of Circumcision, and relieves the wrack
And howls of Jesus whom he holds. How sharp
The burden of the Law before the beast:
Time and the grindstone and the knife of God.
The Child is born in blood, O child of blood.

FOR THE UNION DEAD
"Relinquunt Omnia Servare Rem Publicam."

The old South Boston Aquarium stands
in a Sahara of snow now. Its broken windows are boarded.
The bronze weathervane cod has lost half its scales.
The airy tanks are dry.

Once my nose crawled like a snail on the glass;
my hand tingled
to burst the bubbles
drifting from the noses of the cowed, compliant fish.

My hand draws back. I often sigh still
for the dark downward and vegetating kingdom
of the fish and reptile. One morning last March,
I pressed against the new barbed and galvanized

fence on the Boston Common. Behind their cage,
yellow dinosaur steamshovels were grunting
as they cropped up tons of mush and grass
to gouge their underworld garage.

Parking spaces luxuriate like civic
sandpiles in the heart of Boston.
A girldle of orange, Puritan-pumpkin colored girders
braces the tingling Statehouse,

shaking over the excavations, as it faces Colonel Shaw
and his bell-cheeked Negro infantry
on St. Gaudens' shaking Civil War relief,
propped by a plank splint against the garage's earthquake.

Two months after marching through Boston,
half the regiment was dead;
at the dedication,
William James could almost hear the bronze Negroes breathe.

Their monument sticks like a fishbone
in the city's throat.
Its Colonel is as lean
as a compass-needle.

He has an angry wrenlike vigilance,
a greyhound's gentle tautness;

he seems to wince at pleasure,
and suffocate for privacy.

He is out of bounds now. He rejoices in man's lovely,
peculiar power to choose life and die—
when he leads his black soldiers to death,
he cannot bend his back.

On a thousand small town New England greens,
the old white chruches hold their air
of sparse, sincere rebellion; frayed flags
quilt the graveyards of the Grand Army of the Republic.

The stone statues of the abstract Union Soldier
grow slimmer and younger each year—
wasp-wasted, they doze over muskets
and muse through their sideburns . . .

Shaw's father wanted no monument
except the ditch,
where his son's body was thrown
and lost with his "niggers."

The ditch is nearer.
There are no statues for the last war here;
on Boylston Street, a commercial photograph
shows Hiroshima boiling

over a Mosler Safe, the "Rock of Ages"
that survived the blast. Space is nearer.
When I crouch to my television set,
the drained faces of Negro school-children rise like balloons.

Colonel Shaw
is riding on his bubble,
he waits
for the blesséd break.

The Aquarium is gone. Everywhere,
giant finned cars nose forward like fish;
a savage servility
slides by on grease.

Richard Wilbur (1921-   )

BEASTS

Beasts in their major freedom
Slumber in peace tonight. The gull on his ledge
Dreams in the guts of himself the moon-plucked waves below,
And the sunfish leans on a stone, slept
By the lyric water,

In which the spotless feet
Of deer make dulcet splashes, and to which
The ripped mouse, safe in the owl's talon, cries
Concordance. Here there is no such harm
And no such darkness

As the selfsame moon observes
Where, warped in window-glass, it sponsors now
The werewolf's painful change. Turning his head away
On the sweaty bolster, he tries to remember
The mood of manhood,

But lies at last, as always,
Letting it happen, the fierce fur soft to his face,
Hearing with sharper ears the wind's exciting minors,
The leaves' panic, and the degradation
Of the heavy streams.

Meantime, at high windows
Far from thicket and pad-fall, suitors of excellence
Sigh and turn from their work to construe again the painful
Beauty of heaven, the lucid moon
And the risen hunter,

Making such dreams for men
As told will break their hearts as always, bringing
Monsters into the city, crows on the public statues,
Navies fed to the fish in the dark
Unbridled waters.

Philip Larkin (1922-   )

MR. BLEANEY

'This was Mr. Bleaney's room. He stayed
The whole time he was at the Bodies, till
They moved him.' Flowered curtains, thin and frayed,
Fall to within five inches of the sill,

Whose window shows a strip of building land,
Tussocky, littered. 'Mr. Bleaney took
My bit of garden properly in hand.'
Bed, upright chair, sixty-watt bulb, no hook

Behind the door, no room for books or bags—
'I'll take it.' So it happens that I lie
Where Mr. Bleaney lay, and stub my fags
On the same saucer-souvenir, and try

Stuffing my ears with cotton-wool, to drown
The jabbering set he egged her on to buy.
I know his habits—what time he came down,
His preference for sauce to gravy, why

He kept on plugging at the four aways—
Likewise their yearly frame: the Frinton folk
Who put him up for summer holidays,
And Christmas at his sister's house in Stoke.

But if he stood and watched the frigid wind
Tousling the clouds, lay on the fusty bed
Telling himself that this was home, and grinned,
And shivered, without shaking off the dread

That how we live measures our own nature,
And at his age having no more to show
Than one hired box should make him pretty sure
He warranted no better, I don't know.

Denise Levertov (1923-   )

TWO VARIATIONS

i ENQUIRY

You who go out on schedule
to kill, do you know
there are eyes that watch you,
eyes whose lids you burned off,
that see you eat your steak
and buy your girlflesh
and sell your PX goods
and sleep?
She is not old,
she whose eyes
know you.
She will outlast you.
She saw
her five young children
writhe and die;
in that hour
she began to watch you,
she whose eyes are open forever.

ii THE SEEING

Hands over my eyes I see
blood and the little bones;
or when a blanket covers
the sockets I see the
weave; at night the glare softens
but I have power now
to see there is only gray
on gray, the sleepers, the
altar. I see the living
and the dead; the dead are
as if alive, the mouth of
my youngest son pulls my
breast, but there is no milk, he
is a ghost; through his flesh
I see the dying of those
said to be alive, they
eat rice and speak to me but

I see dull death in them
and while they speak I see
myself on my mat, body
and eyes, eyes that see a
hand in the unclouded sky,
a human hand, release
wet fire, the rain that gave
my eyes their vigilance.

Louis Simpson (1923-   )

LOVE AND POETRY

My girl the voluptuous creature
Was shaving her legs and saying, "Darling,
If poetry comes not as naturally
As the leaves to a tree
It had better not come at all."

"Och," I said, "and the sorra
Be takin your English Johnny!
What, is a poet a thing without brains
    in its head?
If wishing could do it, I'd compose
Poems as grand as physics,
Poems founded in botany, psychology, biology,
Poems as progressive as the effect
Of radiation on a foetus."

She turned on the switch of her razor
And said, "When you talk about poetry
It reminds me of a man in long underwear
Doing barbell exercises.
His biceps bulge. In the meantime
Outside on the gaslit street
His wife, a voluptuous lady,
Elopes with a 'swell' who takes her
To Lindy's for oysters,
From there to the Waldorf, and there
On a bed carved like seashells
They move, while the man with the barbells

By gaslight is marching
And swinging his arms to the tune of the
  Washington Post."

I went to the window. It was night,
And the beautiful moon
Was stealing away to meet someone.
The bitches! They want to feel wanted,
And everything else is prose.

Robert Bly (1926-   )

ROMANS ANGRY ABOUT THE INNER WORLD

What shall the world do with its children?
There are lives the executives
Know nothing of,
A leaping of the body,
The body rolling—and I have felt it—
And we float
Joyfully on the dark places;
But the executioners
Move toward Drusia. They tie her legs
On the iron horse. "Here is a woman
Who has seen our mother
In the other world!" Next they warm
The hooks. The two Romans had put their trust
In the outer world. Irons glowed
Like teeth. They wanted her
To assure them. She refused. Finally they took burning
Pine sticks, and pushed them
Into her sides. Her breath rose
And she died. The executioners
Rolled her off onto the ground.
A light snow began to fall
And covered the mangled body,
And the executives, astonished, withdrew.
The other world is like a thorn
In the ear of a tiny beast!
The fingers of the executives are too thick
To pull it out!
It is like a jagged stone
Flying toward them out of the darkness.

W. D. Snodgrass (1926-   )

APRIL INVENTORY

The green catalpa tree has turned
All white; the cherry blooms once more.
In one whole year I haven't learned
A blessed thing they pay you for.
The blossoms snow down in my hair;
The trees and I will soon be bare.

The trees have more than I to spare.
The sleek, expensive girls I teach,
Younger and pinker every year,
Bloom gradually out of reach.
The pear tree lets its petals drop
Like dandruff on a tabletop.

The girls have grown so young by now
I have to nudge myself to stare.
This year they smile and mind me how
My teeth are falling with my hair.
In thirty years I may not get
Younger, shrewder, or out of debt.

The tenth time, just a year ago,
I made myself a little list
Of all the things I'd ought to know,
Then told my parents, analyst,
And everyone who's trusted me
I'd be substantial, presently.

I haven't read one book about
A book or memorized one plot.
Or found a mind I did not doubt.
I learned one date. And then forgot.
And one by one the solid scholars
Get the degrees, the jobs, the dollars.

And smile above their starchy collars.
I taught my classes Whitehead's notions;
One lovely girl, a song of Mahler's.
Lacking a source-book or promotions,
I showed one child the colors of
A luna moth and how to love.

I taught myself to name my name,
To bark back, loosen love and crying;
To ease my woman so she came,
To ease an old man who was dying.
I have not learned how often I
Can win, can love, but choose to die.

I have not learned there is a lie
Love shall be blonder, slimmer, younger;
That my equivocating eye
Loves only by my body's hunger;
That I have forces, true to feel,
Or that the lovely world is real.

While scholars speak authority
And wear their ulcers on their sleeves,
My eyes in spectacles shall see
These trees procure and spend their leaves.
There is a value underneath
The gold and silver in my teeth.

Though trees turn bare and girls turn wives,
We shall afford our costly seasons;
There is a gentleness survives
That will outspeak and has its reasons.
There is a loveliness exists,
Preserves us, not for specialists.

Allen Ginsberg (1926-   )

AMERICA

America I've given you all and now I'm nothing.
America two dollars and twentyseven cents January 17, 1956.
I can't stand on my own mind.
America when will we end the human war?
Go fuck yourself with your atom bomb.
I don't feel good don't bother me.
I won't write my poem till I'm in my right mind.
America when will you be angelic?
When will you take off your clothes?
When will you look at yourself through the grave?

When will you be worthy of your million Trotskyites?
America why are your libraries full of tears?
America when will you send your eggs to India?
I'm sick of your insane demands.
When can I go into the supermaket and buy what I need with my
    good looks?
America after all it is you and I who are perfect not the next world.
Your machinery is too much for me.
You made me want to be a saint.
There must be some other way to settle this argument.
Burroughs is in Tangiers I don't think he'll come back it's sinister.
Are you being sinister or is this some form of practical joke?
I'm trying to come to the point.
I refuse to give up my obsession.
America stop pushing I know what I'm doing.
America the plum blossoms are falling.
I haven't read the newspapers for months, everyday somebody goes
    on trial for murder.
America I feel sentimental about the Wobblies.
America I used to be a communist when I was a kid I'm not sorry.
I smoke marijuana every chance I get.
I sit in my house for days on end and stare at the roses in the
    closet.
When I go to Chinatown I get drunk and never get laid.
My mind is made up there's going to be trouble.
You should have seen me reading Marx.
My psychoanalyst thinks I'm perfectly right.
I won't say the Lord's Prayer.
I have mystical visions and cosmic vibrations.
America I still haven't told you what you did to Uncle Max after
    he came over from Russia.

I'm addressing you.
Are you going to let your emotional life be run by Time Magazine?
I'm obsessed by Time Magazine.
I read it every week.
Its cover stares at me every time I slink past the corner candystore.
I read it in the basement of the Berkeley Public Library.
It's always telling me about responsibility. Businessmen are serious.
    Movie producers are serious. Everybody's serious but me.
It occurs to me that I am America.
I am talking to myself again.

Asia is rising against me.
I haven't got a chinaman's chance.
I'd better consider my national resources.
My national resources consist of two joints of marijuana millions

of genitals an unpublishable private literature that goes 1400
    miles an hour and twentyfive-thousand mental institutions.
I say nothing about my prisons nor the millions of underprivileged
    who live in my flowerpots under the light of five hundred suns.
I have abolished the whorehouses of France, Tangiers is the next to
    go.
My ambition is to be President despite the fact that I'm a Catholic.

America how can I write a holy litany in your silly mood?
I will continue like Henry Ford my strophes are as individual as
    his automobiles more so they're all different sexes.
America I will sell you strophes $2500 apiece $500 down on your
    old strophe
America free Tom Mooney
America save the Spanish Loyalists
America Sacco & Vanzetti must not die
America I am the Scottsboro boys.
America when I was seven momma took me to Communist Cell
    meetings they sold us garbanzos a handful per ticket
    a ticket costs a nickel and the speeches were free everybody
    was angelic and sentimental about the workers it was all so
    sincere you have no idea what a good thing the party was in
    1835 Scott Nearing was a grand old man a real mensch
    Mother Bloor made me cry I once saw Israel Amter plain.
    Everybody must have been a spy.
America you don't really want to go to war.
America it's them bad Russians.
Them Russians them Russians and them Chinamen. And them
    Russians.
The Russia wants to eat us alive. The Russia's power mad. She
    wants to take our cars from out our garages.
Her wants to grab Chicago. Her needs a Red Readers' Digest. Her
    wants our auto plants in Siberia. Him big bureaucracy run-
    ning our fillingstations.

That no good. Ugh. Him make Indians learn read. Him need big
    black niggers. Hah. Her make us all work sixteen hours a
    day. Help.
America this is quite serious.
America this is the impression I get from looking in the television
    set.
America is this correct?
I'd better get right down to the job.
It's true I don't want to join the Army or turn lathes in precision
    parts factories, I'm nearsighted and psychopathic anyway.
America I'm putting my queer shoulder to the wheel.

Sylvia Plath (1932-1963)

LADY LAZARUS

I have done it again.
One year in every ten
I manage it—

A sort of walking miracle, my skin
Bright as a Nazi lampshade,
My right foot

A paperweight,
My face a featureless, fine
Jew linen.

Peel off the napkin
O my enemy.
Do I terrify?—

The nose, the eye pits, the full set of teeth?
The sour breath
Will vanish in a day.

Soon, soon the flesh
The grave cave ate will be
At home on me

And I a smiling woman.
I am only thirty.
And like the cat I have nine times to die.

This is Number Three.
What a trash
To annihilate each decade.

What a million filaments.
The peanut-crunching crowd
Shoves in to see

Them unwrap me hand and foot—
The big strip tease.
Gentlemen, ladies

These are my hands
My knees.
I may be skin and bone,

Nevertheless, I am the same, identical woman.
The first time it happened I was ten.
It was an accident.

The second time I meant
To last it out and not come back at all.
I rocked shut

As a seashell.
They had to call and call
And pick the worms off me like sticky pearls.

Dying
Is an art, like everything else.
I do it exceptionally well.

I do it so it feels like hell.
I do it so it feels real.
I guess you could say I've a call.

It's easy enough to do it in a cell.
It's easy enough to do it and stay put.
It's the theatrical

Comeback in broad day
To the same place, the same face, the same brute
Amused shout:

'A miracle!'
That knocks me out.
There is a charge

For the eyeing of my scars, there is a charge
For the hearing of my heart—
It really goes.

And there is a charge, a very large charge
For a word or a touch
Or a bit of blood

Or a piece of my hair or my clothes.
So, so, Herr Doktor.
So, Herr Enemy.

I am your opus,
I am your valuable,
The pure gold baby

That melts to a shriek.
I turn and burn.
Do not think I underestimate your great concern.

Ash, ash—
You poke and stir.
Flesh, bone, there is nothing there—

A cake of soap,
A wedding ring,
A gold filling.

Herr God, Herr Lucifer
Beware
Beware.

Out of the ash
I rise with my red hair
And I eat men like air.

Geoffrey Hill (1932-   )

OF COMMERCE AND SOCIETY
Variations on a Theme

———

Then hang this picture for a calendar,
As sheep for goat, and pray most fixedly
For the cold martial progress of your star,
With thoughts of commerce and society,
Well-milked Chinese, Negroes who cannot sing,

The Huns gelded and feeding in a ring.
    Allen Tate: *More Sonnets at Christmas,* 1942

I   THE APOSTLES: VERSAILLES, 1919

They sat. They stood about.
They were estranged. The air,
As water curdles from clear,
Fleshed the silence. They sat.

They were appalled. The bells
In hollowed Europe spilt
To the gods of coin and salt.
The sea creaked with worked vessels.

II   THE LOWLANDS OF HOLLAND

Europe, the much-scarred, much-scoured terrain,
Its attested liberties, home-produce,
Labelled and looking up, invites use,
Stuffed with artistry and substantial gain:

Shrunken, magnified—(nest, holocaust)—
Not half innocent and not half undone;
Profiting from custom: its replete strewn
Cities such ample monuments to lost

Nations and generations: its cultural
Or trade skeletons such hand-picked bone:
Flaws in the best, revised science marks down:
Witness many devices; the few natural

Corruptions, graftings; witness classic falls;
(The dead subtracted; the greatest resigned;)
Witness earth fertilised, decently drained,
The sea decent again behind walls.

III   THE DEATH OF SHELLEY
    i

Slime; the residues of refined tears;
And, salt-bristled, blown on a drying sea,

The sunned and risen faces.
                              There's Andromeda
Depicted in relief, after the fashion.

'His guarded eyes under his shielded brow'
Through poisonous baked sea-things Perseus
Goes—clogged sword, clear, aimless mirror—
With nothing to strike at or blind
                              in the frothed shallows.

ii

Rivers bring down. The sea
Brings away;
Voids, sucks back, its pearls and auguries.
Eagles or vultures churn the fresh-made skies.

Over the statues, unchanging features
Of commerce and quaint love, soot lies.
Earth steams. The bull and the great mute swan
Strain into life with their notorious cries.

IV

Statesmen have known visions. And, not alone,
Artistic men prod dead men from their stone:
Some of us have heard the dead speak:
The dead are my obsession this week

But may be lifted away. In summer
Thunder may strike, or as a tremor
Of remote adjustment, pass on the far side
From us: however deified and defied

By those it does strike. Many have died. Auschwitz,
Its furnace chambers and lime pits
Half-erased, is half-dead; a fable
Unbelievable in fatted marble.

There is, at times, some need to demonstrate
Jehovah's touchy methods, that create
The connoisseur of blood, the smitten man.
At times it seems not common to explain.

V ODE ON THE LOSS OF THE 'TITANIC'

Thriving against facades the ignorant sea
Souses our public baths, statues, waste ground:
Archaic earth-shaker, fresh enemy:
('The tables of exchange being overturned');

Drowns Babel in upheaval and display;
Unswerving, as were the admired multitudes
Silenced from time to time under its sway.
By all means let us appease the terse gods.

VI THE MARTYRDOM OF SAINT SEBASTIAN
Homage to Henry James
'But then face to face'

Naked, as if for swimming, the martyr
Catches his death in a little flutter
Of plain arrows. A grotesque situation,
But priceless, and harmless to the nation.

Consider such pains 'crystalline': then fine art
Persists where most crystals accumulate.
History can be scraped clean of its old price.
Engrossed in the cold blood of sacrifice,

The provident and self-healing gods
Destroy only to save. Well-stocked with foods,
Enlarged and deep-oiled, America
Detects music, apprehends the day-star

Where, sensitive and half-under a cloud,
Europe muddles her dreaming, is loud
And critical beneath the varied domes
Resonant with tributes and with commerce.

Etheridge Knight (1933-   )

THE IDEA OF ANCESTRY

1

Taped to the wall of my cell are 47 pictures: 47 black
faces: my father, mother, grandmothers (1 dead), grand
father (both dead), brothers, sisters, uncles, aunts,
cousins (1st & 2nd), nieces, and nephews. They stare
across the space at me sprawling on my bunk. I know
their dark eyes, they know mine. I know their style,
they know mine. I am all of them, they are all of me;
they are farmers, I am a thief, I am me, they are thee.

I have at one time or another been in love with my mother,
1 grandmother, 2 sisters, 2 aunts (1 went to the asylum),
and 5 cousins. I am now in love with a 7 yr old niece
(she sends me letters written in large block print, and
her picture is the only one that smiles at me).

I have the same name as 1 grandfather, 3 cousins, 3 nephews,
and 1 uncle. The uncle disappeared when he was 15, just took
off and caught a freight (they say). He's discussed each year
when the family has a reunion, he causes uneasiness in
the clan, he is an empty space. My father's mother, who is 93
and who keeps the Family Bible with everybody's birth dates
(and death dates) in it, always mentions him. There is no
place in her Bible for "whereabouts unknown."

2

Each Fall the graves of my grandfathers call me, the brown
hills and red gullies of mississippi send out their electric
messages, galvanizing my genes. Last yr/like a salmon quitting
the cold ocean—leaping and bucking up his birthstream/I
hitchhiked my way from L.A. with 16 caps in my pocket and a
monkey on my back. and I almost kicked it with the kinfolks.
I walked barefooted in my grandmother's backyard/I smelled the
    old
land and the woods/I sipped cornwhiskey from fruit jars with the
    men/
I flirted with the women/I had a ball till the caps ran out
and my habit came down. That night I looked at my grandmother

and split/my guts were screaming for junk/but I was almost
contented/I had almost caught up with me.
(The next day in Memphis I cracked a croaker's crib for a fix.)

This yr there is a gray stone wall damming my stream, and when
the falling leaves stir my genes, I pace my cell or flop on my bunk
and stare at 47 black faces across the space. I am all of them,
they are all of me, I am me, they are thee, and I have no sons
to float in the space between.

Tom Clark (1941-   )

LIKE MUSICAL INSTRUMENTS

Like musical instruments
Abandoned in a field
The parts of your feelings

Are starting to know a quiet
The pure conversion of your
Life into art seems destined

Never to occur
You don't mind
You feel spiritual and alert

As the air must feel
Turning into sky aloft and blue
You feel like

You'll never feel like touching anything or anyone
Again
And then you do

FIVE LYRICS
BY THE BEATLES

The Beatles

ELEANOR RIGBY

Ah, look at all the lonely people.
Ah, look at all the lonely people.
Eleanor Rigby picks up the rice in the church where a wedding
    has been, lives in a dream.
Waits at the window, wearing the face that she keeps in a jar by
    the door,
Who is it for?
All the lonely people, where do they all come from?
All the lonely people, where do they all belong?
Father McKenzie, writing the words of a sermon that no-one will
    hear,
No-one comes near.
Look at him working, darning his socks in the night when there's
    nobody there,
What does he care?
All the lonely people, where do they all come from?
All the lonely people, where do they all belong?
Ah, look at all the lonely people.
Ah, look at all the lonely people.
Eleanor Rigby died in the church and was buried along with her
    name.
Nobody came.
Father McKenzie, wiping the dirt from his hands as he walks from
    the grave.
No-one was saved.
All the lonely people, where do they all come from?
All the lonely people, where do they all belong?

YELLOW SUBMARINE

In the town where I was born,
lived a man who sailed the sea,
and he told us of his life,

in the land of submarines.
So we sailed on to the sun,
till we found the sea of green,
and we lived beneath the waves,
in our yellow submarine.
We all live in a yellow submarine,
yellow submarine, yellow submarine,
we all live in a yellow submarine,
yellow submarine, yellow submarine.
And our friends are all aboard,
many more of them live next door,
and the band begins to play.
We all live in a yellow submarine,
yellow submarine, yellow submarine,
we all live in a yellow submarine,
yellow submarine, yellow submarine,
As we live a life of ease,
everyone of us has all we need,
sky of blue and sea of green,
in our yellow submarine.
We all live in a yellow submarine,
yellow submarine, yellow submarine,
we all live in a yellow submarine,
yellow submarine, yellow submarine.

A DAY IN THE LIFE

I read the news today oh boy
about a lucky man who made the grade
and though the news was rather sad
well I just had to laugh
I saw the photograph
He blew his mind out in a car
he didn't notice that the lights had
changed
a crowd of people stood and stared
they'd seen his face before
nobody was really sure
if he was from the House of Lords.
I saw a film today oh boy
the English Army had just won the war
a crowd of people turned away
but I just had to look

having read the book.
I'd love to turn you on
Woke up, got out of bed,
dragged a comb across my head
found my way downstairs and drank a cup,
and looking up I noticed I was late.
Found my coat and grabbed my hat
made the bus in seconds flat
found my way upstairs and had a smoke,
and somebody spoke and I went into a dream
I heard the news today oh boy
four thousand holes in Blackburn,
Lancashire
and though the holes were rather small
they had to count them all
now they know how many holes it takes
to fill the Albert Hall.
I'd love to turn you on.

THE FOOL ON THE HILL

Day after day, alone on a hill,
the man with the foolish grin is keeping perfectly still.
But nobody wants to know him,
they can see that he's just a fool
and he never gives an answer.
But the fool on the hill sees the sun going down
and the eyes in his head see the world spinning round.
Well on the way, head in a cloud,
the man of a thousand voices talking perfectly loud.
But nobody ever hears him
or the sound he appears to make
and he never seems to notice.
But the fool on the hill sees the sun going down
and the eyes in his head see the world spinning round.
And nobody seems to like him,
they can tell what he wants to do
and he never shows his feelings.
But the fool on the hill sees the sun going down
and the eyes in his head see the world spinning round.
He never listens to them,
he knows that they're the fools.
They don't like him.

The fool on the hill sees the sun going down
and the eyes in his head see the world spinning round.

I AM THE WALRUS

I am he as you are he as you are me and we are all together.
See how they run like pigs from a gun see how they fly,
I'm crying.
Sitting on a cornflake—waiting for the van to come.
Corporation teashirt, stupid bloody
Tuesday man you been a naughty boy you let your face grow long.
I am the eggman oh, they are the eggmen—
Oh I am the walrus GOO GOO G'JOOB.
Mr. City policeman sitting pretty little policeman in a row,
see how they fly like Lucy in the sky—
see how they run
I'm crying—I'm crying I'm crying.
Yellow matter custard driping from a dead dog's eye.
Crabalocker fishwife pornographic
priestess boy you been a naughty girl,
you let your knickers down.
I am the eggman oh, they are the eggmen—
Oh I am the walrus. GOO GOO G'JOOB.
Sitting in an English garden waiting for the sun,
If the sun don't come, you get a tan from standing in the
English rain.
I am the eggman oh, they are the eggmen—
Oh I am the walrus. G'JOOB, G'GOO, G'JOOB.
Expert texpert choking smokers don't you think the joker laughs
at you?
Ha ha ha!
See how they smile, like pigs in a sty, see how they snied.
I'm crying.
Semolina pilchards climbing up the Eiffel Tower.
Elementary penguin singing Hare
Krishna man you should have seen them
kicking Edgar Allen Poe.
I am the eggman oh, they are the eggmen—
Oh I am the walrus GOO GOO GOO JOOB
GOO GOO GOO JOOB GOO GOO
GOOOOOOOOOOOOJOOOOOB.

INDEX OF POETS

INDEX OF POETS

INDEX OF FIRST LINES

INDEX OF FIRST LINES